ACTIONS & GOALS

The Story Structure Secret

Marshall L. Dotson

Actions & Goals: The Story Structure Secret
Copyright © 2016 Marshall Dotson
All rights reserved

No part of this publication may be reproduced, distributed, or transmitted in any form or by any means, including photocopying, recording, or other electronic or mechanical methods, without the prior written permission of the publisher, except in the case of brief quotations embodied in critical reviews and certain other noncommercial uses permitted by copyright law.

Published by Idea Brain Creative Publishing
Printed in the United States of America

Cover Design by Marshall Dotson
Print and Electronic Formatting by Polgarus Studio

ISBN: 978-1537001401

To Charlie:
For the beauty, strength and laughter
You bring me every day.
No words could capture all my love,
But here's four anyway…

Will you marry me?

Contents

Elevator Pitch 1
Spoiler Alert 5
What is an Act? 11
The Evolving Goal 16
The Six Acts 19

ACT ONE: DEALING WITH AN IMPERFECT SITUATION 27
    Goal One: The Initial Goal 33
    Turning Point Catalyst: The Disturbance 39
    Turning Point One: The Dilemma 41
    Act One Summary 50
    Act One Examples 53

ACT TWO: LEARNING THE RULES OF AN UNFAMILIAR
SITUATION 75
    Goal Two: The Transitional Goal 85
    Turning Point Catalyst: The Reality Check 89
    Turning Point Two: The Commitment 91
    Act Two Summary 94
    Act Two Examples 97

ACT THREE: STUMBLING INTO THE CENTRAL CONFLICT ... 109
    Goal Three: The False Goal 116
    Turning Point Catalyst: The Turn 120
    Turning Point Three: The Moment of Truth 122
    Act Three Summary 127
    Act Three Examples 130

ACT FOUR: IMPLEMENTING A DOOMED PLAN 143
   Goal Four: The Penultimate Goal.. 148
   Turning Point Catalyst: The Lowpoint... 152
   Turning Point Four: The Newfound Resolve................................... 154
   Act Four Summary 158
   Act Four Examples... 161

ACT FIVE: TRYING A LONGSHOT 173
   Goal Five: The Ultimate Goal... 179
   Turning Point Catalyst: All is Lost.. 183
   Turning Point Five: The Final Push 185
   Act Five Summary 188
   Act Five Examples.. 191

ACT SIX: LIVING IN A NEW SITUATION 203
   Act Six Summary 207
   Act Six Examples 209

In Conclusion 215

FURTHER EXAMPLES 217
   Avatar 219
   A Game of Thrones (Ned Stark) 235
   A Game of Thrones (Daenerys Targaryen)..................................... 253
   Gravity 269
   Harry Potter and the Philosopher's Stone 283
   Inception 299
   Iron Man 315
   The Lego Movie 331
   Star Trek.. 347
   Star Wars Episode V: The Empire Strikes Back.............................. 365

Quick Reference Guide	381
Glossary	389
Inspirations, Influences and Further Reading	395
Cited Works	397

Elevator Pitch

The structural paradigm you are about to discover has been used by some of the most celebrated novelists and filmmakers of recent decades. From George Lucas to George RR Martin, from JJ Abrams to JK Rowling, successful storytellers have employed this structure to create many of the most revered stories of the modern era.

Yet the structural paradigm contained in these pages has never before been transcribed. You won't find it taught in creative writing workshops or banquet room seminars. While the structure itself has remained immutable, the methods implemented to achieve it have varied greatly from one storyteller to the next. Those who have used this structure with such resounding success have done so either inadvertently or innately. Until now.

Although this structural format is so pervasive, it possesses, at its core, a wholly new approach to structuring stories. Whether you are a writer of novels or screenplays, comic books or video games, the structural method delineated in this analysis is the easiest, most intuitive you are likely to have ever encountered.

But to understand this extraordinary paradigm, we must be willing to release our grip on some of the nebulous structural concepts we have been taught to hold dear. We must take our focus off such ambiguities as *rising actions* and *escalating conflict*, and reverse engineer our favorite stories from the top down to their most readily identifiable and relatable components. Only then can we discover the driving force of story structure in its truest form: the *Actions and Goals* of our characters.

"The most important learning tool in the craft of screenwriting is the written analysis of movies and screenplays." - Daniel Calvisi, professional script analyst and presumably a pretty smart guy

Spoiler Alert

Oh, hello there. I'm the author of the book you're currently reading. Before we initiate the transfer of information from my brain to yours, I would like to draw your attention to the double meaning of this section's title. Metaphorically what follows is a spoiler alert because I will present a synopsis of all the information covered in this book, i.e. a spoiler. Literally, it's a spoiler alert because there will be spoilers of the plots for several popular novels and movies in this analysis of which I will now provide a list. Behold.

- *Avatar* - 2009 film - James Cameron
- *A Game of Thrones* - 1996 novel - George "Rail Road" Martin
- *Gravity* - 2013 film - The director of my favorite Harry Potter film[1]
- *Harry Potter and the Philosopher's Stone* - 1997 Novel - The author of my favorite Harry Potter novel[2]
- *The Hunger Games* - 2008 novel - Suzanne Collins
- *Inception* - 2010 film - Christopher Nolan
- *Iron Man* - 2008 film - Mark Fergus, Hawk Ostby, Art Marcum and Matt Holloway
- *The Lego Movie* - 2014 film - Phil Lord and Christopher Miller
- *The Silence of the Lambs* - 1988 novel - Thomas Harris
- *Star Trek* - 2009 film - Roberto Orci and Alex Kurtzman
- *Star Wars Episode IV: A New Hope* - 1977 film - George Lucas
- *Star Wars Episode V: The Empire Strikes Back* - Leigh Brackett, Lawrence Kasdan and a significantly wealthier George Lucas

---

[1] Alfonso Cuarón (and son).
[2] JK Rowling

- *Titanic* - 1997 film - A soon to be significantly wealthier James Cameron

If you noticed all these stories could accurately be deemed "commercial fiction", you are correct. The structural method enclosed in these pages is primarily applicable to commercial, genre fiction. I'm therefore not holding these stories up as irrefutable works of art, rather as critically and commercially successful stories that have resonated with a wide audience. If it is your sincere belief these stories are the kind of useless dredge ruining our culture and undermining the intellectual growth of society, I will hazard a guess you're unlikely to garner much value from this analysis.

Although I may insert examples from all thirteen of these stories throughout this book (plus a few extra for good measure), in the main section we will focus on only four of these tales: *The Hunger Games* (the novel, not the film), *The Silence of the Lambs* (ditto), *Star Wars* (A New Hope) and *Titanic:* two highly successful novels[3] and two equally successful films. As we reach the end of each component of this structure, we will examine how these four stories utilize the components discussed, so that by the end of this analysis you will have witnessed this structural paradigm demonstrated in full throughout multiple stories. The remaining nine stories are outlined step by step in the appendix for you to reference or ignore as you see fit.

Based on the popularity of the aforementioned novels/movies I hope you have already read/watched them. If you have not read/watched them and would like to, then you should do so before reading further. Otherwise, your reading/watching experience of these novels/movies will be irrevocably spoiled. Thus the alert.

And while the punny title of this chapter tickles me to no hyperbolic end, its greatest power lies in its ability to set the tone for the views and opinions I am

---

[3] Yes, both novels have been adapted into films. Unfortunately, successful novels have a habit of doing that. Those familiar with the differences between the book and the movie will recognize which was analyzed.

about to express. I am confident you will find the content of this book educational. The reason being the theories set forth in this book cannot and will not be found in any other book ever written. When one considers there have been, at my last count, a gagillion books written on writing, this is no small feat. But my goal is to make this book as entertaining as it is educational. Though I may phrase things humorously[4], the subject of this analysis is of direct import to the survival of the human race. More hyperbole, you ask? Not at all.

You see, storytelling is important. Without stories, we wouldn't know about the legendary deeds of Hercules or James Bond or Jesus. That may sound facetious, but I assure you it's not. Without storytelling, there would be no religions or fables or bestselling book series followed by blockbuster film franchises. Without story, there would be no video games or conversation subjects for first dates or Facebook rants about unusually bad customer service experiences at Starbucks. Storytelling is what separates man from beast. Without the desire to recount our experiences, it's likely human language would have never come to exist. And without our spoken language we would be no better than koala bears[5] or trees or nematodes. You don't want to be a nematode, do you?

While I would love to go into a long winded history of story, I assume you aren't reading this book for that. If you are, then I highly recommend you purchase my companion piece, *A Very Long-Winded History of Storytelling and its Impact on Humanity and Civilization throughout the History of Human Civilization*. It's almost as entertaining as the title suggests.

Suffice it to say, regardless of the origins of story, a poorly structured tale is like a badly told joke. It may be the funniest thing since the advent of "yo momma", but if told incorrectly you might as well be giving instructions for loading a dishwasher. You'll get the same response.

---

[4] At least to myself. Your mileage may vary.
[5] Please note: Koalas are not actually bears. It's just more fun to say. Gummy bears aren't really bears either. If we're being technical.

So what makes a well-structured story? Like so many aspiring storytellers before myself, I turned to the existing theories to answer this question. I studied under the masters of the field, amassed a bookshelf full of works on dramatic theory and gained invaluable insight into many different structural paradigms.

And yet, something was missing. My second act still sagged like an elderly breast, and my collection of unfinished manuscripts continued to grow like an elderly prostate. Then I had an epiphany of sorts: so many of these theories are based on archaic ideals. Despite being written before the invention of the wheelbarrow, Aristotle's *Poetics* is still held as an almost biblical examination of story structure. Now I don't presume to decry his insightful philosophical analysis, but surely what makes a good story has evolved since the ancient Greeks danced and sang in Dionysus masks. I mean, they didn't even have toilet paper.

So, much like Aristotle (analogically at least), I armed myself with all I had learned and set myself to the task of dissecting the structure of the modern story from the ground up, by analyzing the most popular and well-received stories of the last few decades. I wanted to see for myself what shared structural patterns are found in most, if not all, critically and commercially successful, modern stories.

I carefully analyzed several dozen movies and novels, outlining their structures, analyzing important events, and dissecting the actions of characters. After nearly a decade of research[6], I unearthed a conclusion so pervasive it seemed impossible it had never been reached. Was there some longstanding and far-reaching conspiracy afoot? Was some Hollywood executive or New York City publisher going to send a team of emotionless, trench coat-clad, silenced-pistol wielding, hitmen after me? Would I be forced to seek out a retired CIA operative who everyone has written off as

---

[6] Which sounds considerably more impressive than seven years.

a crackpot to help exonerate me after revealing this paradigm to the masses[7]?

So what is this simple truth unrealistically warranting my assassination? The structure of stories doesn't arise from such ambiguities as "setup" or "confrontation" or "approaching the inmost cave"[8]. Instead, there is a deeper structure underlying all these narrator-oriented concepts. The true structure of story arises from two simple elements: the evolving *Goals* of the character, and the progressive *Actions* he undertakes to achieve them. Yep, it's that simple.

Now, before we delve into this simple, yet powerful concept, I would like to clarify a few aspects of this book to which some may take issue. Firstly, unless I'm referring to a particular heroine, the central character will always be identified with a masculine pronoun. This is because I wish to provide consistency as opposed to jumping back and forth between *he* and *she*. And since I possess a male reproductive system and its corresponding organs, I defaulted to the pronoun reflective of my gender. I assure you it's nothing personal, ladies. I always picked Chun Li when playing *Street Fighter*, and most of my favorite characters are women: Pippi Longstocking, Murphy Brown, Ross from *Friends*.

Secondly, the focus of this analysis lies exclusively on the structure of physical events within the plot of stories. Therefore, this book is not intended as a comprehensive guide to storycraft. There are many important elements of storytelling not covered in these pages. Topics such as theme and character arc, both cornerstones of storytelling, may be touched upon lightly, but are not the subject of this analysis. This is instead a comprehensive analysis of the physical structure of stories.

---

[7] Probably not, but there's no denying the dramatic appeal.
[8] What does that even mean?!

Lastly, this book is intended as a reference material and not a how-to manual. I say this because the **Plotters** among you may read it and think, oh, I should start here and then do this and then do that. Meanwhile, the **Extemporees** among you may read it and think, I don't need some ridiculous structure book to tell me how to write a story. I cannot be bound by the laws of man! No, this is simply an examination of story structure as it exists. It's an analysis, not a formula. All stories follow some of this structure. Most stories follow most of this structure. Some stories follow all of this structure. Do with it as you see fit.

With that settled, let's get down to the steak and fries. I would like to begin our journey into the great mystery of story structure by posing to you what is perhaps the most important structural question ever posed in the history of the universe…

What is an Act?

"You must unlearn what you have learned."
Master Yoda ~ The Empire Strikes Back

If you are reading this book, I can justifiably assume you are a writer of stories. Because you are a writer of stories, I can also assume you are familiar with the concept of "acts". And while there are many schools of thought concerning structuring stories, in the overwhelming majority of them, the act is so ubiquitous to story structure the two concepts are inseparable. You simply can't have one without the other. If you do, you'll probably die.

But what exactly is an act? This is a serious question I pose to you. Can you define the term? More importantly, can you define it in a way that doesn't rely on more ambiguous terms which themselves require ambiguous definitions?

I ask this question not to be humorous (okay, perhaps a bit), but because with all the literature available on story structure, the concept of the act itself is rarely, if ever, expounded upon. A cursory search of your favorite story structure guidebook or a Bing search[9] for the definition of a literary act will likely provide a definition of each act by explaining the elements it is comprised of. Act One is *The Setup* where the author introduces characters, establishes the storyworld and provides exposition. In Act Two the storyteller does such-and-such and the character does this-and-that. But these definitions fail to define the act itself because they fail to address the universal aspects shared by all acts.

---

[9] Just kidding. Does that still even exist?

For instance, one might describe a Dalmatian as a large white dog with black spots commonly associated with Budweiser commercials and firemen. On the other hand, one might describe a Chihuahua as a tiny dog with pointy ears formerly associated with Taco Bell commercials and Paris Hilton. But you wouldn't use either of these descriptions to define the concept of a dog itself; that is unless you're Paris Hilton. But since chances of that are only 1 in 7,125,000,000, you would likely provide a description of the universal attributes shared by all dogs.

So regardless of the number of acts in the structural paradigm you subscribe to, there have to be some universal elements shared by all acts that clearly distinguish them as acts and not, say, ukuleles or electric toothbrushes. And because the act is so important to so many structural paradigms, before one can truly understand story structure it stands to reason the act itself should be clearly, nay, quantifiably defined.

Searching for the definition of either a literary, screenwriting or theater act in both reference materials and online, these are the best, of the few, I could dredge up.

> *A main division of a play, ballet, or opera*
> *A major division in the action of a play, comprising one or more scenes.*
> *A collection of scenes forming one of the main sections of a script.*
> *A main division within the plot*

So an act is a division of a drama comprised of a collection of scenes. This is similar to how a human being is an inhabitant of Earth made up of a collection of organs[10]. One of the most intelligible definitions I found which at least attempts to explain what *all* acts consist of comes from screenwriting instructor, story consultant and fellow collection of organs, Jennine Lanouette. If I may paraphrase, an act is:

---

[10] An accurate description but woefully vague.

> *A portion of the drama in which a set of specific dramatic tasks are being accomplished.*

Well, at least these divisions are now specific. But ironically, "specific dramatic tasks" is still rather vague. If an act is a set of dramatic tasks, then, what pray tell is a dramatic task and what makes it specific?

Perhaps for that, we should turn to one of the masters. In his seminal book *Screenplay*, Syd Field, one of the godfathers of modern three-act structure, defines an act, indirectly, as a *unit* of dramatic *action*. This seems to line up with Lanouette's definition of an act being a *set* of dramatic *tasks*. From *Screenplay*:

> *Act I, the beginning, is <u>a unit of dramatic action</u>[11] that is approximately twenty to thirty minutes long and is held together with the dramatic context known as the Set-Up.*

While Field's contributions to story structure are vast, this is as close as we come to a definition of an act within his definitive work on the subject. He does say prior to this the dramatic action (as a whole) is the main storyline. Therefore, we can surmise that Act I is a subunit of the dramatic action of the entire story. This first subunit of the dramatic action of the story he appropriately titles, the Beginning/The Set-Up.

But if an act is a unit of dramatic action, what exactly is a dramatic action (or task or any other synonym)? To answer this question let's turn to our dusty, old friend, the dictionary

Knowing the adjective "dramatic" in the instance refers to storytelling and not a Kardashian show or Aunt Judith's behavior at family gatherings, let's set that word aside and focus on the subject word.

---

[11] Emphasis mine.

Action - noun
1. *the act or process of doing something, typically to achieve an aim*
2. thing done; *an act*.

Egad! So, by definition an action is the process of doing something to achieve an aim, and this definition is synonymous with the word act? We can expand upon our use of synonyms and accurately say *an Act is the process of taking action to achieve a goal*.

If we really want to bring drama back into the mix, we can alter our definition to say *an Act is the process of a character within a dramatic work doing something to achieve a goal*. But since the word drama itself derives from the Greek word for "act", let's eliminate the redundancies and simply say, in regard to story, **an Act is the process of a character taking action to achieve a goal.**

There you have it. We have given the act an immutable definition regardless of the media to which it pertains.

Observe there are three important components to this definition: a character, an action he is undertaking, and a goal he is trying to accomplish by undertaking said action. These are all concrete concepts. We have broken the act into something easily identifiable. Within an act, a *character* has a *goal* and takes *action* to achieve it.

Now, I'm sure the naysayers among you are saying nay[12]. You're furrowing your brows and saying to yourselves, "Well if that's the case, isn't the whole story just one long act?! After all, the character has a goal he's trying to accomplish throughout the story, and the story ends when he achieves it!" Or something similar.

Yes, there was once a story written using the structure you've described. I

---

[12] I don't fault you for this. It's simply your lot in life.

believe it was titled *The Novel No One Finished Reading*. You've probably never read it in its entirety.

Instead, as we will see next, the characters of successful modern stories continuously alter their goals and take new actions to achieve them as they acquire new information and learn new skills throughout their stories. This process of having a goal, taking action, learning new things and altering the goal can accurately be termed…

The Evolving Goal

Every story has a primary plot goal the character must accomplish before the story can be resolved. Since this goal is so important, let us call it **The Ultimate Goal** of the story. In the James Cameron film *Avatar,* the Ultimate Goal for Jake Sully is to save the Na'vi from being annihilated by those pesky humans. In *Finding Nemo*, Marlin the clownfish must go on a quest to, um, find Nemo. But neither of these characters begin the story with these specific goals. When these stories begin, Jake just wants to earn some money filling in for his dead brother to get his legs fixed, and Marlin wants to prevent Nemo from being eaten by a barracuda or having any friends.

Now think of your favorite film or novel. Who is the main character and what are they trying to accomplish when the story begins? Now, skip ahead to the end. What is the character trying to accomplish in the big dramatic climax? Is it the same thing?

We can see this evolution of goals in an appearingly simplistic, yet surprisingly complex example: the quintessential, 1980s action film *Die Hard*. In the film, Bruce Willis stars as hard-nosed, New York City cop, John McClane. I think we can all agree John McClane (and by extension, Bruce Willis) is a badass. But his first goal in *Die Hard* is to travel to LA and recapture the affection of his estranged wife, Holly. If that were the extent of the plot then the movie would have been called *Love Hard*, opened on Valentine's Day and would never have spawned a franchise of sequels and countless knockoffs[13]. But John's first Act ends when terrorists take over the building and he receives a new goal to act

---

[13] *Speed* (It's *Die Hard* on a bus!), *Speed 2* (It's Die Hard on a boat!) *White House Down* (It's *Die Hard* in the White House with *Die Hard* references!)

upon. His new goal isn't to take down the terrorists either if that's what you were thinking. No, John's new goal is to call the police. How heroic.

This illustrates how the character begins with a goal (get my wife back), takes actions to achieve it (fly from NY to LA to see her), fails (they have an argument. Way to go, John), gets new information (terrorists are taking over the building) and receives a new or altered goal (alert the authorities). In the subsequent acts, the character's goal continues to evolve as his new course of action fails (the cops think John is a prank caller), is met with resistance (the terrorists thwart John's attempt to use the fire alarm), and he acquires new information (they're executing people to steal bearer bonds). Because of this process, the character must continuously alter his goal and the course of action he takes to achieve it. This process of having a goal, taking action, learning new things and altering the goal is the essence of the **Evolving Goal**.

Each act culminates in the character receiving one final revelation or piece of information that creates an Act Turning Point. These **Turning Points** are decisive moments in the story. That is, at these events the character *makes a decision* to alter his goal and pursue an updated course of action.

It's important to realize that, despite their name, the Act Turning Points are not single points in time, but a scene or series of scenes culminating in the character receiving his new or altered goal. Though often not stated outright, a clearly defined objective is established at the end of each act which the character will attempt to achieve over the course of the next act.

So the flow of the story goes like this:
Act One - A character has an initial goal, takes action, fails or gets new information, reaches a Turning Point and alters his goal.
Act Two - The character devises a new course of action to achieve his altered goal, fails or gets new information, reaches a Turning Point and alters his goal.
Act Such and Such - Rinse. Repeat

But the evolving goals the character pursues throughout the story are not unrelated. All of his Evolving Goals are connected to the Ultimate Goal and drive him toward its realization. In other words, he must *earn* his understanding of the Ultimate Goal's significance by incrementally advancing toward it. In *Avatar*, Jake doesn't arrive on Pandora and set about the task of saving the Na'vi and their preternaturally beautiful, CGI planet from humanity. He could give two expletives about those dirty blue monkeys in their giant treehouses. He only earns his respect for their way of life by pursuing his ever Evolving Goal (fill in for your dead brother, provide intel for the Colonel, learn the ways of the Na'vi, have sex with a Na'vi, etc.). This process, if orchestrated correctly, creates a sense of propulsion that rockets the character, and the audience, through the plot.

So, throughout the story the character's goal is a fluid thing, growing alongside his perceptions of his world as he gathers new information and learns new skills. At the end of each act, the character reaches a Turning Point and receives a new or altered goal. To achieve this new goal, he must perform the action of the subsequent act. This is the Evolving Goal.

Now, you may be asking yourself, couldn't this process just go on forever? Thank you for asking yourself. That astute question brings up the most important aspect of this entire process. For whatever reasons, most successful modern novels and films adhere to the same pattern of actions I like to call…

The Six Acts

A chorus of gasps erupts from the audience.

"Six acts?" exclaims a woman adjusting her monocle. "Heresy!"

"Blasphemy!" agrees a gentleman in a top hat, stroking his handlebar mustache. "There can only be three! Fetch the ropes and the pitchforks and the torches!"

Now let's all calm down, folks. I can assure the skeptics among you the structural layout set forth in this book isn't some arbitrary invention of the author, but a careful extrapolation of structure from an assortment of critically and commercially successful modern stories.

"Three Acts! Three Acts! Three Acts!" responds the lynch mob.

I am in no way questioning the validity of three-act structure. The problem is that, much like a palm reading or daily horoscope, three-act structure is so vague as to almost always be applicable. Of course, every story has a beginning, middle and an end. The pattern of setup, confrontation, and resolution delineated in three act structure can be applied to just about every action every human being has ever undertaken. Ever. Allow me to present a short story to demonstrate.

I woke up in the middle of the night and had to pee (the setup). I got out of my warm, comfy bed to go the bathroom (the conflict). I used the bathroom and went back to sleep (the resolution).

This rather simplistic example illustrates how although three act structure may lie at the foundation of every story, it is far from enough to make a story interesting. Everything we do involves a "setup" of motivation (I'm tired of sitting down). The very act of taking action involves "conflict" (I will defy the force of gravity and stand). And once we have completed the action, the situation is resolved (look ma', I'm standing). So yes, three act structure is a logical derivative of life itself[14], but its shortcoming lies in its inherent vagueness.

Granted, three act structure in stories occurs on a much larger scale, but it remains a gross oversimplification of a complex subject. This can mainly be attributed to a longstanding and arbitrary definition of the act itself. But by thinking of an act as the undertaking of action to achieve a goal, we can see the traditional three acts are not technically acts at all, but **Dramatic Phases** through which the story progresses. While the Dramatic Phases of Setup, Confrontation and Resolution provide the dramatic context of the portion of the story they pertain to, they are narrator focused ideas with no direct impact on the undertakings of the character himself. Instead, in the overwhelming majority of modern stories, the character progresses through six, specific actions that directly influence his, well, actions. These six actions thus divide the story into six acts.

Why six acts, you ask? I have no idea. I didn't invent this structure after all. But, these six, universal actions are the underlying force that drives both the actions of the character and the events of the story unfolding around him.

While this whole Act vs. Dramatic Phase brouhaha may seem like a simple matter of semantics, this small shift in perception can have a profound effect on one's understanding of the way stories are structured. It takes the focus off of actions undertaken by the *storyteller* and instead places it on the actions undertaken by the *character*. This reduces instances of characters doing

---

[14] Which is probably why Aristotle was all like, "Aw snap, there's a pattern here!"

improbable things to accommodate the plot and allows the events of the story to emerge as a logical response to the events unfolding around them.

So without further ado, the Six Acts inherent to modern story are (drumroll please)…

- Act One: Dealing with an Imperfect Situation
- Act Two: Learning the Rules of an Unfamiliar Situation
- Act Three: Stumbling into the Central Conflict
- Act Four: Implementing a Doomed Plan
- Act Five: Trying a Long Shot
- Act Six: Living in a New Situation

Notice all these acts are indeed *actions* (learning, stumbling, etc.). The character undertakes the action of each act in pursuit of a goal. At the end of the act his goal evolves and he must undertake the action of the next act to achieve it.

We can witness a quick glimpse of one of these acts in action by going back to our *Die Hard* example. Observe in Act One the action is *Dealing with an Imperfect Situation*. In the first act of *Die Hard*, John's goal is to reconcile with his estranged wife, Holly. This in itself is quite the opposite of a perfect situation. To complicate things further, Holly now lives on the other side of the country in Los Angeles while John, who fears flying, still lives in New York. How conveniently imperfect. After narrowly surviving a flight to LA, he visits her place of employment and attempts to reconnect with her. It soon becomes clear whatever issues drove them to separate are still unresolved. How can we tell? They argue. All John's actions in the first act are born from his attempts to deal with and improve his Imperfect Situation. It isn't until terrorists take over the building that John receives a new goal to act upon.

Looking at this example we can also see that, though the universal action of Act One is *Living in an Imperfect Situation*, John undertakes specific actions unique to the story of *Die Hard*. He flies out to the coast, hoping to get together with his wife and have a few laughs. He befriends his limo driver and visits the Nakatomi tower. These unique story actions can be called **Story-Specific Actions**. These Story-Specific Actions are (hopefully) what separate one story from every other story ever told.

Unlike in the three-act paradigm, the Story-Specific Actions unique to an individual narrative are *directly influenced* by whichever of the Six Acts they fall under. For instance, John deals with an Imperfect Situation by flying three thousand miles to argue with his estranged wife. The Story-Specific Actions he undertakes in Act One are directly influenced by the Act in which he is. While John's trip to LA does "set up" the initial situation of the story, the dramatic context of The Setup has no immediate influence on John's actions. Instead, it is John's desire to improve his Imperfect Situation that leads him to travel to LA and visit the Nakatomi plaza with a carnival prize teddy bear. In doing so, his actions *set up* the story. Not vice versa.

So the Six Acts function at a level beneath the context provided by the three Dramatic Phases. Conveniently enough, each of the Dramatic Phases is comprised of two acts.

Dramatic Phase One: Set Up

- Act One: Dealing with an Imperfect Situation
- Act Two: Learning the Rules of an Unfamiliar Situation

Dramatic Phase Two: Confrontation

- Act Three: Stumbling into the Central Conflict
- Act Four: Implementing a Doomed Plan

Dramatic Phase Three: Resolution

- Act Five: Trying a Long Shot
- Act Six: Living in an Improved Situation

"Aha!" exclaims a man with bushy muttonchops and an ornate pocket watch chained to his three-piece houndstooth suit. "So this is all just three-act structure spiffied up in decorative knickerbockers and fanciful plimsolls! Fetch the ropes and the pitchforks and the torches!"

I don't want you to think the focus of this analysis is creating radical terminology for existing concepts. All labels in this book exist to reduce ambiguities and enhance the clarity of the concept being addressed. If you prefer to call the traditional Dramatic Phases "acts" and would rather refer to the six acts delineated in this book as segments, or sequences or flubberwumples, then by all means do. So long as by the end of this analysis you understand their validity, purpose, and function within story structure, I will have succeeded in my objective.

And while the above breakdown may make the Dramatic Phases appear to be of remarkable import to structuring stories, for the purpose of this analysis they are superfluous. This is because the actions inherent to each of the Six Acts lend themselves to the context of their respective Dramatic Phases. Learning the Rules of an Unfamiliar Situation naturally denotes an element of "Setting Up" the story, just as Stumbling into the Central Conflict has an inherent implication of "Confrontation", or Living in a New Situation is an intrinsic part of "Resolution". I have included the Dramatic Phases solely for those three-act-structure enthusiasts who would like to use it as a frame of reference, and because it is indeed valid. If you are one of those proponents of the three-acts who feel its abandonment is a blasphemous proposition, feel free to view this paradigm as a structural layer existing beneath them.

Having said that, we will effectively cast aside the context provided by the Dramatic Phases from this point forward. I would, however, like to point out the character's aforementioned Evolving Goal has six stages which correspond to his progression through the Six Acts. As he undertakes the action of each Act, he acquires new information that leads him to alter his goal, and his pursuit of this new goal brings him into the subsequent action of the next Act. The six stages of the character's Evolving Goal that correspond to the Six Acts are…

Act One: Dealing with an Imperfect Situation

- Goal One: The Initial Goal

Act Two: Learning the Rules of an Unfamiliar Situation

- Goal Two: The Transitional Goal

Act Three: Stumbling into the Central Conflict

- Goal Three: The False Goal

Act Four: Implementing a Doomed Plan

- Goal Four: The Penultimate Goal

Act Five: Trying a Long Shot

- Goal Five: The Ultimate Goal

Act Six: Living in a New Situation

- Goal Six: Success/Failure

We will, of course, discuss this in greater detail when we analyze each of the Six Acts individually. The key takeaway at this point is that, though the character will take *Story-Specific Actions* toward a unique *Ultimate Goal*, these actions are directly influenced by whichever of the *Six Acts* they fall under. By aligning the character's Story-Specific Actions with these Six Acts, we can create a cohesive narrative which progresses with logic and momentum.

Now, at last, let us examine each of the Six Acts, step by step, to discern the purpose they serve and how they have been used in some of the highest grossing, and critically acclaimed stories of the last few decades.

ACT ONE: DEALING WITH AN IMPERFECT SITUATION

"It just isn't fair. Oh, Biggs is right, I'm never gonna get out of here."
Luke Skywalker ~ Star Wars, Act One

Approximate Runtime: 20% of the story

Life isn't fair, Luke. And in the first act, we witness the character receiving a crash course in this axiom. When the story begins we quickly come to realize the character's initial situation, in some or many ways, totally blows.

In Act One, the character is shown to be at conflict with the world around him. Try as he might, he seems to be swimming against the proverbial current. This conflict between the character and his world is created by the **Initial Desire** he has at the beginning of the story.

Deep within himself, the character wants something more than anything else in the world. This thing he so desperately craves is often an abstraction, such as *freedom* for Katniss Everdeen or *family* for Harry Potter. The desire may also be motivated by a tangible goal, like John McClane's desire to reconcile with his wife, or Luke's desire to go away to the academy.

Unfortunately for our character, his Initial Desire goes against the desires of those in control of his life. In *Star Wars*, Luke yearns to leave Tatooine and go away to the Imperial Academy, but his uncle needs him to stay and farm moisture. In *Titanic*, Rose craves to break off her engagement to Cal and choose her own path, but her mother needs her to marry the walking enema so she and Rose can continue sipping complimentary mimosas in first class. While the things these characters desire seem logical and warranted to them (and in turn the audience), their desires appear juvenile or unrealistic in the eyes of the powers that be.

It has often been said that conflict is the essence of story. And though this age-old idiom is accurate, it fails to acknowledge that *change* is the wellspring from which a story's conflicts arise. If you'll forgive me the cliché, there are only two types of stories in the world: one in which a character desires to change his initial situation or one in which a character desires not to change his initial situation. Therefore, *conflict created by a desire for change* is the essence of story. The conflicts the character faces are born from his Initial Desire for, or against, changing his initial situation.

If the character desires to change his situation, then he will face opposition in doing so. In Suzanne Collins' *The Hunger Games*, Katniss wants nothing more than to change her poverty-stricken, mud-crusted, medieval life. But her *desire for change* is opposed on all sides by a hedonistic, technologically advanced government. The conflicts Katniss experiences arise from the powerful forces standing between her and change. Notable examples of characters who desire *for change* include Dorothy Gale in *The Wizard of Oz*, Bruce Wayne in *Batman Begins*, Josh Baskin in *Big*, and Peter Parker in *Spider-Man*.

Conversely, if the character desires *not to change*, he will face conflicts with those who desire he should. In *Iron Man*, Tony Stark is contented to go about his awesome life as a jet-setting weapons manufacturer. He desires nothing more than to remain an uninhibited, playboy, genius, which would be fine if everyone around him didn't need him to be a responsible, team-playing, genius. Although things in his life appear perfect to Tony (and perhaps to those of us of the 99%), we can see how Tony's behavior is negatively affecting the people closest to him. The conflicts Tony encounters are born from his *desire to remain unchanged* in the face of those who desire he would. Other famous examples of characters who desire *against change* are Ebenezer Scrooge in *A Christmas Carol*, Marlin in *Finding Nemo*, Woody in *Toy Story* and Frodo Baggins in *The Fellowship of the Ring*.

The Initial Desire for or against changing his situation is the emotional fuel which propels the character through the story. In stories where the character desires change, it is this desire which leads him to abandon his initial situation in search of something greater. Throughout the story, he will frequently draw on his desire to change his situation as inspiration to carry on in the face of adversity. In stories where the character desires not to change his situation, this process is subverted. Over the course of the story, his desire to remain unchanged is slowly eroded as he discovers the importance of changing himself to improve his situation. As the story nears its conclusion, he must draw on this discovery and alter his desire from remaining the same to changing some part of himself (or face the consequences).

The character's Initial Desire and the subsequent opposition he faces in its pursuit combine to create **The Imperfect Situation** he lives in at the beginning of the story. This Imperfect Situation is the heart of the first Act. Everything that happens to the character reflects a deeply ingrained and long-standing sense of imperfection in the world at large. But our character isn't some useless schlub, wallowing in all the tyranny and inequities the powers that be have dumped upon him. Instead, he is an active participant in the conflict of desires created by his Imperfect Situation.

In many cases, the character's Imperfect Situation is a result of his failure to see his own imperfections. In the beginning of *Iron Man*, Tony Stark is willfully obtuse to the negative effects his actions have on the world. He's just being awesome, making a ton of money and helping protect America. But the conflicts he has with those around him arise from the fact he *actually does* need to be more responsible. He is simultaneously an active creator and unjust recipient of his initial conflict.

Contrariwise, the Imperfect Situation may be caused by outside forces of opposition attempting to crush the character's spirit. In *Harry Potter and the*

Philosopher's Stone, Harry tries his best to avoid incurring the wrath of the Dursleys. They are, of course, abusive to him nonetheless, but Harry doesn't stoop his shoulders or sulk at his mistreatment. He stands up for himself when the situation warrants and still manages to achieve the occasional, small success against their tyranny. Though this often results in further punishment, Harry takes an active role in the initial conflict of desires. He may be on the receiving end more oft than not, but his (mostly inadvertent) actions contribute to the injustice he faces. He is actively Dealing with his Imperfect situation.

Significance of *Dealing with an Imperfect Situation*

One of the principal purposes of witnessing the character undertaking this action is it gives the audience the opportunity to *empathize* with him. That is to say, in this act the character must demonstrate his **Likability/Empathy Factors** to the audience. Likability in this sense doesn't mean a "nice person", rather a genuinely interesting character whom we'd *like* to follow through the story. He needn't be a perfect, square-jawed, Dudley-Do-Right who rescues kittens from burning buildings whilst distributing candy to orphaned children, but he should have some degree of relatability. The audience should feel compelled to slip into the character's shoes, losing a portion of their own consciousness to an active engagement in his situation. We must be encouraged to feel what he is feeling. Even if he's unscrupulous, he should be interesting enough to engage us in his plight. We must like him, love to hate him, or at the very least sympathize with him.

Perhaps he is a rich, incorrigible scoundrel such as the aforementioned Tony Stark (you cheeky bastard), or a poor, world-weary teen who must provide for her starving family, such as Katniss Everdeen (you poor dear). The point is, if the audience is expected to go on the story's journey with the character, then there must be some emotional connection established between the audience and the character during the first act. By watching the character struggle against the opposition to his Initial Desire, we can more readily identify with him as someone we'd like to see succeed.

One method of creating audience empathy is by saddling the character with **Undeserved Misfortune**. This concept, dating back to Aristotle, sees a character who is shown to be decent or moral, repeatedly pimp-slapped by the hand of fate. The initial plight of Katniss Everdeen in *The Hunger Games* is an excellent example. After the unexpected death of her father in a coal mining explosion, and the resulting psychological implosion of her mother, the then eleven-year-old Katniss is forced to become the sole provider for her family. This is exacerbated by the fact they live in the poorest region of the poorest District in the country, where food is difficult to come by. Katniss has done nothing to deserve the hardships she faces. The fact her harsh upbringing has turned this resilient, resourceful girl into a cynic unwilling to trust anyone only amplifies the audience's desire to see her succeed.

In addition to allowing the audience to bond with the character, watching him *Dealing with His Imperfect Situation* affords us the opportunity to learn what kind of person he is, both personally and professionally. We get a sense of the things he stands for, his ideals and values as well as his age, profession, physical characteristics and personality.

But the character's personal problems are just the tip of the iceberg. In addition to the conflicts he has with those standing between him and his Initial Desire, the world he lives in has greater conflicts of its own. Another function of the first act is to prepare the audience for the coming events in the story. While we are first introduced to the character dealing with his personal conflicts, we also learn the overall situation of the world he inhabits is just as, or even more imperfect than his own.

This deep, underlying conflict can be seen in both modern and classic stories. In *Star Wars* Luke's personal conflict is with his uncle. But we first discover the entire galaxy is caught in a war between a powerful Empire and a small group of Rebels who purloin data tapes with all the finesse of a teenager swiping a bottle from their old man's liquor cabinet.

Going back further to *Romeo and Juliet*[15], our eponymous hero, Romeo, is initially depressed about his unrequited infatuation for some chick named Rosaline. As it turns out, his little puppy love is small potatoes. He lives in a world so conflicted the story proper begins with a brawl between the servants of Montague and Capulet. These two families dislike each other so much even their maids and butlers are sworn enemies willing to fight to the death.

Because the character's personal conflicts and the external conflicts of the world at large are in full swing before the story begins, let us label the lot of them the **Preexisting Conflict**. All of these conflicts combine to create imperfection of the character's initial situation. But don't feel bad for the guy. If you recall from about thirty seconds ago, the *conflict created by a desire for change* is the essence of story. The more imperfect his situation, the more likely our audience is to root for him to change both his initial situation and the storyworld at large.

But if an act is the process of a character taking *action* to achieve a *goal*, then Dealing with an Imperfect Situation is only the first half of the equation. To have a complete act, the character must also have a goal he is trying to accomplish by Dealing with his Imperfect Situation in the first place. Let us next examine the functions and characteristics of the character's first act goal.

---

[15] I know, I know, I said modern stories, but who isn't familiar with Romeo and Juliet? Cue crickets.

Goal One: The Initial Goal

From the moment the story opens, our character should have a goal he is actively pursuing. After all, he isn't some cardboard cutout who only exists while the book is open or the movie is playing. He should feel like a real person who has a life before the story begins and, unless he dies at the end, a life that continues after the story's conclusion. The story simply begins at a critical juncture his life.

The character's first act goal can accurately be called **The Initial Goal**. The Initial Goal differs from the Initial Desire in that the character's Initial Desire is something he really wants, whether or not he is attempting to get it, while the Initial Goal is something he is actively pursuing.

More often than not, the character's Initial Desire seems so unattainable that his Initial Goal is his only resort. In *The Hunger Games*, Katniss' Initial Desire is for freedom from poverty, but her Initial Goal is to survive her life as a dirt-crusted, mud-farming peasant by hunting squirrels to feed her family. Due to its seemingly unattainable nature, she isn't actively pursuing her Initial Desire for freedom. She's just trying to survive.

Sometimes, however, the character's Initial Goal aligns with his Initial Desire. To return to *Die Hard*, John's Initial Desire at the start of the film is to reconcile with his wife. This is also his Initial Goal. He is taking active steps to achieve his Initial Desire. Good for you, John.

The Initial Goal the character has is another excellent means to imbue him with characterization. The same way you can learn much about a person by the actions they undertake, you can also learn a great deal about them by the things they are trying to accomplish with these actions. In *Die Hard*, John's Initial Goal is to convince his wife to come home to New York. This goal tells us several things about him; the most obvious being he's married. We can also tell he loves his wife, seeing as how he's traveled across the country to see her, but the fact they're separated in the first place implies he hasn't been too great a husband to begin with. The Initial Goal John is trying to accomplish provides the audience with information about his character.

This same demonstration of characterization can be said about the Initial Goal of Dr. Ryan Stone in *Gravity*. In the film, Stone simply wants to fix the thingamabob on the Hubble telescope and return to Earth. We see that while she is inexperienced on space walks (and in space in general), she's determined, focused and knows a great deal from a technical standpoint. Not to mention she even went to space in the first place. I myself am far too claustrophobic.

I feel inclined to reiterate *the Initial Goal is not the Ultimate Goal of the story*. Yes, the character is already doing something to achieve an end, but it isn't the goal he must achieve before the story ends. Keanu Reeves doesn't start the film trying to stop the bus. Shrek doesn't begin the film trying to win Fiona's love. Carraway doesn't arrive in West Egg with a Gatsby fetish. In most cases, the character won't even begin to pursue the Ultimate Goal until near the end of the story (which we'll get to soon enough).

So if the character's Initial Goal isn't the Ultimate Goal, then what is he trying to accomplish when the story begins? As it turns out, there are only two types of Initial Goals: a Normal Routine Goal or a Fish out of Water Goal. The type of Initial Goal the character has depends on at what point in the character's life the story begins.

The Normal Routine Goal

As the name suggests, a character who begins a story with a **Normal Routine Goal** is simply going about his typical, daily routine. In these stories, the Initial Goal exists to demonstrate to the audience what the character's day-to-day life is like. This provides a point of contrast when the character steps out of his initial situation into the primary events of the story.

But routine doesn't necessarily mean boring. His day-to-day life may involve facing death, such as Keanu Reeves' Jack Traven in *Speed*, who's a SWAT officer pursuing an elevator bomber. Or it may involve high-stakes situations, like Dom Cobb and Arthur No-Last-Name in *Inception*, who are attempting to perform an extraction of information from the dream of Tony-Starkish, businessman, Mr. Saito. While these films begin with elaborate action sequences and (what would appear to be) life-or-death stakes, it's all just another day at the office for these characters.

The Normal Routine Goal may also be something a bit more subdued. In George RR Martin's *A Game of Thrones*, Lord Eddard Stark's Initial Goal is simply to be the Lord of Winterfell. Sure, he beheads a guy for desertion, but this is all part of his regular comings and goings. He even brings his seven-year-old son along to watch, seeing as how he'll probably have to do it himself one day. In this world, it's never too early to learn how to lop off a guy's head. Routine, yes, but certainly not boring.

In still other stories, the Normal Routine may be intentionally boring, something as mundane as waking up and going to work (think Lester Burnham in *American Beauty* or Wall·E in, um, whatever the name of that movie was). In fact, *The Lego Movie* has the most exaggerated example of the Normal Routine you're likely to find. Emmet Brickowski wakes up, hops out of bed and literally follows a set of instructions delineating his Initial Goal to fit in, have everybody like him and always be happy[16]. His normal routine plays out comically to establish who he is.

The Fish out of Water Goal

Conversely, we have the **Fish out of Water Goal**. A character with this type of Initial Goal has already had his normal routine interrupted prior to the start of the story. Due to some backstory event, the character was either compelled or forced into doing something far outside his comfort zone. These types of stories begin with the character struggling to adjust to a new and unfamiliar environment.

Die Hard begins with New York City cop John McClane arriving by plane in Los Angeles to reconcile with his wife. He's a long way from New York, and he's not doing his job. His place of residence and his occupation are important components of John's character. In fact, his unwillingness to leave his job in New York is what caused the problems in his marriage in the first place. By beginning the story in LA, John is established to be a fish out of idiomatic water.

Or it may be the character is performing his normal routine in an environment to which he is unaccustomed. In *Gravity*, Dr. Ryan Stone is attempting to fix a piece of equipment with which she is intimately familiar. The only problem is now she must do it... IN SPACE! SPACE! SPACE! SPACE!

It's important to note the fish out of water aspect I am referring to only relates to the character's *Initial Goal*. Many stories have an Ultimate Goal built around the fish out of water concept; the fact the character is so far out of his element is the central premise of the story. But the characters in these stories

---

[16] Brush your teeth, Comb your hair, Don't forget to wear pants: The BCD's of success.

never start out in these situations. These stories begin with the character's normal routine to provide a sense of juxtaposition for the audience when he finally flops out of his bowl into a strange new world.

We can find a good example of this in the 1984 film *Beverly Hills Cop* (what can I say, I'm from the 80s), a Normal Routine Initial Goal story with a similar character situation as *Die Hard*; a hard-nosed, inner city cop finds himself in the decadent world of Los Angeles (County at least). The difference is the entire premise of *Beverly Hills Cop* revolves around a fish out water scenario. It's even in the logline of the original film poster (*Eddie Murphy is a Detroit cop on vacation in Beverly Hills*). But what is Axel Foley doing at the beginning of the movie? He's in his normal element. He goes about his normal routine as a detective in Detroit, engaging in unauthorized sting operations and unintentionally destroying the city in pursuit of criminals. Apparently, that's just what he does. In *Die Hard*, however, John McClane begins the story already out of his element. It isn't until the terrorists attack when he finally finds himself doing what comes naturally to him: machine-gunning bad guys in a blood splattered A-shirt.

Opposition to the Initial Goal: Oppressive Opposition

As the Rolling Stones famously said, "You can't always get what you want," and never has this saying been more applicable than in stories. Every stage of the character's evolving goal will inevitably be met with opposition, and as the character progresses closer to the Ultimate Goal of the story, the strength of this opposition increases.

This increasing opposition is the physical manifestation of conflict within the story. As the character moves through each act, the level of opposition intensifies, creating the "rising stakes", "escalating conflict" or whatever you want to call it. But, by focusing on the opposition to the character's goal, rather than just "conflict" in general, we emphasize how the conflict affects the character's pursuit of his goals.

In the first Act, the character faces **Oppressive Opposition**. That is, his pursuit of the Initial Goal is being oppressed by the world around him. He seems to be on the losing team, held back and stymied by the powers that be.

In *The Hunger Games*, Katniss wants to provide food for her starving family. To do so, we learn she must break the law by sneaking outside the (rarely) electrified fence, use an illegal bow, and sell what little game she can kill to the few people who can afford it. The Capitol is oppressive in a literal sense. Not to mention her best friend Gale intentionally scares away a deer that could have fed both of their families for weeks. Way to go, Gale.

In *Iron Man*, Tony Stark's Initial Desire and Initial Goal of being a super awesome, weapons manufacturing, billionaire, playboy, genius is consistently oppressed by the award-ceremony-holding sticks-in-the-mud he calls friends. Why can't they just let him be super awesome? He is so being oppressed.

The Oppressive Opposition may also be of a more figurative nature. In the first Act of *Gravity*, the opposition Dr. Stone experiences comes from simply being in space. While space may not be intentionally thwarting Stone's goal of fixing the thingamabob, it inflicts hardship and constraints, nonetheless. The disorientation caused by weightlessness makes her feel "like a Chihuahua that's being tumble dried", which in turn makes it difficult for her to do her job.

Sadly for our character (but fortunately for the audience), this Oppressive Opposition is the weakest opposition he will encounter during the story. As his goal evolves, the level of opposition he faces will intensify as well. In *Star Wars* the only opposition Luke faces in pursuit of going away to the Academy is his uncle's insistence he stay on the farm for one more season. But by the end of the next act, Luke is being shot at by Imperial stormtroopers in pursuit of his new goal. The initial opposition he faced in Act One is Bantha poodoo[17] in comparison.

---

[17] A Bantha is a furry, elephant-sized, bison-like creature native to the Star Wars universe. Poodoo is, well, exactly what it sounds like.

Turning Point Catalyst: The Disturbance

As I mentioned earlier, each act culminates in the character reaching a Turning Point where he receives a new goal. But before the character arrives at the Turning Point of the act, there is a preceding event that pushes him toward it. These events are **Turning Point Catalysts**.

Roughly halfway through Act One, the doldrums of the character's imperfect existence are thrown off by an unforeseen event. Just when it seems as though he would go on dealing with his Imperfect Situation forever, something unexpected happens to him. This event is the first Turning Point Catalyst, **The Disturbance**.

As the name suggests, the Disturbance is an interruption to the character's established routine. Something happens to him, or he does something, which shakes up the status quote and pushes him off his comfortable couch of inaction toward the Act One Turning Point. The Disturbance is the canary in the coal mine, a portent to the momentous change coming his way, and as such, often carries an inherent sense of foreboding palpable to the audience. It is the first spark of motivation the character, and the audience, feel pushing him toward an opportunity to step out of his regular existence and into something with greater significance.

The Hunger Games opens with an ominous threat looming over our heroine, Katniss Everdeen; she awakens on the morning of the reaping. The reaping, as we soon discover, is the yearly ceremony where one of her District's minors is essentially selected to die. That's quite a disturbance to one's day-to-day life, especially if you're a minor. While the actual Disturbance, the reaping ceremony, doesn't occur until halfway through the first chapter, its presence is felt from the very first paragraph, and when Katniss and her sister finally attend the ceremony we can feel something important is going to happen.

In *Harry Potter and the Philosopher's Stone*, the Disturbance begins with Harry receiving a letter. While this wouldn't be an unusual occurrence for you or me[18], young Harry's day-to-day life is suddenly interrupted because he has never received a letter in his life. His uncle's fearful reaction upon reading it, and his subsequent forbidding of Harry to read it himself, further fuels the mysteriousness of the letter's arrival. And when more and more of the forbidden letters begin to arrive every day, we get a sense there is an important change coming to Harry's life.

These examples illustrate that while the Disturbance carries an innate implication of coming change for the character, it is only half of the equation. Sure, the reaping is a terrible event, but if your name isn't selected your life pretty much goes back to the way it was. Similarly, having a bunch of magical letters explode out of your chimney is an amazing occurrence, but if they all turn out to be from *Publisher's Clearing House* you don't have much of a story on your hands.
Instead, the Disturbance foreshadows and drives the character toward the coming dilemma he will face about his Imperfect Situation.

The point in time at which the Disturbance takes place in the first act can vary greatly from story to story. It may occur shortly into the act, or it may take place closer to the end, immediately preceding the first act Turning Point. Wherever it lies, it is the first domino that falls for the character and pushes him toward the true Turning Point of Act One.

---

[18] At least if you were born before the year 2000.

Turning Point One: The Dilemma

Approximate Start Time: 15%
Approximate Runtime: 5%

As a result of the Disturbance, the character is placed in a position where he is forced to make a definitive, life-changing decision. Here, he is offered a choice between the inaction he has always known, and taking some new, often radical, course of action. This pickle in which the character finds himself is **The Dilemma**.

A dilemma, by definition, is a difficult or perplexing situation requiring a choice between two or more, typically undesirable, alternatives. The Dilemma as it relates to the Act One Turning Point is a difficult, perplexing situation the character must resolve by making a decision about his initial situation. At this Turning Point he is forced to *choose between remaining who he has always been, and accepting a role in a new, unfamiliar situation.*

One of the most famous examples of the Dilemma in the Information Age occurs in the 1999 talking picture, *The Matrix*. At the Disturbance, Neo's day-to-day work routine is disrupted by a surprise phone call from Morpheus and an equally surprising apprehension at the hands of the agents. At the Dilemma, Morpheus and his leather-clad associates lure Neo to an abandoned apartment building with the promise of revealing the secret of the Matrix. There, Morpheus offers Neo two pills[19] and a choice; take the blue pill and go back to your dead-end job and meaningless existence, or take the red pill and join me in the real world where humanity is enslaved

---

[19] Not roofies, I swear.

by robot overlords who ruthlessly track down and kill anyone who's taken the red pill.

This illustrates why the decision the character faces at this Turning Point is such a Dilemma. Both the options he is presented with are often unpleasant (though admittedly, Morpheus does leave out the whole "robot overlord" thing). The difference is, while one option offers no hope whatsoever, the other offers the thinnest sliver of hope to the character and his world.

If Neo takes the blue pill and goes back to sleep, there is no chance he, or anyone else, will ever escape the Matrix. But if he takes the red pill, if he agrees to abandon the imperfect yet familiar, then maybe, just maybe, humanity will be able to overthrow those robot bastards and take back our position as the supreme life form on the planet.

In *The Hunger Games*, Katniss must choose between watching her sister go off to die in the Games, and volunteering to go die in her place. While both of those choices are terrible, Primrose Everdeen wouldn't last ten seconds in the Games. She might even die on the train ride to the Capitol. Katniss, on the other hand, has skills that lend themselves to survival. Her chances are slim, but slim is better than absolutely no-way-in-hell.

Both the options presented at the Dilemma needn't always be terrible, however. In some instances, the character is offered a choice between the terrible, yet familiar, and the hopeful, yet mysterious. In these cases, the character must choose between leaving his Imperfect Situation behind in exchange for a course of action so fantastic as to be incomprehensible.

At the Dilemma in *Harry Potter and the Philosopher's Stone*, Harry gets the bombshell dropped on him that he's a wizard, and is offered the choice between staying with his horrid family, and going off to a hitherto unfathomable school of wizardry. Going off to magic school is obviously the better option for Harry, but there is a tremendous amount of mystery and danger inherent in this course of action.

While there are a few conflicting schools of thought on the subject, the Dilemma is not what is colloquially referred to as the "Inciting Incident". Instead, for the purpose of this analysis, the **Inciting Incident** is the event that *sets the entire story into motion*, far before the character's participation is required, while the Dilemma is what offers *the character the opportunity to participate* in the story already unfolding around him. Because of this, the Inciting Incident often (but not always) occurs before the story begins.

In the *Harry Potter* saga, the entire series revolves around the fact that, as an infant, our eponymous hero not only survived an attack by Lord Voldemort but seemingly destroyed him in the process. Voldemort's attack on Harry is the Inciting Incident of all the events that occur throughout the series. If Harry had simply died that day, Voldemort would have taken over the world as planned, and there would be no Harry Potter books, movies, or theme parks. I'm going to go out on a limb and say nobody wants to read a seven-book series about a dead infant.

Notice the prologue of Harry Potter begins immediately after this pivotal event. The questions of how and why it happened are the subject of much speculation throughout the novels and aren't fully answered until much later in the series. This illustrates how the Inciting Incident is the all-important piece of the puzzle on which the story hinges. If the reasons behind the Inciting Incident aren't disclosed at the beginning of the story, then the lingering questions it poses will loom over all the events of the story.

But the Inciting Incident doesn't always occur before the story starts. In *Titanic*, the Inciting Incident allowing all the events between Jack and Rose to transpire is when Jack wins a ticket for *Titanic* in a(n) (un)lucky hand of poker. This is the pivotal event on which the narrative (star-crossed lovers on a doomed ship) is built. While Rose was going on the voyage regardless, if

Jack wouldn't have won that ticket, she would have either gone through with her suicide attempt or married Cal. Not only that, but her attraction to Jack revolves around the idea he is the kind of guy who could win a ticket in a game of poker and hop on a ship five minutes later with little more than a few sheets of paper and the air in his lungs. The entire narrative, set against the backdrop of a doomed ship, is about Rose's desire and journey to become that kind of person herself.

So to understand the Inciting Incident is to understand what the story is about. To do this, as storytellers, we must be able to see the story for the fabrication it is. We must understand the story we are trying to tell to determine where it truly begins. If we are the gods of the storyworlds we create, then the Inciting Incident is the "Let There be Light" moment of our stories.

On the other hand, the Dilemma is what brings the *character* into the fold. While the Inciting Incident in *Harry Potter* is the death of Voldemort, it isn't until Harry begins receiving letters from Hogwarts when he's at last presented with a choice to change his Imperfect Situation and step into the wizarding world. Hagrid's offer and Harry's acceptance of it are what send him off on an adventure that would forever change Harry's life and Rowling's tax bracket.

The Dilemma Turning Point can be broken into several stages through which the character progresses. Shortly after the Disturbance, the character reaches the **Presentation of the Dilemma**. Here, he is given the pivotal choice to do something important outside his prototypical course of action. The choice may involve something positive (like learning you're a wizard who's been accepted into a prestigious wizarding academy) or something negative (like having your kid sister's name drawn to participate in a televised death match). Whatever it is, the character is offered a choice to do something he has never done.

At the Disturbance, in the reboot of *Star Trek*, the juvenile-delinquent Kirk gets into a bar fight with a group of Starfleet cadets. But when the cadets' commander, Captain Pike, realizes Kirk is the son of a dead, Starfleet hero, he condemns Kirk for his wasted potential and offers him a choice: enlist in Starfleet, or go back to being the only genius-level, repeat offender in the Midwest. At this point, Kirk is put into a Dilemma. He's been called on his bullshit and must make a decision. Do something meaningful with the life his father died to save, or stay in Iowa chasing skirts and bar brawling.

In *Iron Man*, Tony Stark is captured by terrorists in Afghanistan and offered a choice: build them one of his fancy, new Jericho missiles or die. Tony, of course, chooses a third option by plotting his escape, but only because the situation he is placed in is such a textbook Dilemma. It's a difficult situation requiring a choice between two alternatives so undesirable Tony is forced to devise another option altogether.

In *Inception*, after Dom and Arthur's failed attempt to rob Mr. Saito at the Disturbance, their would-be mark corners them on the roof as they prepare to flee whatever country they're hiding in. But instead of exacting vengeance for their assault on him, Saito offers them a proposition: if they can perform a supposedly impossible inception, not only will he pay them handsomely, he will also fix the legal problems barring Dom from reentering the United States and seeing his kids. Dom is put in a position where he must choose between never seeing his kids (his usual course of action), or entering a new situation by agreeing to do the impossible.

The reason the new course of action offered to the character at the Dilemma seems so radical to him is that inherent to his acceptance of it is a **New Role** he must be willing to assume. The New Role is a function or position in which the character has little experience. Because of this, he is unsure whether he will be able to fulfill the New Role's responsibilities. And he is right for his trepidation. The character's quest to become the best version of whatever the New Role entails will become the force that guides his actions. His assumption and mastery of this New Role will come to define who he is, as well as shape the direction of the narrative.

In *Star Wars*, Luke's Dilemma is between staying on Tatooine and going to Alderaan with Obi-Wan and learning the ways of the Force. What New Role is inherent to this new course of action? Why, becoming Obi-Wan's Jedi pupil, of course. If Luke accepts this course of action and abandons his old life, he will also be agreeing to become Obi-Wan's padawan learner. The entire film (as well as the rest of the original trilogy) revolves around Luke learning to master the Force and becoming a Jedi. It is only through Obi-Wan's tutelage that Luke is able to "use the Force" to sink the winning shot and destroy the Death Star at the film's climax.

In *Star Trek*, if Kirk decides to abandon his cow-tipping, beer swigging life in Iowa and take Pike up on his offer to join Starfleet at the Dilemma, what New Role will he be assuming? Why, that of a Starfleet cadet, of course. Although Kirk pursues an evolving physical goal throughout the film, all the obstacles he encounters serve the purpose of teaching him how to be the best Starfleet officer he can be. And by learning how to be a Starfleet officer he is ultimately awarded command of his own ship at the film's conclusion.

Although the character may believe he is ill-suited to the New Role, fate has been grooming him for this moment all his life. He possesses natural talents that lend themselves to the New Role he has been offered. The New Role is the part he was born to play. Like Patrick Stewart playing Professor Xavier, or Patrick Stewart playing Captain Picard.

In *Star Trek*, Captain Pike comments on Kirk's predilection to "leap without looking" as "something Starfleet's lost". Kirk is a perfect, if unorthodox, fit for leadership in Starfleet. In *Star Wars*, Luke is (unwittingly) the son of a Jedi Knight prophesied to save the galaxy. He was literally born to fulfill the New Role Obi-Wan offers him. In the film *Taken*, Liam Neeson proclaims to his daughter's abductors he has nothing to offer but a "particular set of skills" acquired over a long career, which he will use to hunt them down. These characters were born and bred to fulfill the New Role they are offered in a way no one else possibly could.

In many cases, the New Role the character is offered combines harmoniously with his Initial Desire, creating a logical, new goal for him to pursue. In *Star Wars*, Obi-Wan's proposition for Luke to travel with him Alderaan merges seamlessly with Luke's Initial Desire for adventure. In *Titanic*, the innate sense of freedom Jack offers Rose aligns perfectly with her Initial Desire for independence. In *Avatar*, Jake's Initial Desire for something to fight for is seemingly fulfilled by Colonel Quaritch's request for him to spy on the Na'vi for the Company.

Once the New Role is presented to the character, he may make the logical choice to refuse it. This **Refusal of the New Role** is not found in all stories, but it does serve an important purpose. Most of us have a healthy fear of the unknown, and because of this, the character may be reluctant to accept the New Role outright.

Often, he is simply unready or unwilling to accept such a radical course of action. Perhaps he has duties and responsibilities preventing him from accepting it, like Luke's obligations to his uncle. Or perhaps the very concept of the Proposal seems farfetched, like Captain Pike's offer for Kirk to enlist in Starfleet. Whatever the case, the character may demur initially or he may not, depending on his situation and outlook.

Closely related to, and equally as optional as the Refusal of the New Role is the **Interference to the New Role** the character may encounter. This occurs when the resistance to accepting the New Role comes from someone other than the character himself. While the character may be ready to jump all over the New Role offered at the Dilemma, someone around him attempts to block or dissuade him from accepting it. This can be seen in *Harry Potter* when Harry's Uncle Vernon attempts to forbid Harry from attending Hogwarts.

Of course, Harry wants to go, but the powers that be stand in his way. Similarly, in *Inception*, Dom is eager to accept Saito's too-good-to-be-true offer to fix his stateside issues, but the ever rational Arthur attempts to persuade him to walk away.

If the character has no good reason to accept the New Role, he may receive a **Nudge from Fate** which prompts him to reconsider. In these instances, there is an outside occurrence that drives the character to accept the New Role. At the Dilemma in *A Game of Thrones*, King Robert offers Ned the position of Hand of the King. Because Ned feels obligated to remain at Winterfell, he is set to decline the King's offer. But when he and his wife, Catelyn, receive a letter from her sister warning them the Queen had the last Hand of King murdered, Catelyn urges him to take the position to investigate. The hand of fate gives Ned a push toward the New Role.

Finally, the Dilemma Turning Point ends with the character **Accepting the New Role**. Because the Dilemma is a serious situation that only the character can resolve, he must make a conscious decision to act. His decision at the Dilemma is what lifts him out of the life he has always known and sends him off into the main events of the plot.

This is a decision *only the character can make*. This conscious decision by the character is an important step in the Dilemma. He cannot be a bystander in his own story, but must take an active role. Even in the film *Gravity*, with its tightly focused narrative and emphasis on the character's complete lack of control over her situation, there is a pivotal moment when the recently untethered Dr. Stone acknowledges the severity of her situation and *decides* to act. Hyperventilating and spinning off into space, she catches her breath, attempts to contact Houston and gives Kowalski her precise coordinates.

In stories with no Refusal or Interference, the decision to accept the New Role occurs immediately after it is presented. In *Avatar*, Jake Sully accepts Colonel Quaritch's offer to spy on the Na'vi without a second thought. This is before the Colonel even offers to get his legs fixed in exchange for his services. Talk about Oorah!

It's also possible the character initially refused the New Role, but after taking some time to consider it, comes to realize accepting it is his best interest. This is demonstrated both by the young Jim Kirk in *Star Trek* who realizes there's nothing left for him in Iowa, and the young Luke Skywalker in *Star Wars* who realizes there's nothing left for him on Tatooine after his aunt and uncle are flame broiled by the Empire.

There is a sense of importance underlying the decision the character must make at the Dilemma permeating the entire chain of events. Although the New Role itself may seem limited to the character, the audience can feel it carries a greater implication for the storyworld at large. While he may not recognize the magnitude of what the New Role entails at the time it is presented, the new goal he receives is what propels him off into a world he never knew existed. Navigating this new situation in pursuit of his new goal will fundamentally change who he is and, more often than not, the world he lives in.

In *Star Wars*, lovable, borderline pedophile, Old Ben Kenobi asks Luke to accompany him on an intergalactic adventure and rescue a princess. This seemingly innocuous offer sets off a series of events, culminating in the fall of the Galactic Empire.

In *Harry Potter and the Philosopher's Stone*, lovable, borderline pedophile Hagrid pops up at Uncle Vernon's rickety, seaside shack and officially presents Harry with an invitation to attend Hogwarts. The thwarting of Vold..er, He-Who-Must-Not-Be-Named's seven-year plan for total world domination begins at this moment.

With the character's Acceptance of the New Role, there is essentially a cut-off valve from the normal existence he has always known. By accepting the New Role, he is given a new goal that moves him out of his Imperfect Situation in Act One and into a new and Unfamiliar Situation in Act Two.

Act One Summary

So, the central pillars of Act One are: The Imperfect Situation, the Initial Goal, Oppressive Opposition, the Disturbance, the Dilemma, and the New Role. We can, therefore, summarize Act One as…

A character in an Imperfect Situation faces Oppressive Opposition as he pursues an Initial Goal. But when there is a Disturbance to his routine, he faces a Dilemma regarding his situation, and must assume a New Role.

To witness this process, let's examine the actions undertaken by Tony Stark in the first act of *Iron Man*. In Act One, Tony wants to go about his life as a high-rolling, playboy, billionaire, weapons-manufacturing, genius (the Initial Goal). Let's look at the actions he undertakes in pursuit of this goal.

Flashforward excluded, he plays craps in lieu of attending his Apogee Award ceremony (pursuing the Initial Goal) and is scolded by his best/only friend Colonel Rhodes because of it (Oppressive Opposition). Next, he's accosted by a reporter who accuses him of war profiteering (Oppressive Opposition), but skillfully deflects her question and beds her (pursuing the Initial Goal). Shortly thereafter, he's called out for his overall lack of responsibility by his PA Pepper Potts (Oppressive Opposition), shows up three hours late to his private jets departure to a weapons presentation in Afghanistan (pursuing the Initial Goal) and is scolded, yet again, by his BFF Rhodes (Oppressive Opposition). This is hardly the ideal twelve-hour scenario for a high-rolling, playboy, billionaire, weapons-manufacturing, genius. And here I thought money could buy happiness. So, by simply pursuing his Initial Goal of living a carefree lifestyle in the face of outside resistance, Tony Stark is *Dealing with an Imperfect Situation*.

ACTIONS & GOALS

Finally, near the end of this course of action, Tony is kidnapped by terrorists (the Disturbance), told to build them a missile or die (the Dilemma) and chooses to fight back against them by creating a weaponized suit of armor (the New Role). From this moment forward, Tony Stark's life will never be the same.

Observe how we can use the key elements of Act One to succinctly summarize the first act of *Iron Man*.

Billionaire, weapons-manufacturer, Tony Stark, is saddled with ceremonies and responsibilities (the imperfect situation) and is reprimanded by his closest friends and advisors (oppressive opposition) because he would rather chase skirts and be awesome (the initial goal). But when he flies to Afghanistan to present his new missile to the military and is kidnapped by the terrorist organization the Ten Rings (the disturbance), Tony is forced to either build them a missile or formulate a complex escape plan (the dilemma) by building a weaponized suit of armor (the new role).

The first act accounts for, on average, about 20% of the story. This is an approximation based on the first act's length across multiple stories. There is a degree of variation from story to story, especially between media. The length of each act will vary based on the complexity of the story and the media in which it is being told.

Of all the stories analyzed within this book, the first act of *Star Wars* is by far the longest, taking up a staggering 36% of the film. Hell, we don't even meet Luke and hear his heroic theme music until seventeen minutes into the 120-minute film[20]. So the central character of *Star Wars* isn't introduced until we are 14% into the story.

---

[20] Depending on which of the many edits you are watching.

Meanwhile, the shortest first act belongs to *The Hunger Games*, which takes up a mere 8%. This indicates how novels tend to have shorter first acts than films. This is most likely due to the fact novels must grab your attention quickly lest you set them aside, while films already have your derriere firmly planted in a theater seat thanks to a multimillion dollar marketing campaign of trailers, teaser trailers and licensed Happy Meal toys.

Act One Examples

Now, let's examine how the act of Dealing with an Imperfect Situation is orchestrated in our four example stories. It should be noted that with the exception of the Disturbance and the Dilemma, the act elements in these examples aren't listed in chronological order, but are summarizations of how each element occurs throughout the act.

The Hunger Games
2008 Novel
Written by Suzanne Collins

The success of Suzanne Collins' *The Hunger Games* can, in part, be attributed to the clarity and appeal of the **High-Concept** idea at the core of the story. A televised death match between teenagers? Sign me up. That's about the only way I'd watch reality TV. Even so, it is the psychological complexity of the obstacles our heroine, Katniss Everdeen, faces which elevated Collins' story from an appealing concept to a breakthrough, blockbuster series of novels and films.

Due to the hardships she has endured during her childhood, Katniss has become a self-reliant, but cynical introvert. Her introversion isn't due to shyness but is instead a result of her loss of faith in humanity. Katniss' only concern is keeping enough food on the table to prevent her mother and younger sister, Prim, from starving. Competing in the Games ultimately leads Katniss to reevaluate her mistrust of everyone around her and to realize not only is she capable of helping others, but also that there are people in the world who are willing to help her.

<u>Character</u>
Katniss Everdeen

<u>Ultimate Goal</u>
Win the Hunger Games with Peeta

Total Runtime: 27 chapters

The Hunger Games - Act One: Dealing with an Imperfect Situation

A character in an Imperfect Situation faces Oppressive Opposition as he pursues an Initial Goal. But when there is a Disturbance to his routine, he faces a Dilemma regarding his situation and must assume a New Role.

Katniss Everdeen, an impoverished teen in the poorest region of the country (the imperfect situation), must defy the laws of the Capitol (oppressive opposition) to provide food for her mother and little sister, Prim (initial goal). But when the government holds the reaping (the disturbance), and Prim's name is selected as the tribute for District 12 (the dilemma), Katniss volunteers to take her sister's place in the Hunger Games (the new role).

Runtime: Chapter 1 through Chapter 2 (2 Chapters)
Run Percentage: 2 of 27 Chapters (7.4%)

The Inciting Incident - Something happens, often before the story begins, which if it does not occur would prevent the story as it exists from coming to be.

Decades before the novel begins, the eleven Districts of Panem rebelled against the Capitol. This uprising prompted the government to institute the Hunger Games, an annual event to keep the Districts subjugated, in which two children from each District must compete in a fight to the death for the title of champion.

The Imperfect Situation - The character begins the story in a less than ideal situation he would like to change but seemingly cannot.

We learn in the first chapter Katniss is a poor, mud-crusted peasant. Her family and most other residents of her District live on the brink of starvation. We also learn she has a sweet, innocent kid sister, upon whom she seems to have imparted none of her survival skills.

The Initial Desire - Deep within himself, the character wants one particular thing more than anything else in the world.

Katniss wishes her family were free from poverty, and the world wasn't so damn terrible.

Initial Desire Type - The character's Initial Desire is either for or against changing his situation.

For Change: Katniss wishes she could change her penurious predicament.

Preexisting Conflict - When the story, begins the character is already dealing with personal conflicts as well as the conflicts of the world at large.

The Capitol oppresses all the other Districts due to a long-ago uprising. In Katniss' District, beatings by the "peacekeepers" are a common occurrence. The District is enclosed in an electric fence and leaving is punishable by tongue extraction, death or both[21]. Additionally, Katniss is discontented with her mother, who retreated into herself after Katniss' father died in a mining accident.

Likability/Empathy Factors - The character is shown to be someone the audience would like to see succeed or would be willing to follow on the journey of the story.

---

[21] Presumably in that order.

We can easily sympathize with Katniss' resilience in the face of extreme poverty. Though she is only a teenager, she is the main provider for her family. This demonstrates to the audience her tenacity and competence. She is willing to break the law to keep her family from starving and is shown to be proficient with a bow and arrows. She also loves her helpless sister dearly and is devoted to protecting her.

<u>**The Initial Goal**</u> - When the story opens, the character already has a goal he is actively pursuing.

Katniss wants to hunt squirrels and pick berries with her buddy Gale, so their families don't starve.

<u>**Initial Goal Type**</u> - The character's Initial Goal is either a Normal Routine Goal where he is in his regular environment, or a Fish out of Water Goal where he is already in a situation with which he is unfamiliar.

Normal Routine Goal: The story begins with Katniss attempting to go about her normal routine. Even under the looming threat of the reaping, she completes her day-to-day tasks, sneaking outside the fence to hunt chipmunks, and bartering their carcasses in town.

<u>**Oppressive Opposition**</u> - The character's Initial Desire and/or his Initial Goal are being oppressed by the world around him.

Through Katniss' eyes, we discover the citizens of District 12 live under severe oppression from the Capital. Their lives are kept in a medieval stasis and there is scarcely enough food to go around. Deaths from starvation are common. As a result, Katniss must sneak through the fence constructed by the Capital to access the woods, where she can hunt the abundant, yet illegal game contained within. The Capitol will likely execute her if she is caught, but a gal's gotta do what a gal's gotta do.

ACTIONS & GOALS

Turning Point Catalyst: The Disturbance

<u>The Disturbance</u> - An unexpected event with ominous implications occurs, interrupting the character's normal routine. This event pushes the character toward the Dilemma.

Katniss and the rest of District 12 attend the reaping ceremony in the town square, where one of the District's children will be selected to participate in the 74th annual Hunger Games.

Turning Point One: The Dilemma

Start Time: After 1 of 27 Chapters (3.7%)
Runtime: Chapter 2 (1 Chapter)
Run Percentage: 1 of 27 Chapters (3.7%)

<u>Presentation of The Dilemma</u> - The character is placed in a position where he must choose between life as he has known it or taking a new course of action.

Despite her name only being entered once, Katniss' sister, Prim is selected as tribute for District 12[22]. Katniss is initially too shocked to do anything. She must choose between letting her sister go off to die in the Games, and volunteering to die in her place.

<u>The New Role</u> - If the character takes this new course of action, he will assume a New Role in which he is untested.

If Katniss volunteers to take Prim's place, she will become a tribute in the Games.

<u>Refusal/Interference to the New Role (Optional)</u> - The character may be reluctant, unready or unwilling to leave his Imperfect Situation and accept

---

[22] Because, of course.

the New Role. In other cases, the character may want to accept the New Role, but someone else attempts to prevent him from accepting it.

Interference: The unusualness of having another tribute volunteer causes some confusion. There are some minor formalities to run through with the volunteering process.

Accepting The New Role - The character makes the decision to act by accepting the New Role.

After the formalities are done, Katniss officially becomes the volunteer in Prim's place. Congratulations, Katniss. You're going to the Hunger Games!

ACTIONS & GOALS

The Silence of the Lambs
1988 Novel
Written by Thomas Harris

Thomas Harris' exceptional 1988 novel is as suspenseful as it is cerebral. This is most often attributed to Harris' masterful characterization of Dr. Hannibal Lecter. Dr. Lecter is as suave, refined and intelligent as he is deadly. He is, essentially, the James Bond of psychopathic cannibals.

But it is the young Clarice Starling, an FBI cadet with a troubled past, who takes center stage in the story. As a testament to his storytelling skill, Harris uses the good doctor's remarkable psychiatric insight to tease out the source of Clarice's demons and eventually bring her to the full resolution of her emotional and psychological character arc, all while she races to catch a sadistic serial killer before he makes his next kill.

There is much talk of stoicism throughout the novel. A recurring motif in the story is the need for characters to compartmentalize their feelings to focus on the job at hand. Clarice's superior, Jack Crawford's ability to remain focused on the case while facing the imminent death of his wife, embodies this philosophy. This ties in directly to Clarice's need to learn how to separate her previous experiences from her present situation, lest they cloud her judgment.

Character
Clarice Starling

Ultimate Goal
Stop the serial killer Buffalo Bill before he kills again.

Total Runtime: 61 chapters

The Silence of the Lambs - Act One:
Dealing with an Imperfect Situation

A character in an Imperfect Situation faces Oppressive Opposition as he pursues an Initial Goal. But when there is a Disturbance to his routine, he faces a Dilemma regarding his situation and must assume a New Role.

Clarice Starling, an inexperienced female cadet (the imperfect situation) in the misogynistic world of law enforcement (oppressive opposition), is doing her best to graduate from the FBI Academy (the initial goal). But when her mentor, Jack Crawford, asks her to interview Hannibal Lector at an insane asylum (the disturbance), Dr. Lecter instead offers Clarice an opportunity for advancement by giving her information on a cold case (the dilemma) allowing her to work as an official FBI investigator (the new role).

Runtime: Chapter 1 through Chapter 5 (5 Chapters)
Run Percentage: 5 of 61 Chapters (8.2%)

The Inciting Incident - Something happens, often before the story begins, which if it does not occur would prevent the story as it exists from coming to be.

A serial killer dubbed Buffalo Bill has been kidnapping and murdering heavyset women. FBI agent, Jack Crawford, believes imprisoned serial killer, Hannibal Lecter, knows something about the Buffalo Bill case and devises a plan to use trainee, Clarice Starling, to get him to talk.

The Imperfect Situation - The character begins the story in a less than ideal situation he would like to change but seemingly cannot.

Clarice is an attractive young woman living in a man's world. She has no pull in the world she navigates and is often treated as such. She is hyper-cognizant of this fact.

The Initial Desire - Deep within himself, the character wants one particular thing more than anything else in the world.

Clarice wants to graduate the Academy, become an FBI agent and advance her status in the world.

Initial Desire Type - The character's Initial Desire is either for or against changing his situation.

For Change: Clarice often reflects on the hard-luck the Starling's have experienced. Her enrollment in the FBI academy and her desire to succeed arise from her desire to change her initial situation.

Preexisting Conflict - When the story, begins the character is already dealing with personal conflicts as well as the conflicts of the world at large.

Although he is one of the reasons she decided to join the Academy, Jack Crawford seems to have snubbed Clarice up to this point. Buffalo Bill is killing women on a regular basis, and the FBI is catching hell over it. On top of all this, Crawford and Lecter's conflicted past has spilled into the present.

Likability/Empathy Factors - The character is shown to be someone the audience would like to see succeed, or would be willing to follow on the journey of the story.

We meet Clarice as she responds to an impromptu summons by her superior. Her self-deprecating observations of him reveal she has a knack for analyzing people, including herself. Crawford reveals she's in the top quarter of her class, but also that she doesn't ask for favors, proving she is competent enough to elicit special treatment, but resourceful enough not to need it. Later at the asylum, the director of the facility, Dr. Chilton, propositions her. Clarice deftly rebuffs his advances to focus on the task at hand. She is repeatedly shown to be an underdog and driven, giving us ample reason to root for her success.

The Initial Goal - When the story opens, the character already has a goal he is actively pursuing.

Clarice wants to graduate from the FBI academy and become a special agent. Crawford's request for her to interview Dr. Lecter is supplementary to her Initial Goal of graduating.

Initial Goal Type - The character's Initial Goal is either a Normal Routine Goal where he is in his regular environment, or a Fish out of Water Goal where he is already in a situation with which he is unfamiliar.

Fish Out of Water Goal: Clarice is only a cadet in the FBI, but is sent to interview one of the most dangerous serial killers in FBI history. While she isn't sent to interview Lecter until shortly after the story begins, it happens so quickly it seems to set the tone for her Initial Goal.

Oppressive Opposition - The character's Initial Desire and/or his Initial Goal are being oppressed by the world around him.

Clarice has been completely avoided by Jack Crawford up to this point. She is viewed dismissively due to her sex and attractiveness. Because of this, she is subjected to sexual predation by Dr. Chilton, Barney the orderly, Miggs the schizophrenic and the world in general.

Turning Point Catalyst: The Disturbance

The Disturbance - An unexpected event with ominous implications occurs, interrupting the character's normal routine. This event pushes the character toward the Dilemma.

The novel begins with Jack Crawford summoning Clarice away from her training with an urgent message. This is a literal interruption of her life as an FBI trainee. When she arrives at his office, he tells her he has an errand for her: interview Dr. Hannibal Lecter and get him to fill out a questionnaire. Note how Crawford's request for her to meet Lecter doesn't change her overall objectives and therefore doesn't constitute a Turning Point. The possibility exists nothing will come of her interaction with Lecter, and her life will go back to the way it was.

Turning Point One: The Dilemma

Start Time: After 2 of 61 Chapters (3.2%)
Runtime: Chapters 3 through 5 (3 Chapters)
Run Percentage: 3 of 61 Chapters (5%)

Presentation of The Dilemma - The character is placed in a position where he must choose between life as he has known it or taking a new course of action.

When Clarice visits Lecter, he toys with her for a bit then effectively tells her to beat it. As she's leaving, Lecter's next-door neighbor, Miggs, doses Clarice with a fresh batch of baby batter[23]. This offends Dr. Lecter, prompting him to offer Clarice an opportunity for advancement to change her imperfect situation; he gives her the Raspail lead to follow. Clarice must choose between returning to her studies at Quantico, and following the path Lecter has laid before her.

The New Role - If the character takes this new course of action, he will assume a New Role in which he is untested.

If Clarice takes Lecter up on his offer, she will begin working as an official FBI investigator.

Refusal/Interference to the New Role (Optional) - The character may be reluctant, unready or unwilling to leave his Imperfect Situation and accept

---

[23] i.e. semen.

the New Role. In other cases, the character may want to accept the New Role, but someone else attempts to prevent him from accepting it.

Interference: When Clarice asks Crawford if she can follow up on the Raspail lead, he initially tells her no and instructs her to write up her report like a good little cadet.

<u>**Accepting The New Role**</u> - The character makes the decision to take action by accepting the New Role.

Clarice decides she wants to investigate the lead, but must first consult Jack Crawford. He initially denies her, but ultimately gives her the green-light after reading her report on Lecter.

ACTIONS & GOALS

<u>Star Wars</u>
1977 Film
Written and directed by George Lucas

There are few, if any, stories that have had the cultural impact of George Lucas' 1977 magnum opus. With its (at the time) groundbreaking special effects and seamless blending of humor and epic drama, *Star Wars* forever changed the way movies were made.

While Luke Skywalker, with his quest to save the princess from the sinister Empire, is undoubtedly the central character, the film takes on a more *Odd Couple*, buddy movie feel with the introduction of Han Solo in the second act. This can be seen clearly in Lucas' blending of their individual character arcs to tell a single narrative. While Luke does have the rather amorphous arc of not being such a hothead and "using the Force" or whatever, the film's saving grace comes from Han Solo's arc of realizing there are more important causes to fight for than money. When the realization of their two personal journeys intertwine at the climax of the film, it creates a significant emotional impact befitting the feel of the movie and resonating with the audience in a way few other films have managed to accomplish.

<u>Character</u>
Luke Skywalker

<u>Ultimate Goal</u>
Destroy the Death Star and save the princess.

Total Runtime: 120 minutes

Star Wars - Act One: Dealing with an Imperfect Situation

A character in an Imperfect Situation faces Oppressive Opposition as he pursues an Initial Goal. But when there is a Disturbance to his routine, he faces a Dilemma regarding his situation and must assume a New Role.

Luke Skywalker, an adventurous orphan stuck on a desert farm (the imperfect situation) with his mean old aunt and uncle (oppressive opposition), wants to farm moisture for another season then go away to the Imperial Academy (the initial goal). But when Luke finds a message while cleaning a new droid, removes its restraining bolt and allows the droid to escape (the disturbance), he goes after it, meets Obi-Wan Kenobi and is asked to accompany him to Alderaan (the dilemma) and become a Jedi (the new role).

Runtime: 43 minutes
Run Percentage: 43 out of 120 minutes (35.8%)

The Inciting Incident - Something happens, often before the story begins, which if it does not occur would prevent the story as it exists from coming to be.

The Rebels steal the plans for the Death Star from the Empire, prompting Vader's mission to recover them, the interception of Leia's ship and the droid's escape to Tatooine.

The Imperfect Situation - The character begins the story in a less than ideal situation he would like to change but seemingly cannot.

Luke hates living in the middle of nowhere with his aunt and uncle. Meanwhile, the Empire controls the galaxy with an iron fist[24]. They are on the verge of completing a planet-destroying, superweapon that will give them even more power.

The Initial Desire - Deep within himself, the character wants one particular thing more than anything else in the world.

---

[24] Or whatever metal alloy Darth Vader's robotic limbs are constructed of.

Luke wants to run away from Tatooine and join the academy. He wants adventure.

<u>Initial Desire Type</u> - The character's Initial Desire is either for or against changing his situation.

For Change: Luke wishes to escape his life on the farm and go zipping through space.

<u>Preexisting Conflict</u> - When the story begins, the character is already dealing with personal conflicts as well as the conflicts of the world at large.

Luke argues with his uncle over his responsibilities on the farm and when he will finally be able to leave. Meanwhile, the Rebels and the Empire are locked in conflict over the fate of the galaxy. Vader and Princess Leia would seem to share a longstanding disdain for one another.

<u>Likability/Empathy Factors</u> - The character is shown to be someone the audience would like to see succeed, or would be willing to follow on the journey of the story.

We sympathize with the fact Luke is stuck on a farm in the middle of the desert while all his friends have gone off to have adventures. Even his Aunt Beru seems to understand he wasn't born for their nerf herding lifestyle. Also, it's revealed Luke never knew his birth parents, and his aunt and uncle are unwilling to discuss them in any detail.

<u>The Initial Goal</u> - When the story opens, the character already has a goal he is actively pursuing.

Luke wants to farm moisture for one more season then leave his aunt and uncle for good.

Initial Goal Type - The character's Initial Goal is either a Normal Routine Goal where he is in his regular environment, or a Fish out of Water Goal where he is already in a situation with which he is unfamiliar.

Normal Routine Goal: Farming moisture and dreaming of zipping off on space adventures is what Luke does on a daily basis.

Oppressive Opposition - The character's Initial Desire and/or his Initial Goal are being oppressed by the world around him.

Luke's butthead uncle makes him do chores and stuff, rather than letting him hang out with his friends. Later, R2D2 runs away, which will only get Luke in trouble. When Luke goes after him, Sandpeople interrupt his simple task of bringing the runaway droid home.

Turning Point Catalyst: The Disturbance

The Disturbance - An unexpected event with ominous implications occurs, interrupting the character's normal routine. This event pushes the character toward the Dilemma.

Luke finds a portion of Princess Leia's message in R2D2. This prompts him to remove the droid's restraining bolt, allowing R2 to run off in the night.

Turning Point One: The Dilemma

Start Time: 33 of 120 minutes (27.5%)
Runtime: 10 minutes of 120 minutes (8.3%)

Presentation of The Dilemma - The character is placed in a position where he must choose between life as he has known it or taking a new course of action.

ACTIONS & GOALS

After Obi-Wan saves Luke from the Sandpeople, he asks Luke to accompany him to Alderaan to learn the ways of the Force and help the princess. Luke must choose between farming moisture Tatooine or following a crazy old man across the galaxy to learn the Force.

The New Role - If the character takes this new course of action, he will assume a New Role in which he is untested.

If Luke accepts, he will become Obi-Wan's Padawan learner.

Refusal/Interference to the New Role (Optional) - The character may be reluctant, unready or unwilling to leave his Imperfect Situation and accept the New Role. In other cases, the character may want to accept the New Role, but someone else attempts to prevent him from accepting it.

Refusal: Luke declines Obi-Wan's offer due to his responsibilities on his uncle's farm and also because it's batshit crazy.

Nudge From Fate (Optional) - In instances where the character has every reason to decline the New Role, he may receive influence from an outside force that drives him to accept it.

Luke's aunt and uncle are killed by the Empire, leaving him no reason to remain on Tatooine.

Accepting The New Role - The character makes the decision to take action by accepting the New Role.

After Luke discovers his aunt and uncle's charred remains, he decides to take Obi-Wan up on his half-baked offer after all.

Titanic
1997 Film
Written and directed by James Cameron

James Cameron's *Titanic* was a box-office phenomenon. While it might not have had the massive cultural impact of *Star Wars*, it raked in an unprecedented box-office total, becoming the first film ever to reach the billion-dollar mark. The film also lifted Cameron from an above average, action movie director, to a respected, Academy Award-winning big shot.

The plot of *Titanic* is essentially a run-of-the-mill star-crossed love story. In fact, Cameron even pitched it to the studio as "Romeo and Juliet on the *Titanic*". But the film's emotional resonance comes as much from the burgeoning relationship of the fictional Jack and Rose, as from the meticulous historical detail and groundbreaking special effects used to recapture the grandeur of the eponymous ship and its catastrophic demise.

<u>Character</u>
Rose Dawson

<u>Ultimate Goal</u>
Survive the ship and live life on her terms.

Total Runtime: 187 minutes

Titanic - Act One: Dealing with an Imperfect Situation

A character in an Imperfect Situation faces Oppressive Opposition as he pursues an Initial Goal. But when there is a Disturbance to his routine, he faces a Dilemma regarding his situation and must assume a New Role.

ACTIONS & GOALS

Rose Dawson, who is betrothed to a man she despises (the imperfect situation) at his and her mother's insistence (oppressive opposition), struggles to come to terms with the arranged marriage (the initial goal). But when Cal and her mother continually insist on controlling her life, Rose runs to the back of the ship to commit suicide (the disturbance), meets the roguish Jack while contemplating her decision (the dilemma), and decides to befriend him instead of killing herself (the new role).

Runtime: 45 minutes
Run Percentage: 45 out of 187 minutes (24.1%)

The Inciting Incident - Something happens, often before the story begins, which if it does not occur would prevent the story as it exists from coming to be.

Lowly vagabond, Jack, wins a ticket aboard the Titanic in a lucky hand of poker, setting the events of the story into motion.

The Imperfect Situation - The character begins the story in a less than ideal situation he would like to change but seemingly cannot.

Rose is being forced into marriage with a man she dislikes. She is bored with her life and fed up with the stuffy rules governing her existence. If only she had been born poor.

The Initial Desire - Deep within himself, the character wants one particular thing more than anything else in the world.

Rose wants to get out of marrying the boorish Cal and be free to make her own decisions.

Initial Desire Type - The character's Initial Desire is either for or against changing his situation.

For Change: Rose wants to escape the constraints imposed on her by her mother and Cal, and follow her own path.

Preexisting Conflict - When the story begins, the character is already dealing with personal conflicts as well as the conflicts of the world at large.

Rose and Cal have a disagreeable relationship. Rose's mother is forcing her to marry him, and Rose resents her for it. On a grander scale, the rich and the poor are at odds over their different statuses and treatment.

Likability/Empathy Factors - The character is shown to be someone the audience would like to see succeed, or would be willing to follow on the journey of the story.

Rose is shown to be treated unjustly, having no control over her life. She has the foresight to recognize the artistic skill of a then unknown Picasso, while Cal refers to his works as "finger paintings". She isn't impressed with the money Cal flaunts. She's also familiar with Freud and uses his theories to imply the ship's designer, Mr. Ismay, has a tiny pecker. Burn.

The Initial Goal - When the story opens, the character already has a goal he is actively pursuing.

Rose is being forced to marry Cal against her will. She doesn't want to but sees no way out of it.

Initial Goal Type - The character's Initial Goal is either a Normal Routine Goal where he is in his regular environment, or a Fish out of Water Goal where he is already in a situation with which he is unfamiliar.

Normal Routine Goal: Rose has lived her whole life in the first-class section. Upon seeing the Titanic *for the first time, she is unimpressed and remarks it doesn't look any bigger than the Mauretania, implying she's no stranger to luxury cruises. The Titanic is just another ship to her.*

ACTIONS & GOALS

<u>Oppressive Opposition</u> - The character's Initial Desire and/or his Initial Goal are being oppressed by the world around him.

Cal is a douchebag to Rose every chance he gets. He criticizes her taste in art. He orders her food for her and snatches cigarettes out of her mouth. I'm pretty sure if he had a mustache he'd twirl it. Meanwhile, her mother refuses to listen to any of Rose's objections to marrying Cal, insisting he is a "good match" because he's rich.

Turning Point Catalyst: The Disturbance

<u>The Disturbance</u> - An unexpected event with ominous implications occurs, interrupting the character's normal routine. This event pushes the character toward the Dilemma.

Over dinner, Rose has a sudden realization how the rest of her life will play out. This prompts her to run to the back of the ship to commit suicide by jumping overboard.

Turning Point One: The Dilemma

Start Time: 36 of 187 minutes (19.2%)
Runtime: 9 minutes of 187 minutes (4.8%)

<u>Presentation of The Dilemma</u> - The character is placed in a position where he must choose between life as he has known it or taking a new course of action.

Jack shows up and attempts to convince Rose that jumping into the Atlantic Ocean is a horribly stupid idea. She must choose between her terrible life, and heeding the advice of this charming, dirt-poor stranger.

<u>The New Role</u> - If the character takes this new course of action, he will assume a New Role in which he is untested.

If Rose takes Jack up on his offer, she will become friends with a hobo. Eww!

Refusal/Interference to the New Role (Optional) - The character may be reluctant, unready or unwilling to leave his Imperfect Situation and accept the New Role. In other cases, the character may want to accept the New Role, but someone else attempts to prevent him from accepting it.

Rose is initially dismissive of Jack's interference and commands him to leave her be.

Accepting The New Role - The character makes the decision to take action by accepting the New Role.

Jack offers Rose his penniless, lice-ridden hand, and she accepts it.

ACT TWO: LEARNING THE RULES OF AN UNFAMILIAR SITUATION

"Do you think you can explain to me why I'm dressed like this? And what those big words in the sky were all about? And, like, where we are... in time?"
                                    Emmet Brickowski - **The Lego Movie**, *Act Two*

Approximate Start Time: 20% into story
Approximate Runtime: 20% of the story

Though the character's initial situation in Act One was imperfect, at least he understood the way it worked. Coming into Act Two, however, the character finds himself transported to a strange and unfamiliar world. In the immortal words of the Fresh Prince, his life got flipped, turned upside down.

As a result of the unprecedented nature of the New Role he accepted at the Dilemma, the character is extracted from his comfort zone and dropped deep into unfamiliar territory. This great unknown he must navigate is **The Unfamiliar Situation**. No matter how much training he's received, no matter how skilled he thinks he is, no matter how easy he believes it will be, he's still prodigiously ill-equipped for the new situation he has entered.

In some stories, this transition to the Unfamiliar Situation is the focal point of the narrative, with the entire premise built around the character's foray into, and exploration of, a magical new world. This is exemplified by Alice tumbling through the rabbit hole into Wonderland, or the Pevensies stumbling through the wardrobe into Narnia. Both of these tales revolve around the characters' attempts to navigate strange and magical worlds completely unlike their own.

We can find a more contemporary example of this in *Avatar*. In the opening act, Jake arrives on the planet Pandora for the first time. Though the planet is decidedly alien, Jake's initial experience in Act One lends it an almost Earth-like quality. There are paved roads and concrete structures and people going about their daily business. There are crops being grown in orderly, garden rows and avatar drivers shooting hoops.

But while Jake only experiences the human side of life on Pandora from behind the walls of the compound in Act One, in the second act he ventures outside the walls on his first expedition into the Pandoran wilderness. In this new, Unfamiliar Situation we discover the similarities between Earth and Pandora witnessed in the first act were manufactured. The true Pandora is wild and unkempt. The fauna and flora of the Pandoran jungle are unlike anything Jake has ever seen, and we are given the opportunity to experience this strange and incredible planet through his eyes as he explores it.

In other instances, the character may discover an unfamiliar side of his world he never knew existed. Katniss' excursion through the twelve Districts to the mysterious Capitol in *The Hunger Games* or Harry's first foray into the hidden wizarding world of *Harry Potter* are both felicitous examples. In these stories, the characters discover the worlds they live in are actually much larger places than they had been led to believe. The new worlds they stumble into have been right under their noses all along, but it is only by accepting the New Role at the conclusion of Act One that they are ultimately granted access.

The scope of the Unfamiliar Situation will depend on the genre and style of story being told. In more down-to-earth stories, the character's world itself doesn't change, rather his situation within it does. In *Gravity*[25], Dr. Stone begins Act Two tumbling through space after being separated from the *Explorer* by a debris field. She's still in the same arena of space, but her situation is now unlike anything she could have ever anticipated.

---

[25] I know, I said down-to-earth. You know what I meant

ACTIONS & GOALS

This type of changing situation can also be seen in *Inception*, where Dom and Arthur go from performing routine extractions[26] to trying to figure out how to perform a complex inception. They're still operating in a world where they have copious experience, but they are now out of their depth in the scale of what they are trying to accomplish.

Whatever the case, the Unfamiliar Situation the character enters into finds him struggling to adjust. This is primarily because he is inexperienced in the New Role he accepted at the Dilemma. Though the character has existing skills that lend themselves to his New Role, he must find new ways to use them if he is to succeed in the Unfamiliar situation.

In *The Hunger Games*, Katniss goes from being a povertous[27], small-game hunter in Act One to a full-fledged tribute in the Games by Act Two. By mastering the art of survival in District 12, she has gained many skills that lend themselves to her new predicament. She is proficient with a bow, knows how to hunt and track game, and is accustomed to foraging for food. While these skills will be applicable when she ultimately enters the arena, they are not enough to complete the New Role she has inherited. This is because her new role involves not only survival but murder, an action with which she is woefully unfamiliar. If she is to survive the Hunger Games, Katniss must learn how to apply her existing skills as a huntress to her New Role as a killer.

Likewise, in *The Silence of the Lambs*, Clarice accepts the New Role by investigating the cold case given to her by Dr. Lecter. In doing so, she steps out of her initial role as an FBI trainee and into a New Role as a card-carrying (albeit temporarily) FBI investigator. Though she has learned a great deal in training and is said to have excelled in her classes, she must now actively apply this knowledge to the performance of field work.

---

[26] Much like your family dentist.
[27] I am aware this is not a word. But since no word was a word until it became a word, I figured I'd throw it out there.

Often, when the character steps into the Unfamiliar Situation, his ignorance of its inner workings comes to the forefront of the narrative. He simply doesn't understand the rules governing the world he has entered. In some cases, this causes him to come across as a clueless, bumbling oaf to the new world's inhabitants. In *Avatar*, Neytiri and the rest of the Na'vi chastise Jake for having all the tact and grace of a drunken toddler. Because this new situation is so foreign to him, he must quickly learn the rules governing his new situation or suffer severe consequences.

In stories with life or death stakes, the character will likely face his first threat of death in this act. This is because the new world he has entered is a dark and dangerous place. Often, the character enters into the Unfamiliar Situation underestimating the dangers he will face there. He steps into the new world bolstered by the confidence of naiveté, only to discover just how dangerous the situation is.

In the famous cantina scene in Act Two of *Star Wars*, Pignose and his equally unattractive associate are ready to kill Luke just for being alive. The situation he has entered in his New Role as Obi-Wan's Padawan is filled with dangers he failed to foresee. Luke quickly learns in this new world you either sink or swim.

If the character has a **Mentor**, they will either be introduced in this act or, if they were introduced in Act One, will now become a focal point of the narrative. This is because the character now needs guidance more than ever and will eagerly soak up the Mentor's lessons. Going back to *Star Wars*, Obi-Wan goes from simply telling Luke about the Force in the first act, to demonstrating it to him in the second. How so? He Jedi mind tricks stormtroopers, lops off the arm of an ill-humored bar patron and negotiates their passage aboard a smuggler's starship. This demonstrates to Luke (and the audience) that this old coot isn't just blowing smoke. Maybe there's something to this Jedi business after all.

Learning from the Mentor also allows the character to serve as an **Audience Surrogate**. This makes it possible to provide exposition and delineate world mechanics to the audience as it is taught to the character. In Act Two of *The Matrix*, Morpheus explains to the audience and the perpetually clueless Keanu Reeves what the Matrix is, how it came to be and how it works. Likewise, in *Harry Potter and the Philosopher's Stone*, Hagrid explains the workings of the wizarding world to Harry as he takes him to and through Diagon Alley for the first time. Through the use of a mentor, the backstory is presented to these characters in a logical manner without the need for a random and inexplicable **Infodump**.

Significance of Learning the Rules of an Unfamiliar Situation

In Act Two, we begin to get a sense of what our character is made of. Because he is thrown into an uncomfortable and dangerous situation, we are given the opportunity to learn who he is by watching him react and adjust to it. Having been introduced to him in his Imperfect Situation of Act One, in this act we get to see his *true nature* in action. This true self the character displays is an important component of his character arc and comes to the foreground of the narrative in Act Three.

In *Titanic* the first act established Rose is unhappy with the strict monotony of her life; however, we only receive a superficial glimpse of the reasons for her internal conflict. It isn't until Act Two when we begin to understand exactly why she is so unhappy with the stuffy exterior she must present to the world and are given a glimpse into the kind of person she is on the inside. She confides to Jack she wishes her life could be more like his. She wants to learn to ride like a cowboy and spit like a man. She lets her hair down[28] at a party, chugs a few brewskies and has some fun for possibly the first time in her life. We see her true, free-spirited, fun-loving nature as she adjusts to the Unfamiliar Situation she has entered into with Jack. Rose's character arc over

---

[28] Literally. James Cameron, you sneaky bastard.

the course of the film revolves around her becoming the kind of person she demonstrates she is in this act.

Watching the character operate outside his comfort zone also gives us the opportunity to see what skills he possesses. We learn much about Jake Sully when he's pursued by the giant space panther in Act Two of *Avatar*. Even after losing his trusty machine gun, he escapes the death beast by diving headlong into a waterfall, survives into nightfall, and takes on a pack of snarling space wolves in true, Cro-Magnon fashion. We observe from this that Jake is tough and resourceful. Behind the paralyzed exterior we were introduced to in the first act lies the essence of a true warrior. We can get behind a guy like this for the next seven hours and hope he's able to find a way to transfer his consciousness from his useless human body into the strong, virile, Avatar body our future children's tax dollars have paid for.

In Act Two of *Iron Man*, Tony Stark adjusts to the Unfamiliar Situation of being imprisoned in an Afghan cave by terrorists. He is forced to demonstrate to the audience not only his engineering skill by building a miniature arc reactor to keep the shrapnel out of his heart[29], but also prove he has a heart by befriending and caring about the opinions of his fellow captive, Yinsen. This is something he has been unable or unwilling to do throughout the story to this point.

By witnessing the character deal with his Unfamiliar Situation, we learn who he is and what he is capable of accomplishing. We also get a prelude to the plot events that will occur to lead the character to this realization himself. Because of this, there is often a great deal of foreshadowing in Act Two, as we begin to get a sense of the moral lessons the character must learn, as well as the physical obstacles he will face in doing so.

In *Harry Potter and the Philosopher's Stone*, Hagrid takes Harry to Gringotts where he retrieves a mysterious package for Dumbledore. This package turns out to be

---

[29] With a box of scraps!

the Philosopher's Stone, which as the title suggests, is vital to the plot; Harry spends a good portion of the story in its pursuit. Also in the second act, Harry meets a pretentious, unnamed fellow student to whom he takes an immediate disliking. This snobby boy is later revealed to be Draco Malfoy, who goes on to become Harry's principal rival at Hogwarts throughout the series.

A particularly useful form of foreshadowing is the employment of **Setups, Callbacks, and Payoffs**. This technique involves providing a seemingly innocuous piece of information to the audience (the Setup) that is later shown to have greater significance (the Payoff). While often used for humor and dialogue, Setups and Payoffs can be used to give stronger meaning to any event that comes later in the story. Although the implementation of Setups isn't confined to the second act, there are often many introduced here to be paid off in the later acts.

In the second act of *Inception*, Arthur informs the team's financier, Mr. Saito, there is "no room for tourists on these jobs", foreshadowing the life-threatening gunshot wound Saito sustains in the following act. Additionally in this act, Ariadne follows Dom into his private dream, discovers Mal is trying to keep Dom in Limbo with her (which is a pivotal part of the climax in act five), and is startled by the sudden appearance of a rumbling freight train while riding the elevator (which is brought to fruition in Act Three).

In Act Two of *The Lego Movie*, Emmet, Vitruvius and Wyldstyle go into Emmet's mind. There, Emmet reveals his idea for a double-decker couch, as well as the vision where he glimpsed The Man Upstairs. When he finally builds his couch in Act Three and sees The Man Upstairs in Act Five, these Setups are paid off in full. This gives these events more meaning than if they would have simply occurred with no previous reference, and creates a sense of cohesiveness in the narrative.

A Payoff can be further strengthened and prolonged by implementing a Callback between the Payoff and the Setup. In this method, the Setup is called back to, prior to the true Payoff. This often creates a false sense of completion for the Setup, increasing the effectiveness of the true Payoff.

Iron Man employs a clever Setup and Callback using Tony Stark's arc reactor prototype to Payoff his relationship with his personal assistant Pepper. After she helps him remove the old reactor from his chest in Act Two, Tony gives her a speech about his lack of sentimentality and tells her to incinerate it lest it fall into the wrong hands. This exchange would seem to be paid off in Act Three, when it is revealed that, instead of destroying the reactor, Pepper had it englassed[30] as "proof that Tony Stark has a heart". Upon seeing it, Tony smiles, sentimental music plays, and the studio audience releases a collective "aww." This little Setup appears to have been paid off in full by Tony's reaction. He has gone from a heartless narcissist to someone with a heart.

But this is not the true Payoff. The Mark One reactor proves itself more than an ornamental keepsake in Act Four when Obadiah steals Tony's new reactor. Pepper's saving of the old reactor out of sentimentality becomes instrumental to the plot. In doing so, she inadvertently saves Tony's life, allowing him to save her from Obadiah in Act Five. This skillful storytelling probably had something to do with Disney's $4 billion acquisition of Marvel the year after the film's release.

Also in this act, the audience is introduced to the **Hooking Premise** of the story. The Hooking Premise is the unique idea separating an individual story from every other story ever told. It is the attractive concept, the distinctive selling point which piqued the audience's interest in the story in the first place, and in Act Two the character enters into this unique premise.

The Hooking Premise generally revolves around the "what if" scenario at the heart of the story. The audience pays to see, read or listen to a story to learn

---

[30] Yet another word that isn't a word. I'm willing to bet you know what it means, though.

the answer to this question, and everything that happens from this act forward serves to provide that answer.

In the film *Jurassic Park*, the Hooking Premise centers on "what if dinosaurs were brought back into existence after millions of years of extinction?" The desire to see (realistic) dinosaurs and man side by side is the hooking idea that sent us scrambling to the multiplex in droves. While the existence of these dinosaurs is alluded to in the first act, it isn't until Act Two that Drs. Alan Grant and Ellie Sattler arrive at the titular park, and we get our first glimpse of living, breathing dinosaurs. The full delivery of the Hooking Premise is skillfully withheld until the moment when it will provide the greatest impact, and everything that happens from this point forward answers the question put forth by the Hooking Premise.

In the movie *Wreck-it-Ralph*, the Hooking Premise of "what if video game characters could leave their own games and go to others?" is posed in Act Two, when Ralph abandons his game to visit Hero's Duty in hopes of winning a medal. The answer to this hypothetical question is explored over the course of the next four acts as we see how Ralph's actions affect the games he enters as well as his own game he's left behind. In *Die Hard*, Act Two begins after the terrorists attack Holly's Christmas party. It is at this point that the Hooking Premise of "what if a hard-nosed cop is unwittingly locked in a building with a gang of terrorists and becomes the only hope to stop them?" comes to fruition. The answer is played out to the audience in real time as John demonstrates exactly what would happen in the proposed scenario[31], which is exactly what we came to see.

Because the Hooking Premise is realized during Act Two, a film's logline or a novel's blurb often revolve around the events of this act. When the average person describes what the story is about, they will generally focus on the events initiated in Act Two, because it is here where we learn what the physical events

---

[31] Well, at least in a movie.

of the story are built upon. In fact, you can often summarize the story using only this act. If you're familiar with the below films, I'm sure you can easily identify them based on these general descriptions of the characters and the actions they undertake in Act Two.

1. A newly imprisoned man takes up rock chiseling and tax accounting to adjust to life in prison.
2. A depressed middle-aged man finds a new purpose in life by pursuing his teenage daughter's best friend.
3. A reclusive monster attempts to rescue a princess to get his land back from the king.
4. Two men start an underground social group where men can beat the snot out of each other for recreation.
5. A betrayed soldier is sold into slavery and forced to fight other slaves to the death for sport.

Now check your answers[32].

The fact is, most of the time you can provide a basic explanation of the story to people who have yet to experience it by summarizing Act Two, all while remaining confident you haven't provided any unintentional spoilers. Although the character's goal may change slightly as the story progresses, the ideas introduced here are what set the backdrop for the coming events.

It is important to note that while a majority of the world building and exposition takes place in Act One, there is still key information being introduced in this act which will set up the plot. The character and the audience are still gaining necessary information and being introduced to key characters who will play a vital role. The roots of the central conflict are still being set up as well, but after this act is completed, the stage will truly be set.

---

[32] 1. The Shawshank Redemption, 2. American Beauty, 3. Shrek, 4. Fight Club, 6. Gladiator

Goal Two: The Transitional Goal

Because the character existed in a state of such heavy inertia in Act One (and likely, long before), the goal he accepts at the Dilemma must be powerful and purposeful enough to spur him into action. This is because his Act Two goal is a **Transitional Goal**, breaking him free of his lifelong stasis and yanking him into a world he has either purposely chosen to ignore or never realized existed. By accepting this goal, he transitions away from the familiarity of the imperfect world he has inhabited, into an unfamiliar world filled with both danger and hope.

The character's goal in this act is often the goal most sane individuals would have chosen to pursue were they placed in his shoes; it just makes sense. Of course Jake Sully wants to spy on the Na'vi for the Colonel. He gets to do some Marine work *and* he gets his legs fixed. Of course Luke Skywalker will help Obi-Wan take the droids to Alderaan. His aunt and uncle just got flambéed by the Empire, and he's always wanted to get off that godforsaken rock anyway.

For the first time in his life, the character has a goal to pursue with some kind meaning to him. Lester Burnham pursues his teenage daughter's friend in *American Beauty* despite himself because, after so many years of feeling dead inside, he finally feels alive. Harry Potter prepares to attend a school of magic and revels in the fact he will finally be free of his horrible family. Katniss Everdeen boards a train to the Capitol aware she may never return to District 12. These characters transition out of the mundane lives they've always known in pursuit of goals brimming with significance.

But while the character's goal in this act is laden with purpose, it still doesn't *feel* like the Ultimate Goal of the story, and the audience can tell there is something bigger the character must accomplish. Looking at what the character is trying to achieve in this act you can easily tell, whether or not he succeeds, the story wouldn't be over. If you were to explain the character's goal in this act to a friend or random hobo on the street, said friend/hobo would likely ask, "Well, what does he do next?"

For instance, in *A Game of Thrones*, Ned Stark's Transitional Goal in Act Two is to travel to King's Landing as the newly appointed Hand of the King and investigate the circumstances of his mentor's death. There is no finality in this goal. There will still be more to do once he figures out how and why his friend died. Is Ned going to kill his murderer? Make him stand trial? So the Transitional Goal isn't an end, but a means to an end. And by pursuing this goal, the character transitions into a New Role, in an Unfamiliar Situation.

The purpose of the Transitional Goal is to bring the character into the external, Preexisting Conflicts of the story. While, he may have had conflicts of his own in Act One, the character was either willfully or unintentionally ignorant of the conflicts raging around him in the world at large. The Transitional Goal he pursues in Act Two brings him out of the periphery and into the story proper. Just as this goal transitions him from inaction to action, it also transitions him from a mere spectator on the sidelines to a true player in the game.

Opposition to the Transitional Goal: Incidental Opposition

Although the Transitional Goal has a grand sense of purpose, the character suffers from the delusion its attainment will be easy. In pursuit of what he believes to something simple, he soon learns there are greater forces in the new world standing between him and his goal. But the resistance the character faces to his Transitional Goal is **Incidental Opposition**. That is, the forces of opposition in this act aren't out to thwart the character's goal specifically, rather he attempts to accomplish his goal in a manner that places him at odds with the way the new world operates.

In Act Two of *Avatar*, Jake goes out into the Pandoran wilderness with the simple intention of gaining intel on the Na'vi so the Colonel can blast them to smithereens. Soon after arriving in the jungle however, Jake stumbles upon a herd of space rhinos going about their space rhino business and finds himself on the receiving end of a territorial threat display. This, in turn, leads to him being pursued by an oily, six-legged, space panther who's just out looking for a snack. Neither of these creatures has the specific intentions of stopping Jake from spying on the Na'vi. This is all just basic Pandoran animal behavior that takes place in response to Jake's naiveté about the new world he has entered. Maybe he should have read the manual instead of cryosleeping the whole trip to Pandora.

In *The Silence of the Lambs*, Clarice must contend with her class schedule and lack of free time as she investigates the Raspail lead given to her by Dr. Lecter. Because she is now working as an investigator for the FBI, she faces the Incidental Opposition it entails: overly ambitious reporters, sexist police officers and the red tape typical of a bureaucratic organization. None of these things are out to thwart her pursuit of the Raspail lead specifically; it's just part of the job.

In Act Two of *The Lego Movie*, Emmet and Wyldstyle navigate the "Old West" to rendezvous with Vitruvius. True to form, it is a wild and dangerous place, and the hapless Emmet is threatened with violence by the patrons of the saloon they visit. While Emmet faces obstruction from the inhabitants of this new world, none of these people (or mini-figures or whatever) are interested in whether or not he meets up with Vitruvius. They just don't like his face.

Though the opposition the character faces in this act may be incidental, the force of it is much stronger than he experienced pursuing his Initial Goal in

Act One. The Incidental Opposition clearly establishes the stakes of the new world to the character. This serves as a wake-up call for him and is often the precipitating event that leads him to the Turning Point Catalyst of the second act.

Turning Point Catalyst: The Reality Check

The character enters into Act Two harboring a gross underestimation of what he has gotten himself into by accepting the New Role in Act One. But as he nears the end of this act, he receives a dose of reality when his simple plan of action hits a major roadblock and fails. This event and the resulting failure of the character's plan is the second Turning Point Catalyst, **The Reality Check.**

As implied by the idiom, the Reality Check is an intrusion of reality upon the delusions the character brought into his new situation. Here, the character and the audience finally realize he is waaaay out of his depth, and the situation he's stepped into is far more severe than he initially concluded. The stakes inherent to achieving his Transitional Goal become clear to him for the first time, and whatever misconceptions he had regarding the Unfamiliar Situation are laid to rest as the new world reveals its inherent dangers.

In *Iron Man*, the head terrorist, Raza, wisely grows suspicious of Tony's mysterious actions and pays him a visit. Though Raza doesn't know Tony is plotting his escape, he threatens to kill Yinsen and gives Tony one day to finish the missile he was supposed to have been working on. This is Tony's Reality Check. He underestimated the consequences of the terrorists discovering his secret project, but the severity of his situation, as well as consequences for failure, are now made clear.

In *Avatar*, Jake is separated from the rest of his avatar team, and they are forced to call off the search for him when night falls. He's now left alone to fend off a pack of viperwolves MacGyver style, with a stick and a lighter.

Though Jake initially underestimated the dangers of Pandora, this Reality Check makes it clear to him that his failure to acknowledge the severity of his situation may very well lead to his death (or at least the death of his billion-dollar Avatar).

Similarly, in Act Two of *Gravity*, Stone and Kowalski discover their fellow astronaut Shariff is catastrophically dead, the space shuttle *Explorer* is catastrophically damaged and they are the only survivors. They now find themselves 250 miles above Earth, adrift in space, with no means of contacting Mission Control in Houston. That's a Reality Check I hope to never receive.

The Reality Check leads the character to realize the Unfamiliar Situation he is dealing with is far more complicated than he initially thought. As a result of this realization, the character must next make a resolution to persevere in the face of this adversity at the Act Two Turning Point.

Turning Point Two: The Commitment

Approximate Start Time: 35%
Approximate Runtime: 5%

At the end of the second act, approximately a third of the way into the story, the character makes the decision, or has the decision made for him, *to fully commit himself to his New Role and take part in the events unfolding around him.* This decision by the character to willingly participate in the external conflicts of his world is **The Commitment**.

At this Turning Point, the insights and information the character has gained over the course of Act Two cause his Transitional Goal to transmute into something more elaborate. He finally begins to understand his place in the new world and realizes the plan of action he had coming into it was inadequate. This leads him to alter his strategy and commit himself to the active pursuit of a greater goal. In layman's terms, he goes from being reactive in the first two acts, to being proactive moving forward.

In Act Two of *Iron Man*, Tony Stark's Transitional Goal is to escape imprisonment by the Ten Rings. In pursuit of this seemingly straightforward goal he discovers the terrorists are in possession of a large cache of his weapons, which they are using for stereotypical terrorist purposes. He also gains and promptly loses a new friend who helps him come to terms with the error of his narcissistic ways. This all culminates in Tony's action-packed escape, return to the US and announcement to the world that Stark Enterprises will no longer produce weapons. He obtains, through this Turning Point, a more powerful goal of building the ultimate weapon for himself, and using it to dispense justice on behalf of 'Murica! The Commitment he makes at this Turning Point is a pivotal, life-changing event for Tony.

The Commitment is sometimes the result of the forces of antagonism gaining the upper hand on the character. In *Star Trek*, the Romulan Captain, Nero, spares the *Enterprise* in exchange for Captain Pike. Nero's ship has just laid waste to the Starfleet armada dispatched to save the Vulcan planet, Vulcan[33], and Kirk et al. are essentially left at his mercy. This demonstration of force by the antagonist is what galvanizes Kirk, Spock and the crew of the *Enterprise* to commit to their new goal of thwarting Nero's plans.

The Commitment Turning Point may also come in the form of **Superior Position**, where the audience learns something has altered the character's goal before he realizes it himself. In *Star Wars*, Luke and Obi-Wan have a simple enough Transitional Goal of taking the droids to Alderaan. But while they are en route, we witness the destruction of the planet by the Death Star and realize our would-be heroes are now on a collision course with the Empire. They have unknowingly committed themselves to a showdown with the very forces they have been trying to avoid.

It may also be the character receives a vital piece of information that changes his perspective, such as Clarice Starling learning her mentor, Jack Crawford's initial request for her to meet with Lecter had a greater motive than a simple, homicidal maniac questionnaire. Crawford's revelation and subsequent request for her to question Lecter again, prompts Clarice to commit herself to the investigation.

These examples illustrate how the character's Commitment is closely tied to his New Role. In fact, the Commitment the character makes at this Turning

---

[33] And Vulcans say humanity is narcissistic? At least we don't live on the planet Human. Aren't there any other species on their planet?

Point revolves around his decision to become the epitome of whatever his New Role is. He essentially makes a decision that, if he must be a "such-and-such", he is going to be the best, damn "such-and-such" he can be.

In the second act of *The Empire Strikes Back*, Luke finds himself on Dagobah in search of Jedi Master, Yoda. The New Role Luke has assumed in this act is that of an aspiring Padawan. When Luke finally realizes who Yoda is, the little, green puppet declines his request to be trained. It is only at Obi-Wan's insistence that Yoda relents. But before he does, he solicits a Commitment from his would-be pupil. Luke's promise to devote himself to Yoda's teachings is a clear Commitment to perform his New Role as a Padawan to the best of his ability[34].

Act Two of Harry Potter and the Philosopher's Stone finds Harry preparing for and arriving at Hogwarts in his New Role a wizarding student. This act culminates in the Sorting Hat's separation of each student into one of the four Houses. When the hat suggests Harry would be a nice fit for Slytherin, Harry balks. This outright rejection of Slytherin is based on Harry's realization that if he's going to fill his New Role (i.e. a wizarding student), then he's going to be the best student he can be (i.e. not a Slytherin). As a result, he is assigned to Gryffindor. From this moment forward, Harry is unquestionably committed to his new house, with the ever-present contest for the House Cup there to remind us.

In *Die Hard*, John realizes if he's the only one who can fight the terrorists, he's gonna be the best damn terrorist fighter he can be. In *Avatar*, Jake decides if he's going to spy on the Na'vi, he's going to throw himself into the role completely by joining the clan and becoming one of the people. As a result of the character's Commitment to his New Role, he receives an updated, more involved goal which, as we will discover in the next act, is what pulls him into the Central Conflict of the story.

---

[34] Even though he doesn't. But we'll get to that.

Act Two Summary

So, the central pillars of Act Two are: The Unfamiliar Situation, the Transitional Goal, Incidental Opposition, the Reality Check and the Commitment. We can, therefore, summarize Act Two as...

> *The character Learns the Rules of an Unfamiliar Situation and faces Incidental Opposition in pursuit of a Transitional Goal. But when he receives a Reality Check, he makes a Commitment to his New Role.*

To demonstrate this, let's examine the actions undertaken by James T. Kirk in Act Two of *Star Trek*. Jim begins the second act in his New Role as a cadet in the Starfleet Academy. This is an extremely Unfamiliar Situation for the freewheeling and ruleless Kirk. He literally has to learn the rules governing Starfleet if he is to achieve his Transitional Goal of graduating the Academy and becoming the awesomest Starfleet captain in the history of both Starfleet and awesomeness.

Consequently, the Incidental Opposition Kirk faces in this act arises from his lack of knowledge of Starfleet's rules and his inability to follow them. He cheats on the intentionally unbeatable Kobayashi Maru exam and earns himself a disciplinary hearing (in front of the entire Academy for some reason). Notice neither Spock nor Tyler Perry are out to thwart Kirk's dream of becoming a Starfleet captain, but the methods he uses to pursue his goal put him at odds with the way Starfleet operates.

Because of this, Kirk finds himself on academic suspension and grounded when the fleet is mustered to investigate a distress call from Vulcan. This serves as Kirk's Reality Check where he begins to realize the plan of action he had coming into this act isn't working out how he envisioned. But his Reality Check doesn't end there. To board the *Enterprise*, McCoy has to inject him with the Melvaran mud flea vaccine, giving him all its ridiculous symptoms. See what happens when you break the rules, Kirk?

Next, comes the Act Two Turning Point, the Commitment. Up to this point, Kirk's only objective has been to graduate the Academy and be awesome. His goal remains unchanged even when the fleet is deployed to Vulcan, and he stows aboard the *Enterprise*. But as the ship approaches the planet, Kirk discovers Vulcan is under attack by the same Romulans who killed his dad in the prologue of the film. When he shares this revelation with the Captain, he is inexplicably promoted from suspended cadet to First Officer and tasked with leading an away team to the planet's surface to disable the Romulans' drill. His goal of graduating now becomes an afterthought as he receives a new goal to act upon; stop the Romulans at all costs.

This marks Kirk's first official action as a member of Starfleet. It is at this point when he truly accepts his New Role as a Starfleet officer, by Committing himself to being the baddest sumbitch in the fleet (a newly minted First Officer who singlehandedly saves a planet). In doing so, he also commits to his new goal of stopping the Romulans. It is the pursuit of this goal that pits the crew of the *Enterprise* against the crew of the *Narada*, creating the Central Conflict of the next act.

Using the key points of Act Two, we can summarize the second act of *Star Trek* as such.

> *Kirk goes to Starfleet Academy (the unfamiliar situation) where they have an abundance of things called rules (incidental opposition) in hopes of graduating from simply being super awesome to being super awesome in space (the transitional goal). But when the fleet is mustered while he is on academic suspension, and he's forced to stow aboard the* Enterprise *(reality check), he is*

recruited by Captain Pike (again) to lead an away team tasked with stopping Romulans from destroying the planet Vulcan (the commitment).

The second act begins, on average, about 20% into the story and typically runs for another 20%. If you're a math whiz, then you realize Act Three, kicks off at about 40%. Again, these percentages are averaged across multiple stories. They aren't rules etched into stone tablets and brought down from a mountaintop by Moses or Aristotle or any other thickly bearded historical figure.

Act Two Examples

The Hunger Games
2008 Novel
Written by Suzanne Collins

Character
Katniss Everdeen

Ultimate Goal
Win the Hunger Games with Peeta

Total Story Runtime: 27 chapters

The Hunger Games - Act Two:
Learning the Rules of an Unfamiliar Situation

The character Learns the Rules of an Unfamiliar Situation and faces Incidental Opposition in pursuit of a Transitional Goal. But when he receives a Reality Check, he makes a Commitment to his New Role.

Katniss sees how others live as she passes through the other Districts to the Capitol (the unfamiliar situation) and bumps heads with her coaches and fellow tributes (incidental opposition) as she begins learning how to survive the Games (the transitional goal). But when she has a botched scoring session with the Gamemakers and thinks Peeta is trying to manipulate her (the reality check), he confesses his love for her in an interview and locks her into their star-crossed love angle (the commitment).

Start Time: After 2 of 27 Chapters (7.4%)
Runtime: Chapter 3 through Chapter 9 (7 Chapters)
Run Percentage: 7 of 27 Chapters (25.9%)

Learning the Rules of an Unfamiliar Situation - The character now finds himself in a situation unlike anything he's ever experienced.

Katniss is swept away in a train and taken toward the strange and mysterious Capitol. She sees a side of life and the world she has never before seen. She also begins to prepare for her fight to the death with people she doesn't know (and one she does).

The Hooking Premise - The unique premise at the heart of a story, often involving an intriguing "what if" scenario that piques the audience's interest.

What if once a year, 24 subjugated children from around the country were brought together to compete in a death match for the entertainment of a self-indulgent plutarchy?

The Transitional Goal - The character receives a new goal that transitions him out of his initial state of inertia and into the main events of the story.

Katniss begins learning how to survive the Hunger Games.

Incidental Opposition - The character learns there are greater forces of opposition in this new world that may not be out to thwart him specifically, but still stand between him and his new goal.

Katniss bumps heads with Haymitch (who thinks she and Peeta will pretty much roll over and die), Effie (who thinks Katniss is being ungrateful for the wonderful opportunity she's been presented with), Peeta (with whom she has a complicated history), and the "Careers" (tributes from the wealthier Districts who are just dying to kill someone). With the exception of the Careers, none of these people are out to thwart Katniss' success. In fact, they are trying to help her.

ACTIONS & GOALS

Turning Point Catalyst: The Reality Check

The Reality Check - The plan the character had coming into this act hits a major roadblock, and either fails completely or has unintended negative consequences.

Frustrated by their inattentiveness, Katniss fires an arrow at the Gamemakers during her scoring session. This earns her an unprecedented tribute score of 11 and makes her a target for the careers. Soon after, she learns Peeta has asked to be coached separately.

Turning Point Two: The Commitment

Start Time: After 8 of 27 Chapters (29.6%)
Runtime: Chapter 9 (1 Chapter)
Run Percentage: 1 of 61 Chapters (3.7%)

The Commitment - The character commits, or finds himself committed, to becoming the epitome of the New Role he accepted at the Dilemma. In doing so, he becomes an active participant in the Central Conflict.

During her interview with Caesar, Katniss feels a resurgence of her resolve when she recalls the promise she made to Prim that she would win the Games. She makes an internal commitment to her New Role as a tribute.

During Peeta's interview, he reveals to Caesar the girl he is in love with from District 12 came to the Games with him. Though Katniss is initially furious at this revelation, Haymitch explains to her that Peeta has made her appear desirable, something she has been unable to do on her own. Now, Peeta and Katniss become the epitome of tributes in the games. The star-crossed love angle, which Katniss is inadvertently committed to, makes them an audience favorite.

MARSHALL L. DOTSON

<u>The Silence of the Lambs</u>
1988 Novel
Written by Thomas Harris

<u>Character</u>
Clarice Starling

<u>Ultimate Goal</u>
Stop the serial killer Buffalo Bill before he kills again.

Total Runtime: 61 chapters

The Silence of the Lambs - Act Two:
Learning the Rules of an Unfamiliar Situation

The character Learns the Rules of an Unfamiliar Situation and faces Incidental Opposition in pursuit of a Transitional Goal. But when he receives a Reality Check, he makes a Commitment to his New Role.

Clarice begins working as a federal investigator under Crawford's direction (the unfamiliar situation) but faces time constraints and bureaucratic stonewalling (incidental opposition) as she investigates the Raspail lead given to her by Lecter (the transitional goal). But when Buffalo Bill kidnaps senator Martin's daughter, Catherine (the reality check), Crawford tells Clarice that Bill, not Raspail, killed Klaus, that he believes Lecter knows who he is, and that he wants her to talk to him again (the commitment).

Start Time: After 5 of 61 Chapters (8.2%)
Runtime: Chapter 6 through Chapter 18 (13 Chapters)
Run Percentage: 13 of 61 Chapters (21.3%)

ACTIONS & GOALS

<u>Learning the Rules of an Unfamiliar Situation</u> - The character now finds himself in a situation unlike anything he's ever experienced.

Clarice begins working as a federal investigator under Crawford's direction. Despite her aptitude, this is something for which she is still in training. The fact she is not fully qualified for the job is a source of contention throughout this act specifically and the novel in general.

<u>The Hooking Premise</u> - The unique premise at the heart of a story, often involving an intriguing "what if" scenario that piques the audience's interest.

What if a notorious, imprisoned serial killer who will only talk to an inexperienced FBI cadet is the only person who knows the identity of a new serial killer preparing to kill his next victim?

<u>The Transitional Goal</u> - The character receives a new goal that transitions him out of his initial state of inertia and into the main events of the story.

With Crawford's blessing, Clarice begins to investigate the Raspail lead given to her by Lecter.

<u>Incidental Opposition</u> - The character learns there are greater forces of opposition in this new world that may not be out to thwart him specifically, but still stand between him and his new goal.

With her class schedule, Clarice only has a total of three hours and forty-five minutes of free time to trace Raspail's car. Chilton denies her access to Lecter after Lecter's neighbor, Miggs commits suicide (at Lecter's suggestion). The executor of Raspail's estate barely makes it to the storage lot in time due to having just returned from a week long business trip. When she finds a body in Raspail's car, she must contend with a news crew trying to force their way onto the scene. This gets her taunted by her fellow trainees when it's shown on the news.

Later, Crawford sends her to interview Lecter for the second time. Crawford then takes Clarice to West Virginia to print a floater[35]. There, he uses a sexist ploy at Clarice's expense to talk to the sheriff alone.

Turning Point Catalyst: The Reality Check

<u>The Reality Check</u> - The plan the character had coming into this act hits a major roadblock, and either fails completely or has unintended negative consequences.

Just when it would seem as if the FBI has gotten a handle on things, Buffalo Bill kidnaps Senator Martin's daughter, Catherine.

Turning Point Two: The Commitment

Start Time: After 16 of 61 Chapters (26.2%)
Runtime: Chapter 17 through 18 (2 Chapters)
Run Percentage: 2 of 61 Chapters (3.2%)

<u>The Commitment</u> - The character commits, or finds himself committed, to becoming the epitome of the New Role he accepted at the Dilemma. In doing so, he becomes an active participant in the Central Conflict.

Crawford tells Starling that Bill, not Raspail, killed Klaus, and he believes Lecter knows who he is. Because Clarice is the only one Lecter talks to, he asks her to question him again. Clarice agrees, committing herself to fulfilling her New Role as an investigator to the best of her ability.

---

[35] Which, surprisingly, isn't a euphemism for using the toilet.

Star Wars
1977 Film
Written and directed by George Lucas

Character
Luke Skywalker

Ultimate Goal
Destroy the Death Star and save the princess.

Total Runtime: 120 minutes

Star Wars - Act Two: Learning the Rules of an Unfamiliar Situation

The character Learns the Rules of an Unfamiliar Situation and faces Incidental Opposition in pursuit of a Transitional Goal. But when he receives a Reality Check, he makes a Commitment to his New Role.

Luke accompanies Obi-Wan to the scummy and villainous Mos Eisley (the unfamiliar situation) and faces dimwitted stormtroopers and bar patrons (incidental opposition) while trying to find a pilot to take them to Alderaan (the transitional goal). But when some guy in an elephant mask reveals their location to the stormtroopers (the reality check), they become fugitives on the run from the Empire, trying to make it to a planet that has been destroyed by the Death Star (the commitment).

Starting Percentage: 43 of 120 minutes (35.8%)
Runtime: 16 minutes of 120 minutes (13.3%)

Learning the Rules of an Unfamiliar Situation - The character now finds himself in a situation unlike anything he's ever experienced.

Luke follows Obi-Wan to Mos Eisley and gets a crash course on scum, villainy, the Force, and just how dangerous the Empire is.

<u>The Hooking Premise</u> - The unique premise at the heart of a story, often involving an intriguing "what if" scenario that piques the audience's interest.

What if the unwitting son of a space wizard teams up with an aging space wizard and a space pirate to rescue a space princess from a powerful Empire?

<u>The Transitional Goal</u> - The character receives a new goal that transitions him out of his initial state of inertia and into the main events of the story.

Luke and Obi-Wan attempt to find a ship and pilot to take them and the droids to Alderaan.

<u>Incidental Opposition</u> - The character learns there are greater forces of opposition in this new world that may not be out to thwart him specifically, but still stand between him and his new goal.

In the Cantina, Luke is accosted by some ruffians for breathing up their air. Meanwhile, the stormtroopers are looking for the droids. This demonstrates the incidental nature of the Act Two Opposition. The Empire isn't looking for Luke or Obi-Wan at this point.

Turning Point Catalyst: The Reality Check

<u>The Reality Check</u> - The plan the character had coming into this act hits a major roadblock, and either fails completely or has unintended negative consequences.

Stormtroopers nearly find the droids who are hiding in a closet. The elephant man follows Luke and Obi-Wan and snitches on them to the stormtroopers. The troopers arrive and open fire just as the gang boards the Falcon. *A shoot-out ensues with the* Falcon *taking off and jumping to lightspeed just in the nick of time. Maybe this whole droid delivery service wasn't such a smart business move after all.*

ACTIONS & GOALS

Turning Point Two: The Commitment

Start Time: 54 of 120 minutes (45%)
Runtime: 5 minutes of 120 minutes (4.1%)

The Commitment - The character commits, or finds himself committed, to becoming the epitome of the New Role he accepted at the Dilemma. In doing so, he becomes an active participant in the Central Conflict.

Obi-Wan and Luke are initially just going to Alderaan to deliver the droids. But when the planet is destroyed by the Death Star, the duo inadvertently become the last hope for delivering the plans hidden in R2 to the Rebel Alliance. Luke himself is now placed at direct odds with the Empire.

Titanic
1997 Film
Written and directed by James Cameron

Character
Rose Dawson

Ultimate Goal
Survive the ship and live life on her terms.

Total Runtime: 187 minutes

Titanic - Act Two: Learning the Rules of an Unfamiliar Situation

The character Learns the Rules of an Unfamiliar Situation and faces Incidental Opposition in pursuit of a Transitional Goal. But when he receives a Reality Check, makes a Commitment to his New Role.

Rose learns about life on the other side from Jack (the unfamiliar situation) and is berated by her mother and Cal (incidental opposition) for trying to get to know him (the transitional goal). But when Cal reveals he had Lovejoy follow her, and her mother forbids her from seeing Jack again (the reality check), Jack sneaks back into first class and convinces Rose to be herself and have an affair with him (the commitment).

Starting Percentage: 45 of 187 minutes (24.1%)
Runtime: 38 minutes of 187 minutes (20.3%)

Learning the Rules of an Unfamiliar Situation - The character now finds himself in a situation unlike anything he's ever experienced.

Jack enters Rose's privileged but strict world, and Rose enters Jack's poor but carefree world.

ACTIONS & GOALS

<u>The Hooking Premise</u> - The unique premise at the heart of a story, often involving an intriguing "what if" scenario that piques the audience's interest.

What if two young people from conflicted backgrounds fall in love with each other aboard a doomed ocean liner?

<u>The Transitional Goal</u> - The character receives a new goal that transitions him out of his initial state of inertia and into the main events of the story.

Rose begins to get to know Jack, however, they haven't begun a relationship in earnest yet.

<u>Incidental Opposition</u> - The character learns there are greater forces of opposition in this new world that may not be out to thwart him specifically, but still stand between him and his new goal.

Rose's mother shows up while she and Jack are hanging out on the decks. Her mother's disdain for Jack is palpable. Later, Jack goes to their fancy dinner party and, much to Cal's dismay, charms everyone at the table (except Rose's mother, of course). Afterward, Lovejoy follows Rose to Jack's party and reports his findings to Cal.

Turning Point Catalyst: The Reality Check

<u>The Reality Check</u> - The plan the character had coming into this act hits a major roadblock, and either fails completely or has unintended negative consequences.

The next day, Rose faces the reality of the world in which she lives. Over breakfast, Cal tells her he knows where, and with whom, she went the previous evening. He flips out and flips the table to demonstrate it visually. He demands that as his wife in training, she will honor him. Rose's mother arrives shortly thereafter and reveals to the audience that Rose's father has left their family penniless. They argue over her engagement to Cal and who is the selfish one in their relationship.

Turning Point Two: The Commitment

Start Time: 74 of 187 minutes (19.2%)
Runtime: 9 minutes of 187 minutes (4.8%)

The Commitment - The character commits, or finds himself committed, to becoming the epitome of the New Role he accepted at the Dilemma. In doing so, he becomes an active participant in the Central Conflict.

The same morning, Jack returns to first class to find Rose but is turned away by Mr. Lovejoy. Undissuaded, Jack sneaks Rose into a room and confesses his feelings for her. Despite herself, she tells him to leave her alone. Over lunch, she remembers how boring her life will be when she sees a little girl being forced to be a lady by her mother. This prompts Rose to go find Jack on the bow of the ship. He gives her his patented "king of the world" treatment and Rose commits to her New Role by beginning a love affair with Jack. Her decision to be with Jack brings the new couple into the Central Conflict with Cal.

ACT THREE: STUMBLING INTO THE CENTRAL CONFLICT

"Yes, the girl from District 2, ten yards away, running toward me, one hand clutching a half-dozen knives. I've seen her throw in training. She never misses. And I'm her next target."

Katniss Everdeen - The Hunger Games, Act Three

Approximate Start Time: 40% into the story
Approximate Runtime: 20% of the story

In the third act of our tale, there is a proverbial convergence of the shit and the fan. Though the character may have been on the periphery of the conflict, or dealt with it indirectly in some way, his actions in this act lead him into the crosshairs of the antagonist. The decision he made at the Commitment to participate in the events of the story propels him into the Central Conflict.

The Central Conflict can be thought of as the algebraic problem at the heart of the story the character must solve to resolve the story. The character (y) wants to do something (x), but an antagonist force (z) stands in his way. So y - z = x. Or something. It's just an analogy. Math isn't my strong suit.

In *Gravity*, Dr. Stone (y) wants to get back to Earth (x), but space (z), by nature, wants all life exterminated. So if Stone (y) overcomes space (-z) then she can return to Earth (=x). In order for her to achieve her goal of returning to Earth, space must be eliminated from the equation.

In *Star Wars*, Luke (y) wants to save the princess (x), but the Empire (z) wants her and the Rebels dead. If Luke can defeat the Empire, he will save the princess. Y-z=x.

Regardless of the genre or media of the story, the Central Conflict can almost always be boiled down to two parties pursuing **Mutually Exclusive Goals**. For one side to be successful, the other side must fail. In *A Game of Thrones*, Ned Stark's third act goal is to gather proof of the Lannister's attempted murder of his son, Bran, as well as their actual murder of his friend Jon Arryn. Contrarily, the Lannister's goal is to control the Iron Throne for as long as possible by any means necessary; obviously being tossed into the Black Cells for murder is going to throw a monkey wrench in their objectives. So the goals of the Starks and the goals of the Lannisters are mutually exclusive.

Similarly, in *The Lego Movie* Emmet's third act goal is to assemble the Master Builders and attack Octan Tower. Meanwhile, Lord Business' goal is to capture and enslave the Master Builders and kill Emmet. There is no scenario in which both sides can get what they want.

While there are several types of "conflict" regarding storytelling (man vs. self, man vs. nature, man vs. flying spaghetti monster), and the character most often has some kind of internal conflict to resolve within himself, the Central Conflict I'm referring to here is *always* external. It is a visible, identifiable conflict between a clearly established force of protagonism and a clearly established force of antagonism. In the first two acts, this conflict is introduced and established, but in Act Three it takes center stage as the character's pursuit of his new goal puts him at direct odds with the antagonist.

Notice the action of this act is not *Entering* into the Central Conflict or *Merrily Jumping* into the Central Conflict, but *Stumbling* into it. The stumbling aspect is important. The character doesn't actively seek out the Central Conflict at this point, rather he stumbles toward it like a curious toddler, waddling toward the edge of an unsupervised swimming pool. He is simply a trouble magnet, pulled into the mix by the ineluctable draw of fate.

While he may have some inkling as to the danger of the situation, and quickly comes to realize just how diametrically opposed his goal is to that of the antagonist, he enters into this act oblivious to the full extent of the conflict, or unsure how to proceed.

In Act Three of *Iron Man*, Tony begins working on his new and improved suit, oblivious to the state of Stark Enterprises, or the fact Obadiah is the one who tried to have him killed. He simply stumbles along in pursuit of his goal. Although he isn't seeking out the conflict, his actions in this act ultimately bring him into the center of the conflict taking place around him.

In *The Hunger Games*, Katniss officially enters the Games. She knows she must compete, yet after escaping the cornucopia still stumbles aimlessly through the arena. She is well aware of the severity of the Central Conflict but is unsure how to proceed.

Because he enters into the Central Conflict in this act, the character must now make a personal commitment to fight. After observing the dichotomy of opinion in the first two acts, he realizes that, like it or not, he's standing in the middle of a literal or metaphorical war and must choose a side.

It is in Act Three of *Star Wars* where Luke first learns of the Death Star and realizes the Rebel Alliance is the only hope of stopping it. Based on this information, he firmly aligns himself with the side of the rebellion by sneaking into the detention area to rescue the princess.

Similarly, in Act Three of *Titanic*, Rose and Jack officially begin their love affair. They are well aware Cal and Rose's mother will be displeased, but it doesn't stop Rose from leaving Jack's nudie drawing of her in Cal's safe along with a taunting message. Now, Cal is also made aware of the conflict and given the opportunity to implement his own devious plan. Oh yeah, and the ship dings a bit of ice.

Significance of Stumbling Into the Central Conflict

The third act clarifies the Central Conflict of the story to the audience. Here, a line is drawn in the sand, and it is made clear what stakes the opposing sides are playing for and why.

At its heart, the Central Conflict revolves around a **Conflict of Ideals**. An ideal in this sense is a conception of perfection being strived for. Each side of the Central Conflict is pursuing their ideal of a perfect world (or galaxy or whatever), and much like their mutually exclusive goals, these two ideals stand in stark contrast to one another.

For simplicity's sake, let us label these two opposing sides the **Superior Ideal** and the **Inferior Ideal**. This isn't to imply that one ideal is good and the other is evil. Instead, the Superior Ideal is the one ultimately proven correct within the context of the storyworld, while the Inferior Ideal is proven false. This duality should never be something as vanilla as "Good vs. Evil". Nothing in life is every so black and white, which is why it's generally a bad idea to have a mustache-twirling, hand-wringing antagonist who just loves being "Eeeeeeevil". Instead, the duality created by deeply rooted, conflicted ideals gives the Central Conflict a sense of purpose. Because the opposing ideals are so sharply conflicted, only one of them can be proven true at the story's conclusion.

Even *Star Wars* with its "menacing" empire and "righteous" band of freedom fighters, has a Conflict of Ideals running deeper than a simple battle between good and evil. Sure, the Galactic Empire is ruthless, but they aren't just pursuing evil for the sake of "Eeeeeeevil". What the Empire idealizes over all else is order and control. This contrasts with the Rebel Alliance who idealizes autonomy and independence. Their two ideals are irreconcilable.

The Empire isn't interested in wanton destruction. Darth Vader's personal goals excluded, the Empire's one objective throughout the entire original trilogy is to neutralize a terrorist organization disrupting the order and control they have established. Considering Princess Leia's plan was to deliver the stolen Death Star schematics to her home planet of Alderaan, it stands to reason there was indeed a significant Rebel presence on the planet. While the Empire's reaction may have been extreme, it certainly coincides with their ideology of maintaining order and control above all else; they destroyed a terrorist breeding ground and sent a message to the galaxy just how far they are willing to go to maintain order. Put into this context, we can see the actions of the Empire, though ruthless, are motivated by a commitment to an ideological system. They aren't just going around blowing up planets for fun.

In *Avatar*, the money-grubbing Company idealizes wealth and technological advancement, while the tree-hugging Na'vi idealize nature and heritage. This Conflict of Ideals comes to a head when the company wants to use their advanced technology to excavate the reservoir of invaluable **MacGuffin** buried beneath the Na'vi's ancient, ancestral treehouse. Because their Conflicted Ideals converge around a single, mutually exclusive, physical goal, the two sides can no longer coexist.

The Conflict of Ideals can also be found in stories without a physical antagonist. The ideal Dr. Stone pursues in the film *Gravity* is life itself. The antagonistic force she encounters through the film comes from space, which is the quintessence of the absence of life. As the title card informs us at the beginning of the film, "Life in space is impossible." How much Dr. Stone wants to survive is rivaled by how very few damns space gives whether she does. Space idealizes nothingness. Life vs. no life. Conflicted ideals.

It is important to understand the Conflict of Ideals pertains to the Central Conflict first and the character second. When the story begins, the Conflict of Ideals already exists, but the character only has a weak attraction to one of the ideals. In *Avatar*, Jake begins the film with loosely the same ideals as the company for which he works. He just wants to make a little money and maybe machine gun some blue aliens in the process. It is only by learning the ways of the Na'vi that he comes to understand the attractiveness of their ideological system.

In other instances, the character begins the story with no personal interest in the Superior or Inferior Ideal. It is only by undertaking the events of the story that he slowly comes to understand the importance and appeal of the Superior Ideal. In *Star Trek*, the Central Conflict is between the crew of the *Enterprise* and the crew of the *Narada*. This conflict arises from the conflicted ideals held by the two sides. Starfleet idealizes peace and justice, while the Romulans idealize destruction and revenge. However, when the film begins, Kirk has no interest in any of these ideals. The only thing he appears to value is the freedom to do whatever the hell he wants. It is only by aligning himself with Starfleet that he slowly comes to accept their ideals as his own.

While the Superior Ideal is more often than not the morally correct ideological choice the character makes in the end, this needn't always be the case. Because the Superior Ideal is simply *the ideal proven true within the context of the storyworld*, it can be morally deficient as long as it is ultimately proven to be the way in which the storyworld operates. In tragic stories, the character's demise often arises from his pursuit of the Inferior Ideal for what he believes to be righteous reasons. In *A Game of Thrones*, Ned Stark's morally correct pursuit of honor and righteousness is proven to be inferior within the context of the world he lives in, making it the Inferior Ideal.

We can find a similar example of subverted ideals in Brian DePalma's 1993 masterpiece (at least to me), *Carlito's Way*. In the film, Al Pacino stars as the eponymous Carlito Brigante, a former drug lord and lifelong criminal recently exonerated from a thirty-year prison sentence thanks to a deft reexamination of his case by his lawyer. While Carlito is committed to abandoning his former life, he still abides by a strict "code of the streets", a Superior Ideal with an amoral implication, which has kept him alive all these years. But when he deviates from this ideal by doing something morally correct (the Inferior Ideal), sparing the life of an upstart rival against his better judgment, he sets into motion a chain of events culminating in his demise.

A common storytelling technique used to amplify the two sides of the Central Conflict is to make the main antagonist a mirror of the character's ideological choice. A **Mirror Antagonist** is similar to the character in many regards, often sharing his profession or position, but differs from the character by his pursuit of the opposite ideal. The Mirror Antagonist is who the character is in danger of becoming if he sets aside the Superior Ideal and embraces the Inferior (or vice versa). The character and the Mirror Antagonist are two sides of the same coin.

In *Iron Man*, the principal antagonist, Obadiah Stane, is similar to Tony Stark in many respects. Like Tony, he's a jet-setting, billionaire, weapons manufacturer. The only difference between them lies in their morality (well, that and their IQ's). Obie is willing to sell weapons to anyone with a big enough bank account (i.e. terrorists), while Tony feels a moral responsibility to keep his weapons out of the hand of those who would use them for malevolence (i.e. terrorists). They are two characters in similar positions who have chosen opposing sides of an Ideal.

The original *Star Wars* trilogy revolves heavily around the Mirror Antagonist premise. Luke is in ever-increasing danger of becoming like his Force-wielding father. If he gives into hate, if he lets his feelings control his action, he will lose the thin sliver of morality differentiating him from Vader. His evolution from hapless farm boy to the last Jedi Knight is predicated on the duality that exists between him and his father.

The Payoffs we discussed in Act Two may also continue to be Set Up in this Act. In the third act of *Gravity*, Dr. Stone nearly knocks herself unconscious while using a fire extinguisher to fight an electrical fire aboard the ISS. This teaches Stone (and the audience) about the propellant force of the extinguisher's gasses in space. This knowledge is called back to in Act Five when Stone intentionally uses a fire extinguisher to propel herself from the derelict Soyuz to the Chinese Space Station.

Goal Three: The False Goal

The goal the character pursues in the third act is a mirage: a big, juicy carrot dangling from a string just beyond his reach. He may feel if he can just achieve this goal then all will be set right in the world. But as he soon learns, this is **The False Goal**. It gets both the character and the audience's hopes up. As the character navigates this act, he comes to realize there is still something bigger he must accomplish before the conflict can be resolved.

The reason this goal is so deceptive is because it *feels* like it could be the Ultimate Goal. This is because the False Goal has an inherent and logical endpoint which, if reached, would signify success for the character and bring the story to a logical, albeit simplistic, conclusion.

Jake's third act goal in *Avatar* is to convince the Na'vi to leave Hometree under the guise of learning their ways. This is a straightforward goal with a definitive endpoint. If Jake succeeds in this objective, the Na'vi pack up and leave, the humans get their unobtanium, and the story is resolved. Both the character and audience are justified in believing the accomplishment of this goal would signify the end of the story. But as it turns out, due to the Conflict of Ideals, the accomplishment of this goal is impossible. Not only will the Na'vi never leave Hometree, the fact of the matter is they shouldn't be made to. This is something Jake learns for himself over the course of the third act.

In *Gravity* Stone and Matt's third act goal is to reach the ISS and use a Soyuz to return to Earth. This is a clearly defined goal with a clearly defined endpoint. If their pursuit of this goal is successful, it would logically conclude the story. The problem is it would conclude the story in the most boring and anticlimactic fashion imaginable. Fortunately for us, the dramatic deck of cards is stacked against astronauts Stone and Kowalski, and when they reach the station, Matt's jetpack is out of fuel. This leads him to sacrifice himself to save Stone. Additionally, they discover the ISS's Soyuzes have been irreparably damaged, and they can't use them to get to Earth. The goal they have been pursuing throughout this act proves to be a pipe dream.

So in his pursuit of the False Goal in Act Three, the character realizes it will never come to fruition and it is not the Ultimate Goal of the story. In some cases, this is the result of the character being duped by an erroneous belief. In *Avatar*, Jake doesn't initially realize the complexity of the Na'vi way of life or that they'll never leave Hometree for blue jeans and light beer. He believes the human way of doing things is not only the right way but the only way. His goal in this act is false because it is based on a flawed belief.

Most often, however, the character simply comes to realize the goal he has been pursuing is small potatoes in the grand scheme of things, and he has underestimated the scope of what he needs to accomplish. In *Titanic*, Rose's third act goal is simply to have a relationship with Jack. But when the ship hits an iceberg, they both realize there are greater events unfolding than their burgeoning love affair. They even attempt to set aside their differences with Cal in light of this development (though Cal, of course, doesn't reciprocate the sentiment). So Rose's Act Three goal is false because it is based on an underestimated objective.

Opposition to the False Goal: Intentional Opposition

By Stumbling into the Central Conflict in this act, the character, often unintentionally, makes the antagonist aware of his existence. The forces of antagonism discover who he is and what he's after. Because the antagonist now recognizes the character as a threat to his plans, he makes a concentrated effort to eliminate him from the picture. This **Intentional Opposition** is the realization of the Central Conflict which pits the character and antagonist against each other.

In Act Two of *The Hunger Games*, Katniss met the antagonistic Careers who didn't like her because they're all contestants in an imminent death match. The most they did at that point was throw snide remarks and menacing glares in her direction, but in the third act, the Games officially begin. Now, not only do they want to kill her because that's the name of the game, but all her showmanship in the second act has made her their primary target. Once the initial chaos of the Cornucopia abates, the Careers rally together behind a unified objective of hunting her down and killing her. Katniss' third act goal of winning the Games *alone* is now opposed by a bloodthirsty mob working *together* with lethal intentions.

In *Inception*, Dom and his motley crew of would-be thieves spent Act Two scraping together the plan for their heist under the nose of their mark. Up to this point, Robert Fischer wasn't trying to stop them because frankly, he didn't even know they existed. But in this act, Don's team enters a dream world unexpectedly populated by Fischer's subconscious projections, who are armed, aware of their presence, and systematically hunting them down. The opposition shifts from being Incidental to being Intentional, with both sides now made aware of the threat the other side poses.

Another clear example of this shift from Incidental to Intentional Opposition can be found in *The Silence of the Lambs*. Clarice spends the second act contending with routine oppression to her goal of investigating the Raspail lead given to her by Lecter. The majority of her problems are bureaucratic in nature. But in Act Three, the opposition she faces is directed at her specifically. Dr. Chilton, the director of the insane asylum where Lecter has reluctantly taken up residence, goes from propositioning her for a date in Act Two, to trying to manipulate her into wearing an illegal wire to record Lecter in Act Three. When she declines, Dr. Chilton, ever the twit, records their conversation anyway. He reveals the phony offer from the FBI to Senator Martin, turning her against Starling. Based on Chilton's interference, the Senator concludes the bureau is gambling with her kidnapped daughter's life by sending a trainee to negotiate, and effectively shuts down the whole operation. The opposition to Clarice's goal is Intentional now. Chilton wants the credit for Lecter's revelations for himself, and Senator Martin wants Clarice off the case.

The Intentional Opposition of Act Three serves the purpose of clearly defining the two sides of the Central Conflict. The audience now knows all the major players in the game and, with the exception of any intentional misdirection by the storyteller, where their allegiances lie.

Turning Point Catalyst: The Turn

Near the end of the third act, there is a drastic turn of events that exponentially complicates things for the character. Something happens to destabilize the already turbulent situation and amplify the Central Conflict. If the Reality Check in Act Two was a firecracker, **The Turn** is a stick of dynamite. It is a major revelation, plot twist or complication that raises the stakes for the character and his allies. This event is often surprising, coming as a shock to both the character and the audience.

Gravity has a particularly poignant Turn. After Stone and Matt overshoot the ISS and narrowly avoid drifting past it thanks to Stone's foot getting caught in a parachute cable, Matt realizes his added weight is going to pull her loose[36]. This leads him to untether himself and heroically float away to his death for Stone to survive. This turn of events complicates things greatly for Stone. Matt had been the pillar of calm and experience throughout the film. Without his guidance, the task of returning to Earth would seem to have become impossible.

Inception uses a powerful, drawn out, and escalating Turn. Almost immediately after entering Fischer's dream, a freight train smashes through downtown, Fischer's subconscious is revealed to have been militarized, Saito is critical wounded, and Dom admits he failed to mention that if any of them die they'll be stuck in Limbo for eternity. In a matter of minutes, things get a lot more complicated for the team.

---

[36] The scientific basis for this has been refuted, but Hollywood physics = drama. Physics be damned.

After decimating the Starfleet armada in *Star Trek*, the Romulan captain Nero creates a black hole at the center of Vulcan, destroying the planet, and causing Trekkies the world over to release a collective groan. The crew of the *Enterprise* is left helpless after this drastic event. The Turn they face is further exacerbated by the fact Nero and his black hole device are now headed straight for Earth.

The severity of the Turn forces the character to again reevaluate his plan of action and leads him into the Act Three Turning Point. Though he made a Commitment to participate at the end of the second act, he must now take it a step further and make a decision to fight tooth and nail for what he believes is right.

Turning Point Three: The Moment of Truth

Approximate Start Time: 55%
Approximate Runtime: 5%

Having Stumbled into the Central Conflict and faced the subsequent Intentional Opposition to his False Goal from the forces of antagonism, the character now comes to the Act Three Turning Point, **The Moment of Truth**.

As the name implies, this is a crucial moment in the story for the character. Here, he is presented with a pivotal, life-changing choice. *He must look within himself to determine his true nature, and make the decision to fight for the things he believes in.* He weighs all the information he has acquired and decides not only which side of the conflict he is on, but how far he is willing to go to ensure the right side prevails.

After his experiences in Act Three, the character finally realizes his objectives and the antagonist's objective are zero sum. There can only be one. May the best man win. Yada yada yada. If the character went from being reactive to proactive at the end of Act Two, then at this Turning Point he goes from being proactive, to going on an all-out offensive.

In *The Hunger Games*, Suzanne Collins demonstrates skillful usage of the Moment of Truth. Katniss takes her first offensive actions against the other tributes, dropping a tracker jacker nest on the careers as they sleep. It is in this moment she first chooses to fight back.

As a result of a tracker jacker sting she receives, Katniss suffers a hallucinatory self-reflection where she is confronted by her worst memories and greatest fears. She is forced to look within herself at the things she has been trying to avoid: the death of her father and the potential death of her sister. Added into this is the revelation of Peeta's true allegiances when he saves her before the Careers have time to regroup. When Katniss finally awakens from the venom, not only has she faced her fears and learned the truth about Peeta, she now has a bow and arrows and commits herself to fighting back against the other tributes. Observe her internal dialogue upon this realization:

"The weapons give me an entirely new perspective on the Games. I know I have tough opponents left to face. But I am no longer merely prey that runs and hides or takes desperate measures. If Cato broke through the trees right now, I wouldn't flee, I'd shoot. I find I'm actually anticipating the moment with pleasure."

She has gone from a participant to a warrior. All these elements combine to give Katniss' Moment of Truth a sense of resonance rarely seen.

To Change or Not To Change

This Turning Point is a critical juncture in the character's arc, revolving around his need to change himself in some way. Similar to the two types of Initial Goal types from Act One, there are two types of Moments of Truth at the character's disposal. He can either make the decision to change some critical facet of himself to become a better person, or he can make the decision not to change, in the belief he is already the ideal version of himself. The Moment of Truth Turning Point often culminates in this decision.

While closely related to the character's Initial Desire for or against changing his *external* initial situation, the change that takes place at this Turning Point is an *internal* change occurring within the character himself. In stories where the character desired to change his initial situation, it is here where he makes a shift in his outlook that gives him the psychological tools to do so. In stories where the character desired not to change his situation, it is here where he realizes he must change some aspect of his attitude or perspective to become a better version of himself.

Because of this, there is often a moment of intense self-examination for the character at this Turning Point. Having come this far, he knows what the consequences will be if he fights, but he feels he must act in accordance with the true nature he has discovered lying dormant within himself. He is forced to make a decision about the type of person he will be moving forward. Everything that happens from this point on hinges on his decision and, once he makes it, he will no longer be able to go back to the way things were. If he makes the right decision at this Turning Point, the story will end happily. If he makes the wrong decision, the story will end in tragedy.

In *A Game of Thrones*, Ned Stark's Moment of Truth occurs when he discovers the truth about Queen Cersei's incestuous relationship with her brother Jamie, and that none of the children she bore are legitimate heirs to the throne. He ponders what he has learned and weighs his options before sending a message for Cersei to meet him in the godswood. There, he reveals he knows the truth about her relationship with her brother and grants her the opportunity to leave the city before King Robert returns. It is this decision not to change, to unwaveringly adhere to his code of honor, despite the protestations of those around him, that allows Cersei's to assassinate the king and ultimately results in Ned following his friend to the grave. He makes the wrong decision at The Moment of Truth and pays the ultimate price for it in the end. This is one of the elements that lends so much authenticity to George R.R. Martin's series. Characters who make poor decisions are forced to pay the price, and the "right" answer morally, isn't always the right course of action to take.

Similarly, in *The Empire Strikes Back*, The Moment of Truth occurs after Luke has a vision of Han and Leia being tortured in the Cloud City at the

Turn. He makes the hasty decision to rocket off into the conflict and square off with the Empire to save the lives of his friends. Both Yoda and Obi-Wan attempt to talk him out of it, reasoning *he* is the one the Emperor wants. By walking away from the Jedi path he has chosen in favor of saving his friends, Luke makes the decision not to change. Sure, he makes the "right" decision from a moral standpoint, but he still pays dearly for it by the film's conclusion. It's also interesting to note his arrival at Cloud City changes nothing regarding the fates of Leia and Han. In fact, *she's* the one who has to turn around and rescue him as he dangles from an antenna beneath the city. My, how the tables have turned since *Episode IV*.

Of course, the Moment of Truth applies to stories with the more "Hollywood" style endings to which most of us are accustomed. The vast majority of stories revolve around the character making a conscious decision to change who he is. In stories that end with the character actually, you know, becoming a hero, The Moment of Truth is where he first comes to realize there is heroic potential lying dormant inside him and chooses to change himself by accepting it. After all he's been through during the first half of the story, he now sees the error in his ways and resolves to do something meaningful with his life.

At The Moment of Truth in *The Lego Movie*, Emmet makes the decision to finally be himself by building his double-decker couch while everyone else scrapes together a submarine. Though he is initially ridiculed, this is a pivotal moment for Emmet and the Emmettes. His couch ends up saving all their lives when the submarine implodes, and galvanizes the remaining Master Builders to rally behind Emmet and his unorthodox (read: terrible and dumb) ideas.

Jake Sully spends the first half of *Avatar* learning about the Na'vi and their ways. He begins to feel like being inside his avatar body is when he's truly awake while being inside his human body is all blue-tinted and depressing. This leads him to the realization at the Moment of Truth that humanity is stupid and dumb while being a Na'vi is where it's at. When the humans bulldoze Willow Glade, Jake makes the slipshod decision to act against them by destroying the video camera guiding their equipment. In this moment, he has chosen to change even if he doesn't fully realize it yet.

At the Moment of Truth, the character is forced to be *truthful* with himself about who he is and what he must become. This leads him to the realization he has either been pursuing the wrong goal and must now pursue something greater, or that he will adhere to his existing ideology no matter what anyone around him opines. Either way, this decision propels him into the next act with a renewed sense of purpose.

Act Three Summary

So, the central pillars of Act Three are: The Central Conflict, the False Goal, Intentional Opposition, the Turn and the Moment of Truth. We can, therefore, summarize Act Three as…

The character Stumbles into the Central Conflict and faces Intentional Opposition in pursuit of a False Goal. But when there is a grave Turn of events, he has a Moment of Truth.

To witness this act in action let's examine Christopher Nolan's masterful, mind-bending, science-fiction, epic *Inception*. Despite its unconventionality and multiple time layers, *Inception* follows a very basic structure (don't worry it's fully delineated in the appendix).

In the third Act, Leonardo DiCaprio's Dom Cobb and his team finally implement the cockamamie plan they cooked up in Act Two by kidnapping Robert Fischer and entering the first dream layer. Their goal is to kidnap Fisher (again) inside the dream and take their sweet time breaking him down until he tells him what they want to know. Easy peasy, right?

But as we soon learn, this is a False Goal. Sure their overall objective remains the same, but their little plan quickly goes to excrement when Dom and his team Stumble into the Central Conflict. Unbeknownst to them, Fischer's subconscious has been militarized as a contingency for just such an occasion. The team almost instantly comes under gunfire from Fischer's ruthless, subconscious projections, and now has an unending stream of heavily armed assailants Intentionally Opposing their goal of sweet-talking Fischer into accepting the inception. Their original goal becomes subservient to the act of staying alive.

As a result of this opposition, their billionaire backer, Mr. Saito, takes a life-threatening bullet to the chest, confirming the foreshadowed line that there is, indeed, no room for tourists on these jobs. But, as we learned in the first act if you die in a dream you just wake up, right? Wrong. We next find out the chemist who cooked up the team's Nyquil made it so strong the good old fail-safe of dying is ineffective. Instead, if any member of the team dies they will slip into Limbo, the unconstructed dream space where seconds last for years and you slowly shrivel into a wrinkly, prune version of your former self. This revelation is The Turn. Things just got infinitely more complicated for our lovable band of dream thieves. They are surrounded by an army who wants to kill them, and they can't, under any circumstances, die.

The Turn precipitates the Moment of Truth, where the character is finally truthful with himself about who he has become. Immediately following the revelation that everyone will spend eternity in Limbo if the die, Ariadne confronts Dom about his guilt over Mal and the instability he has brought into their shared dream. At her insistence, he vows to do something he has been unable to do until this point: admit Mal is not real. This is a pivotal, life-changing moment for Dom.

But the character must also make a decision to fight for what he believes in at the Moment of Truth. In *Inception* Dom has been recklessly committed to the cause from its, um, inception, but in a testament to Nolan's storytelling genius, it is in this moment when we receive the big reveal of *why* he has been so willing to risk everything and fight to return to his children. We learn what events transpired between him and Mal that led to his banishment. The depth of his resolve is firmly established. It's all or nothing at all.

The third act of *Inception* can be effectively summarized using the central pillars of Act Three.

> *Cobb and the team enter into Fischer's protected dream world (the central conflict) and must contend with his unexpectedly weaponized subconscious (intentional opposition) to implement their simple plan for the inception (the false goal). But when Saito is shot, and it is revealed Fischer's subconscious has been militarized to protect itself from extraction (the turn), Cobb realizes the only way to survive to is to complete the mission and comes clean to Ariadne about how Mal died (the moment of truth).*

Again, notice the character's Story Specific Actions coincides with the universal action of the act. Dom and his team Stumble into the Central Conflict by learning of the existence of Fischer's militarized projections and realizing they must fight them if they are to succeed in their task. Their foray into the conflict is not intentional, but a consequence of their naiveté in pursuing their False Goal.

Act Three begins, on average, about 40% into the story and, like the previous two acts, tends to run about 20%. So, when this act ends, we should be approximately 60% into the telling of our tale.

Act Three Examples

The Hunger Games
2008 Novel
Written by Suzanne Collins

Character
Katniss Everdeen

Ultimate Goal
Win the Hunger Games with Peeta

Total Runtime: 27 chapters

The Hunger Games - Act Three: Stumbling into the Central Conflict

The character Stumbles into the Central Conflict and faces Intentional Opposition in pursuit of a False Goal. But when there is a grave Turn of events, he has a Moment of Truth.

After the Games begin, Katniss tries to survive the attacks of the other tributes (the central conflict) who want to kill her (intentional opposition) before she can win the Games alone (the false goal). But when she discovers Peeta is working with the careers, and severely burns her leg (the turn), she uses a tracker jacker nest to attack the careers, is saved by Peeta and obtains a bow and arrows enabling her to fight back (the moment of truth).

Starting Percentage: After 9 of 27 Chapters (33.3%)
Runtime: Chapter 10 through Chapter 15 (6 Chapters)
Run Percentage: 6 of 27 Chapters (22.2%)

Stumbling into the Central Conflict - The character learns more about the storyworld and develops a new goal that is diametrically opposed to the goal of the antagonist.

Katniss faces the external conflict of the other tributes in the Games, as well as the internal conflict of her feelings toward Peeta. She's not just battling the other tributes; she's battling to maintain her humanity.

The Conflict of Ideals - The two sides of the Central Conflict are pursuing opposing ideals of perfection.

Freedom (Superior Ideal) vs. Subjugation (Inferior Ideal)

The False Goal - The character receives a new goal he feels will set everything right in his world. Sadly, this isn't the case, and there is still something bigger he must accomplish.

Katniss attempts to Survive the Games alone, but this is not the Ultimate Goal. If Peeta were to die in the arena, it would likely haunt her forever.

Intentional Opposition – As a result of his decision at the Commitment, the character comes to the attention of the forces of antagonism. They now begin opposing him with the specific intention of thwarting his plans.

Now that the Games have begun, "The Girl on Fire" is an, ahem, hot target for both the Gamemakers and the other tributes.

Turning Point Catalyst: The Turn

The Turn - There is a major turn of events that raises the stakes for the character and his allies and makes his situation far more complicated than it had been up to this point. This event is often surprising, coming as a shock to both the character and the audience.

Katniss discovers Peeta is working with the careers to hunt her down. What a douche. Shortly thereafter, her leg is severely burned, and she bumps into the Careers who chase her up a tree like a pack of bloodthirsty hounds.

Turning Point Three: The Moment of Truth

Start Time: After 13 of 27 Chapters (48.1%)
Runtime: Chapters 14 through 15 (2 Chapters)
Run Percentage: 2 of 27 Chapters (7.4%)

<u>The Moment of Truth</u> - As a result of the Turn, the character must reevaluate his strategy, analyze who he is, and decide to be truthful with himself about the type of person he must become. In figuring out his true nature, he makes the decision to fight for the things he believes in.

Thanks to Rue who she befriended in training, Katniss sees and plots to use a tracker jacker nest against the Careers. She saws off the nest and drops it on the unsuspecting careers, proving to herself she is willing to kill to survive. She is stung by the tracker jackers in the process but manages to grab a bow and arrows before she succumbs to the venom. Peeta also reveals his true nature by shaking her awake and telling her to run while the Careers are distracted.

When Katniss awakens from the venom, she realizes Peeta saved her life. More importantly, she has a bow and arrows and decides to fight back against Cato and the Careers. She teams up with Rue, and the two concoct an offensive plan; they will destroy the supplies the Careers have horded to make them hungry, seeing as it's the Hunger Games *and all.*

<u>To Change or Not to Change</u> - At the Moment of Truth, the character faces the decision to either change his perspective and who he has been or retain the same outlook in the face of all which has transpired.

To Change: Katniss makes the decision to fight back against the Careers and control her fate by killing other tributes so she may survive.

The Silence of the Lambs
1988 Novel
Written by Thomas Harris

Character
Clarice Starling

Ultimate Goal
Stop the serial killer Buffalo Bill before he kills again.

Total Runtime: 61 chapters

The Silence of the Lambs - Act Three: Stumbling into the Central Conflict

The character Stumbles into the Central Conflict and faces Intentional Opposition in pursuit of a False Goal. But when there is a grave Turn of events, he has a Moment of Truth.

Clarice pursues Buffalo Bill (the central conflict) and deals with interference to her investigation (intentional opposition), in attempt to convince Lecter to reveal Bill's true identity (the false goal). But when Chilton reveals to Lecter that Clarice lied about the deal with the Senator, and has him extradited to Tennessee (the turn), Starling asks Crawford for permission to go after him (the moment of truth).

Start Time: After 18 of 61 Chapters (29.5%)
Runtime: Chapter 19 through Chapter 31 (13 Chapters)
Run Percentage: 13 of 61 Chapters (21.3%)

Stumbling into the Central Conflict - The character learns more about the storyworld and develops a new goal that is diametrically opposed to the goal of the antagonist.

Clarice faces off with everyone standing between her and Buffalo Bill.

The Conflict of Ideals - The two sides of the Central Conflict are pursuing opposing ideals of perfection.

Justice and Self-Sacrifice (Superior Ideal) vs. Death and Self-Importance (Inferior Ideal)

The False Goal - The character receives a new goal he feels will set everything right in his world. Sadly, this isn't the case, and there is still something bigger he must accomplish.

Clarice attempts to convince Lecter to reveal Bill's true identity.

Intentional Opposition - As a result of his decision at the Commitment, the character comes to the attention of the forces of antagonism. They now begin opposing him with the specific intention of thwarting his plans.

As Jame Gumb prepares Catherine for slaughter, Crawford's sends Clarice to interview Lecter a third time. Chilton attempts to make her wear a wire. Lecter's more intrusive and cryptic than ever. He toys with her and gets her to reveal the juicy details of her father's murder. Nom, nom, nom.

Afterward, Clarice realizes Crawford is intentionally manipulating her. She returns to Lecter with Crawford's made up offer of relocation. Lecter extracts more information from her in exchange. Clarice tells him about her life after her father's death and that he was really a "night marshal" not an actual policeman. She also tells him about the slaughterhouse she was sent to as a child. Chilton intentionally opposes the FBI's plan and contacts Senator Martin after hearing the whole thing on an illegal wiretap.

Turning Point Catalyst: The Turn

The Turn - There is a major turn of events that raises the stakes for the character and his allies and makes his situation far more complicated than it had been up to this point. This event is often surprising, coming as a shock to both the character and the audience.

Chilton reveals to Lecter he eavesdropped on his conversation with Clarice, and there is no deal with the Senator. Crawford learns Chilton and the senator have had Lecter extradited to Tennessee in exchange for information on Buffalo Bill.

Turning Point Three: The Moment of Truth

Start Time: After 29 of 61 Chapters (47.5%)
Runtime: Chapter 30 through 31 (2 Chapters)
Run Percentage: 2 of 61 Chapters (3.2%)

The Moment of Truth - As a result of the Turn, the character must reevaluate his strategy, analyze who he is, and decide to be truthful with himself about the type of person he must become. In figuring out his true nature, he makes the decision to fight for the things he believes in.

Having learned of Chilton's manipulations, Clarice is fighting mad and asks Crawford for permission to go after him. Crawford gives her lessons on not letting her emotions get the best of her. Starling decides he is right and to focus her attention on stopping Buffalo Bill and saving Catherine Martin. She sees this decision through to the end of the narrative, even in the face of being recycled in the Academy.

To Change or Not to Change - At the Moment of Truth, the character faces the decision to either change his perspective and who he has been or retain the same outlook in the face of all which has transpired.

To Change: Upon hearing the news of what transpired between Senator Martin and Dr. Chilton, Clarice's natural reaction is for retribution. Crawford gives her a stirring lecture on the importance of stoicism...

"This is the hardest time, Starling. Use this time and it'll temper you. Now's the hardest test—not letting rage and frustration keep you from thinking...

"I want you to freeze something now. Freeze this business with Chilton. Keep the information you got from Lecter and freeze the feelings. I want you to keep your eye on the prize, Starling. That's all that matters... Take the knowledge of Buffalo Bill you got from Lecter and keep it. Freeze the rest. The waste, the loss, your anger, Chilton. Freeze it. When we have time, we'll kick Chilton's butt up between his shoulder blades. Freeze it now and slide it aside. So you can see past it to the prize, Starling. Catherine Martin's life. And Buffalo Bill's hide on the barn door. Keep your eyes on the prize. If you can do that I need you."

This lesson is something Crawford has been trying to instill in Clarice throughout the story. His words here lead to a shift, however subtle, in her perspective, enabling her to focus on the task at hand.

Star Wars
1977 Film
Written and directed by George Lucas

Character
Luke Skywalker

Ultimate Goal
Destroy the Death Star and save the princess.

Total Runtime: 120 minutes

Star Wars - Act Three: Stumbling into the Central Conflict

The character Stumbles into the Central Conflict and faces Intentional Opposition in pursuit of a False Goal. But when there is a grave Turn of events, he has a Moment of Truth.

The Empire destroys Alderaan in pursuit of the Rebels (the central conflict) and captures the Millennium Falcon (intentional opposition) while Luke and the gang are on their way to deliver the droids (the false goal). But when they are caught by the Death Star's tractor beam and pulled inside (the turn), Luke discovers Princess Leia is onboard and must convince Han and Chewie to rescue her before she is executed (the moment of truth).

Starting Percentage: 59 of 120 minutes (49.1%)
Runtime: 13 minutes of 120 minutes (10.8%)

Stumbling into the Central Conflict - The character learns more about the storyworld and develops a new goal that is diametrically opposed to the goal of the antagonist.

Luke and the Rebels, vs. the Empire's Death Star. It is in this act that Luke and the gang discover and contend with the Death Star.

The Conflict of Ideals - The two sides of the Central Conflict are pursuing opposing ideals of perfection.

Autonomy and Freedom (Superior Ideal) vs. Order and Control (Inferior Ideal)

The False Goal - The character receives a new goal he feels will set everything right in his world. Sadly, this isn't the case, and there is still something bigger he must accomplish.

Luke and the gang attempt to escape the Death Star.

Intentional Opposition - As a result of his decision at the Commitment, the character comes to the attention of the forces of antagonism. They now begin opposing him with the specific intention of thwarting his plans.

The Falcon *gets caught in the Death Star's tractor beam and brought on board. The Emperor's minions search the ship, and Luke's crew sneaks into the control room under the noses of their enemies.*

Turning Point Catalyst: The Turn

The Turn - There is a major turn of events that raises the stakes for the character and his allies and makes his situation far more complicated than it had been up to this point. This event is often surprising, coming as a shock to both the character and the audience.

Leia is to be executed immediately. Meanwhile, the Death Star catches the Falcon *in a tractor beam and pulls it into the base.*

Turning Point Three: The Moment of Truth

Start Time: 68 of 120 minutes (57%)
Runtime: 4 minutes of 120 minutes (3.3%)

<u>The Moment of Truth</u> - As a result of the Turn, the character must reevaluate his strategy, analyze who he is, and decide to be truthful with himself about the type of person he must become. In figuring out his true nature, he makes the decision to fight for the things he believes in.

R2 reveals Leia is on the Death Star and is scheduled to be terminated[37]. When Luke realizes this, he wants to go save her. Han initially refuses, but Luke convinces him he will receive a huge reward if they rescue her. Luke comes up with a plan to gain access to the detention area, making the decision to fight for what he believes is right.

<u>To Change or Not to Change</u> - At the Moment of Truth, the character faces the decision to either change his perspective and who he has been or retain the same outlook in the face of all which has transpired.

To Change: Up to this point, Luke has been little more than a farmhand at best, and the Robin to Obi-Wan's Batman at worst. It is only when he discovers Princess Leia is being held on the Death Star that he decides to take a course action outside of who he has always been and change his stars.

---

[37] Because apparently there is already a termination schedule on this newly constructed space station.

Titanic
1997 Film
Written and directed by James Cameron

Character
Rose Dawson

Ultimate Goal
Survive the ship and live life on her terms.

Total Runtime: 187 minutes

Titanic - Act Three: Stumbling into the Central Conflict

The character Stumbles into the Central Conflict and faces Intentional Opposition in pursuit of a False Goal. But when there is a grave Turn of events he has a Moment of Truth.

Rose shuns and infuriates Cal (the central conflict) who sends Lovejoy after her (intentional opposition) for starting an all-out relationship with Jack (the false goal). But when the ship strikes an iceberg and Cal frames Jack for the theft of the heart of the ocean diamond (the turn), Rose realizes Jack is innocent and turns her back on Cal and her mother to rescue him (the moment of truth).

Starting Percentage: 83 of 187 minutes (44.4%)
Runtime: 35 minutes of 187 minutes (18.7%)

Stumbling into the Central Conflict - The character learns more about the storyworld and develops a new goal that is diametrically opposed to the goal of the antagonist.

Rose and Jack square off with Cal, Lovejoy, and the sinking ship.

ACTIONS & GOALS

The Conflict of Ideals - The two sides of the Central Conflict are pursuing opposing ideals of perfection.

Freedom and Happiness (Superior Ideal) vs. Wealth and Control (Inferior Ideal)

The False Goal - The character receives a new goal he feels will set everything right in his world. Sadly, this isn't the case, and there is still something bigger he must accomplish.

Rose attempts to have a relationship with Jack

Intentional Opposition - As a result of his decision at the Commitment, the character comes to the attention of the forces of antagonism. They now begin opposing him with the specific intention of thwarting his plans.

Cal orders Lovejoy to find Rose, and she and Jack narrowly evade his pursuit. Cal finds the drawing of Rose in his safe and comes up with the awesome idea to frame Jack for a crime[38].

Turning Point Catalyst: The Turn

The Turn - There is a major turn of events that raises the stakes for the character and his allies and makes his situation far more complicated than it had been up to this point. This event is often surprising, coming as a shock to both the character and the audience.

The lookouts spot an iceberg. After much communication throughout the ship to turn, they hit it anyway. Cal tells a steward he has been robbed and to fetch the master of arms. Rose and Jack overhear what is going on with the iceberg and resolve to tell Cal and her mother. When they return Cal orders Jack searched, and they find the diamond Lovejoy planted on him. Jack pleads with Rose to

---

[38] Seeing as how he's a filthy peasant and all.

believe him. She doesn't. Mr. Andrews tells the captain the ship will sink in an hour or two at most.

Turning Point Three: The Moment of Truth

Start Time: 108 of 187 minutes (57.7%)
Runtime: 10 minutes of 187 minutes (5.3%)

<u>The Moment of Truth</u> - As a result of the Turn, the character must reevaluate his strategy, analyze who he is, and decide to be truthful with himself about the type of person he must become. In figuring out his true nature, he makes the decision to fight for the things he believes in.

Back in their stateroom, Cal slaps Rose to demonstrate what their married life will be like. Meanwhile, Lovejoy leaves Jack to die in the slowly flooding detention area of the ship.

While they make their way to the lifeboats, Cal and Rose's mother make saucy remarks about the state of the ship. Rose tells her mother to shut up and that half the people on the ship will die. Cal tells Rose Jack's drawing will be worth more in the morning, prompting her to realize he set Jack up. Rose bids her mother a final goodbye. Cal tries to stop her but she spits in his face[39] and flees. She now realizes the person she must be moving forward and makes the decision to fight against adversity for what she believes is right.

<u>To Change or Not to Change</u> - At the Moment of Truth, the character faces the decision to either change his perspective and who he has been or retain the same outlook in the face of all which has transpired.

To Change: After waffling on her relationship with Jack during the Turn, Rose has a change of heart at the Moment of Truth and decides he is innocent. She fully commits herself to her newfound perspective on money and its effect on happiness in life.

---

[39] A Payoff from the Setup of Jack teaching her how to spit in Act Two.

ACT FOUR: IMPLEMENTING A DOOMED PLAN

"So that's it, then? We failed... It's a shame; I really wanted to know what was going to happen in there. I swear we had this one."

Eames, the forge - Inception, Act Four

Approximate Start Time: 60% into the story
Approximate Runtime: 20% of the story

Because the character committed to fighting for what he believes in at the Moment of Truth, he enters into the fourth act with a righteous cause and a newfound desire to do something purposeful with his life. Motivated by his new goal, he devises a plan to achieve it, launching a full-on assault against the forces of antagonism in the process. Unfortunately for him, his plan, be it planned out to the millisecond or improvised on the fly, is destined to have disastrous results. This is **The Doomed Plan**.

In most instances, the plan the character implements is well-thought-out and carries a reasonable likelihood of success. Though his plan may encounter some initial difficulties, he has a justified level of confidence and is able to think on his feet to work through whatever hiccups he encounters. But just when he is on the verge of success, there is a sudden and shocking reversal of fortune that shoves a big, fat monkey wrench in the cogs of his scheme. Though the character comes close to achieving his goal, he is ultimately denied its attainment.

In Act Four of *A Game of Thrones*, Ned Stark plans to depose the Lannisters from the Iron Throne by soliciting the aid of the often dubious Master of

Coin, Petyr "Littlefinger" Baelish to pay off the City Watch and bring them to his cause. When the big moment arrives and Ned orders the Lannister's arrested, Littlefinger reveals his betrayal and instead has Ned apprehended by the City Watch as the Lannisters look on. As a result of his Doomed Plan, Ned is imprisoned for treason (and ultimately beheaded) by the very people he sought to overthrow. Fail.

In Act Four of *The Lego Movie*, Emmet and the gang implement his surprising intricate plan to sneak into Octan tower and destroy the Kragle. They hit a few snags requiring improvisation along the way but ultimately come within capping distance of their objective. Just when we're all ready to break out the party hats and noisemakers, Wyldstyle gets captured, Emmet hesitates, and the whole plan falls apart.

A similar Doomed Plan can be found in *Gravity*. Dr. Stone has every reason to be optimistic about her plan to use the ISS's escape pod to fly to the Chinese station. It was Kowalski's last suggestion after all, and he always seemed to know what he was doing. In implementing her plan, she, of course, faces complications: the ISS catches fire, the Soyuz is tangled in the wreckage, the debris field returns, et cetera, et cetera, et cetera. While these things can all be managed, when she realizes en route that the Soyuz is out of fuel and she's adrift in space, the monkey wrench of fate once again rears its ugly head.

In some cases however, the character's plan succeeds but has grave, unanticipated consequences. At the Moment of Truth in *Star Wars*, Luke firmly commits to fighting for the rebellion by making the decision to rescue the princess. In Act Four he demonstrates this commitment by implementing his plan to march into the detention area with Han and Chewie. Though they are able to (narrowly) escape the detention block with the princess, (narrowly) escape the garbage compactor, and do indeed rescue the princess, they also lose the most valuable, knowledgeable and powerful member of their motley little crew in the process: Obi-Wan "the last Jedi in the galaxy" Kenobi. Not only that, but we also learn at the end of the act the Empire placed a tracking device on the *Falcon* and are following them to the Rebel base. So yeah, fail.

In other stories, the character's plan is obviously doomed from the onset. After his feed is killed while trying to come clean to the Omaticaya at the Moment of Truth, Jake reenters his avatar in Act Four to convince them to leave Hometree before Quaritch and his fleet of gunships level it. This in itself is a huge improbability. It has already been established in Act Three the Na'vi will never leave Hometree. When you add on the fact Jake was in on the whole "blow-up-Hometree" thing all along, his chances of success plummet from infinitesimal to absolute zero.

Significance of Implementing a Doomed Plan

Storytelling is all about ups and downs, (or rising and falling actions if you prefer to obfuscate). And Act Four is all about playing off the audience's expectations of the upward momentum provided by the Moment of Truth. At this point, everything is set up for the character's grand success. After witnessing him realize the error of his ways and make a resolution to change at the Moment of Truth, we are rooting for his success. He has a reasonable plan in place and a team of people around him he trusts to help accomplish it. The audience can *feel* the character has success within his grasp.

But this ain't your grandpa's nickelodeon. The character must now demonstrate his commitment to fight when his dedication to his new cause is tested. Before he can accomplish his goal, he must first face a catastrophic defeat. It is only through the devastating failure resulting from Implementing his Doomed Plan in Act Four that he comes to the realize he must be willing to sacrifice himself, if need be, to ensure the side of right is victorious.

In Act Four of *Avatar*, Jake now knows the company is bad, m'kay. He appeals to Selfridge's sense of morality to allow him and Grace to at least attempt to get the Na'vi to leave Hometree before the Colonel and his war machines destroy it. While Selfridge allows it, Jake's attempt to reason with the Na'vi fails. As a result, the Na'vi turn their backs on him, the company turns its back on him, Hometree is destroyed, and Jake and the avatar team are thrown in the brig. We wanted Jake to be successful in this act, but his expectations and our own are left unfulfilled. It is only through being kicked down to where he no longer has anything left to lose (except his life) that Jake realizes he must be willing to risk it all (i.e. his life). Now we are behind him more than ever.

Because the character is knocked down so low in this act, the momentum of the story takes a hard shift from the side of the character to that of the antagonist. The audience receives a clear glimpse of just how powerful the forces of antagonism are, and how far *they* are willing to go to ensure their sinister (though hopefully justifiable) plan succeeds.

We learn in Act Three of *Iron Man* that Obadiah is a no-good, money-grubbing shyster who's been dealing arms to both sides under the table. While this is deplorable behavior, it's not flat-out malevolent. I mean, he's a businessman in a multibillion-dollar, war-based industry. Let's be honest, the public perception is that this is customary behavior for someone in his position. But in Act Four, we learn not only is Obie in cahoots with the Ten Rings, he's the one giving them orders, specifically the order to kill Tony at his weapons presentation in Afghanistan. In this act we watch Obie kill off the red herring terrorist leader, threaten to kill Pepper and attempt to kill Tony[40]. We witness the full power of his, um, power in action as well as how far *he* is willing to go to maintain his position. Act Four goes to the antagonist.

In stories with tragic endings, Act Four serves as the prelude to the character's downfall. As such, there is often a certain amount of hubris to his actions in this act. People close to the character try to warn him against the error of his

---

[40] In an admittedly, Bond villain, "let me explain the genius of my evil plan then leave you to die slowly" fashion.

ways, but his overconfidence in his belief system in this act ultimately leads him to his demise.

In Act Four of *A Game of Thrones*, Ned implements his plan to install Stannis Baratheon as king against the advice of *everyone* around him who would rather he imprison or execute the Lannisters immediately. The ultimate failure of his plan occurs because he erroneously believes his code of honor is beyond reproach.

Goal Four: The Penultimate Goal

Though the character learned the basic idea behind the Ultimate Goal at The Moment of Truth, he isn't thinking big enough in the goal he pursues into Act Four. At this point, he almost has it figured out, but his goal still is too small. He is pursuing **The Penultimate Goal**.

As the name suggests, the Penultimate Goal is closely related to, but a step removed from the Ultimate Goal of the story. By pursuing this goal, the character will come to realize exactly what it is he needs to do to end the conflict once and for all (or, at least until the sequel).

The Penultimate Goal is often the Ultimate Goal on a smaller scale. In *Avatar*, the Ultimate Goal is for Jake to save the whole of Pandora from those obtuse Sky People with their flying doohickeys and explosive doodads, but his Penultimate Goal in Act Four is only to save Hometree and the Omaticaya clan. Similarly, in *Star Wars* Luke's Penultimate Goal in Act Four is to save the princess from the Death Star. This is closely related, though smaller in scale, to his Ultimate Goal of saving the entire galaxy (starting with the princess on Yavin 4) from the Death Star in the next act.

Because the overall action of Act Four is *Implementing a Doomed Plan*, the character's pursuit of the Penultimate Goal will either fail outright or have disastrous consequences he failed to foresee. One of the reasons the Penultimate Goal so often fails is because it doesn't involve the character confronting the main antagonist head-on. His Doomed Plan attempts to circumvent the antagonist in a path of least resistance.

In *Inception*, the Penultimate Goal for Dom is to get Fischer into the inception room and implant the inception. But when the principal antagonist, Mal, murders Fischer as he enters the room, Dom realizes that in order to implant the inception he must confront his projection of Mal in Limbo and free himself from the guilt he feels over her suicide. This confrontation with Mal is intrinsic to the achievement of his Ultimate Goal.

In stories where the character made a decision to change at the Moment of Truth, the resulting failure of his Doomed Plan is often the final tipping point of his arc. Although he resolved to change, he does so in a manner requiring the least amount of effort on his part. He believed he could keep a part of his old self intact and only change superficially. The price he pays for the failure of his Doomed Plan in this act leads him to realize he must change completely. In doing so he finally understands the scale of his objective and learns the Ultimate Goal of the story.

At the Moment of Truth in *The Lego Movie*, Emmet finally commits himself to believing he is the Special. But when his plan to sneak into Octan tower fails and the prophecy of the Special is revealed to have been made up by his mentor, Vitruvius, Emmet questions the internal change he has undergone. It is only through his realization he can still take action, regardless of whether or not he is the Special, that he actually becomes the Special. By (seemingly) sacrificing himself, Emmet saves all the other Master Builders and becomes a martyr for the others to rally behind.

Because the character pays such a heavy price for trying to achieve The Penultimate Goal, he realizes at the end of this act what the Ultimate Goal is and why it is so important. This understanding of the Ultimate Goal can only be obtained by the character passing through the crucible of the Act Four Turning Point. Only then will he truly understand what it is he is fighting for and why it is so imperative he succeeds.

Opposition to the Penultimate Goal: Self-Inflicted Opposition

Because the character made the decision to engage the forces of antagonism at the Moment of Truth, he now becomes a willing contributor to the Central Conflict in Act Four. By intentionally seeking out the antagonist in this act, he also becomes the primary cause of the opposition he faces. All the bad things that befall him are a result of his intentional attack on the antagonist. This is the **Self-Inflicted Opposition**.

In this act, the character shoots himself in the foot, so to speak. His willingness to seek out a confrontation with the antagonist backfires, and he must deal with the repercussion brought about by his course of action.

In Act Four of *The Lego Movie*, Emmet and the gang implement their doomed plan to infiltrate Octan Tower and cap off the Kragle. While their objective is (of course) not to get caught, they intentionally risk bringing the opposition of the laser, sharks, and laser sharks guarding the Tower onto themselves. The opposition they face in this act is a direct result of their attempt to attack the forces of antagonism.

In *The Empire Strikes Back*, Luke travels to Cloud City to rescue Han and Leia against the logical protests of Yoda and Obi-Wan. Don't be a fool, they tell him. It's you and your abilities the Emperor wants, to which Luke replies, "Whatevs." Because Luke enters into this situation knowing it's a trap, the subsequent opposition he faces, the shoot-out with Boba Fett and the Imperial guards, and his duel with Darth Vader, are inflicted by his own desire to square off with the Empire and rescue his friends.

The Self-Inflicted Opposition is exacerbated by the fact the plan the character implements in this act is doomed from the onset. While the character may think he has what it takes to defeat the forces of antagonism at this point, he is gravely mistaken. This is often because he overestimates his abilities or underestimates the physical or tactical superiority of the forces of antagonism.

It is generally in this act that the antagonist gives the character a demonstration of his full power.

In Act Four of *Iron Man*, Tony is flying high after his successful attack on the Ten Rings in Gulmira. But we soon learn Obadiah is the murderous Iron Monger who masterminded Tony's kidnapping in Afghanistan and has built a suit of his own. Using a sonic taser to paralyze Tony, he elaborates on his superiority in an evil monologue detailing his plan. Tony underestimated the ruthlessness of his adversary and nearly pays the ultimate price for it.

In *Empire*, Luke underestimates both Vader's strength in the Force and the nature of their relationship. Not only is he bested in (one) armed combat, he also gets the bombshell dropped on him that he's one of Darth Vader's sperms. And oh yeah, he doesn't save Han or Leia from anything. Failed them he has.

Turning Point Catalyst: The Lowpoint

Whether the character's plan has some initial success or is doomed from the onset, there comes a point in the fourth act where he realizes, unequivocally, his plan has failed. This realization brings with it a sense of complete hopelessness and failure. This is **The Lowpoint**.

Here, the character's worse fears are realized as his seemingly foolproof plan unravels, and he is dealt a terrible loss at the hands of the antagonist. At this point, the character is effectively taken back to ground zero, and it appears all his actions over the course of the story have been for naught. Much like the Moment of Truth, the Lowpoint is a time of deep self-examination for the character. He looks back over everything that has transpired, and all the actions he has taken over the course of the story and feels, justifiably, that he has lost.

Jake reaches his Lowpoint in *Avatar*, when his plan to reenter his avatar and convince the Na'vi to leave Hometree before the Colonel destroys it fails completely. Despite his sincere efforts to confess his sins to the Omaticaya and renounce his foolish ways, he is excommunicated from the tribe (by his new wife, nonetheless) and cut off from the only thing in his life ever to give him purpose. In the wake of this, Hometree is destroyed by the company and Jake arises from the ashes in "the place the eye does not see". Cue sad music.

In *Star Trek*, the Lowpoint occurs when Kirk goads Spock into revealing his emotional instability over the loss of his mother and planet. Spock takes the bait and nearly kills Kirk to death in a fit of uncontrollable rage. This leads Spock to realize he has failed as both a Vulcan and a Starfleet officer, and he is no longer capable of commanding the *Enterprise*. Cue sad music.

In *The Lego Movie*, Vitruvius reveals to Emmet the prophecy was all made up, and Emmet was never really "the Special". And then he dies. All of Emmet's Master Builder buddies are apprehended by Lord Business who jubilantly informs Emmet that not only is he unspecial, he is a thousand billion times more unspecial than Lord Business is himself. Emmet must now watch helplessly as his nemesis implements the final phase of his plan to Kragle the universe. Cue sad music.

The Lowpoint, as the name implies, is the lowest point the character will reach in the story. Though he will still face hardships in Act Five, the Lowpoint gives him a taste of what the consequences will be should he truly fail to defeat the antagonist. The failure he faces here will provide him with the motivation to succeed regardless of the adversity he encounters moving forward.

Turning Point Four: The Newfound Resolve

Approximate Start Time: 75%
Approximate Runtime: 5%

With the devastating failure of Doomed Plan at the Lowpoint, the character is often knocked lower than where he was when he started. But it is only from this viewpoint of near defeat that he is finally able to see the big picture. By implementing his Doomed Plan and suffering such a heavy loss, the character finally earns his understanding of the Ultimate Goal. With nothing left to lose, *he realizes he must defeat the forces of antagonism, whatever the cost*. This realization is the Turning Point of Act Four: **The Newfound Resolve**.

There is an element of death and rebirth implicit to this Turning Point and its Catalyst analogous to the mythical phoenix. In modern times the phoenix has become synonymous with death and rebirth. While this isn't wholly inaccurate, it downplays some aspects of the original mythology. In the legends of old, the phoenix didn't just die to be born again. Instead, it constructed a pyre, set itself afire, burned to dust and rose anew from its ashes. The fourth act is metaphorical of this process.

The character enters into Act Four on fire, so to speak, from his decision at the Moment of Truth. He knows what he faces in the forces of antagonism and though he is outmatched, still believes he has a legitimate shot at success. However, when the forces of antagonism close in, the plan he hatches becomes the self-constructed pyre that will ultimately consume and destroy him at the Lowpoint.

The character's actions at the Lowpoint culminate in death, either literal or symbolic. In stories with life or death stakes, someone or several people close to him may die, or he may come to the edge of death himself. This death or near death at the Lowpoint reinvigorates the sense of purpose he discovered at the Moment of Truth. At the Newfound Resolve, he rededicates himself to his cause with a much clearer understanding of its significance. Much like the phoenix, the character rises from the ashes of defeat a stronger and fully actualized version of his former self.

In other stories, the character will face a metaphorical death. In a romantic comedy, the Lowpoint comes when our two attractive leads break up over some ridiculous and completely avoidable misunderstanding. This "death" of their relationship often leads to a period of mourning for the two lovers, as they meander around in their pajamas, eating ice cream out of the carton while criticizing men/women with their man/woman-hating best friend[41].

But just when the character has lost all hope whatsoever of succeeding, something leads him to finally realize the Ultimate Goal he has been unable to recognize up to this point. There is often a final revelation at the Newfound Resolve that illuminates to the character exactly what he needs to do to achieve the Ultimate Goal of the story. The lessons and themes have been repeatedly beat over his head, but it isn't until this moment that the character is finally able to see what everyone has been trying to teach him. After all this time, he finally "gets it".

This "getting" of "it" may be a literal revelation of information. After Katniss loses Rue at the Lowpoint of *The Hunger Games*, the Gamemakers make the sudden and surprising announcement that, should two tributes from the same District be the only remaining survivors, they can win the Games together.

---

[41] It's interesting to note that Rom-Coms diverge from this structural method at this point, as the character spends Act Five in pursuit of the Newfound Resolve and reconciliation which typically occurs at the "rush to the airport in a taxi" climax of the fifth act.

Their announcement is unprecedented, something that has never occurred in the seventy-four years the Hunger Games have been held. This revelation fills Katniss with a newfound hope she couldn't have imagined moments before. But for the audience, the fact that Peeta is her ally is something we've been rooting for the self-reliant Katniss to "get" for the entire story.

In *The Silence of the Lambs,* Clarice is sent back to Quantico after being scapegoated for Lecter's escape at the Lowpoint. Here at her lowest, she discovers a note from Lecter among his personal things. This revelation of information leads her to realize that Buffalo Bill lives in Belvedere, Ohio. This is something Lecter has been slyly attempting to lead her to all along. After all this time, Clarice finally "gets" what he's been trying to tell her.

Because of the "ah-ha" nature of the Newfound Resolve, there is a deep feeling of reinstilled emotional vigor that occurs at this Turning Point. As chock full of hopelessness and despair as the Lowpoint was, the Newfound Resolve is filled with an equal and opposite sense of hope and encouragement. It is an epiphany moment for the character where he finally realizes he's more than just a hapless schlub at the mercy of fate. He has a say in his destiny, and though he has suffered a terrible loss, he won't be counted out just yet.

The grandness of the revelation at this Turning Point often involves a huge Payoff for the audience that was Set Up earlier in the story. In *Iron Man,* the Newfound Resolve occurs when Tony Stark, having had his chest reactor removed by Obadiah at the Lowpoint, crawls into his lab to retrieve the old reactor Pepper saved against his orders. His robot arm thingy hands it to him, Tony smashes the glass casing on the ground, and the crowd goes wild.

In Act Two of *Avatar,* Neytiri explained to Jake the significance of Toruk Makto and the big flying monster he rides. This setup it is paid off at the Newfound Resolve when the excommunicated Jake shows up at the Na'vi sacred place as Toruk Makto, riding the big flying monster and fulfilling the prophecy. The Na'vi literally have no choice but to respect him and obey whatever he says. He has gone from reviled as a pariah at the Lowpoint, to revered as the chosen one at the Newfound Resolve.

Although the character made the decision to fight at the Moment of Truth in Act Three, at this Turning Point he must take it one step further. If the Moment of Truth turned him into a willing warrior for his cause, the Newfound Resolve turns him into a willing martyr. Having realized the Ultimate Goal of the story, he must abandon his selfish desires and resolve to destroy the forces of antagonism at any cost, even if it means sacrificing his life. By coming to realize his cause is greater than himself, he achieves a level of transcendence only attainable through *clarity of purpose*.

In *The Silence of the Lambs*, upon Clarice's discovery that Buffalo Bill lives in Belvedere, Ohio, she makes the decision to go there, knowing it will likely end with her being recycled, or worse, expelled from the academy. Throughout the story, the importance of graduating has been shown to be an integral part of who Clarice is. But with the revelation she receives at this Turning Point, she makes the decision to set aside her personal desires and risks sacrificing her future, in exchange for the future of Catherine Martin.

At the Lowpoint of *Titanic*, Rose agrees to enter one of the last remaining lifeboats at Jack's urging. As the boat is slowly lowered, Celine Dion's flute arrangement makes us feel like no one in the world will ever be happy again. But as Rose looks up at Leo's dashing mug, she realizes she can't and won't ever leave him. She jumps out of the lifeboat back onto the ship. She makes the decision to stand by Jack, knowing their next few moments together may be their last. She has obtained clarity of purpose.

Act Four Summary

So the central pillars of Act Four are: The Doomed Plan, the Penultimate Goal, Self-Inflicted Opposition, the Lowpoint and the Newfound Resolve. We can, therefore, summarize Act Four as…

The character Implements a Doomed Plan and faces Self-Inflicted Opposition in pursuit of a Penultimate Goal. But when an unthinkable Lowpoint occurs, he pulls himself together and discovers a Newfound Resolve.

Now let's examine how this act was skillfully orchestrated in the 2014, feature-length commercial, *The Lego Movie*. Motivated by the success of Emmet's unorthodox ideas at the Moment of Truth, his Rebel friends enter into Act Four confident in their ability to achieve their Penultimate Goal of stopping Lord Business before he can use the Kragle.

Emmet devises a Doomed Plan to sneak into Octan Tower and put the cap on the Kragle, delineating it in an **Unfolding Plan Montage** as his team implements it. Though their plan is doomed by the nature of this act, his team still comes close to success. They gain entry to the building, deactivate the laser shield around the Kragle and come within centimeters of placing a literal and metaphorical cap on Lord Business' scheme. But when Wyldstyle is unexpectedly captured, a distracted Emmet misses his opportunity to destroy the Kragle, and all his allies are apprehended in short order. Emmet and the Master Builders bring this Self-Inflicted Opposition onto themselves by willingly entering into Lord Business's lair to thwart his plan.

Also of note, Lord Business uses a penny to decapitate Vitruvius (which has to be cinematic first), leaving Emmet mentorless. Before succumbing to his injuries however, Vitruvius confesses to Emmet and everyone in attendance, that the prophecy was made up. The loss of his mentor and the revelation he is not the Special begins the Lowpoint for our hapless protagonist. Emmet wallows in defeat and Lord Business gloats over just how unstoppable his sinister plan is. Just to prove it, he sets a timer to keep the Master Builder alive long enough to watch while he goes off to attend to his evil business. At this point, it would appear success is no longer attainable for Emmet and his pitiful little band.

Having come to terms with his colossal failure and imminent death, Emmet is visited by the ghost of his recently deceased mentor[42]. Vitruvius explains to Emmet that just because the prophecy was made up, it doesn't mean it isn't true. He can still be the Special if he only believes he is. Inspired by this, Emmet discovers a Newfound Resolve. He throws himself and the 9-volt battery powering Lord Business' death machine out the window of the infinitieth floor, successfully disabling the device. This seeming self-sacrifice by Emmet inspires Wyldstyle to formulate a plan to rally the citizens of the universe and stop Lord Business. The audience cheers their collective approval, and the story rolls into Act Five with a renewed sense of hope for our heroes.

Observe the summarization of Act Four of *The Lego Movie* using the key points of the fourth act.

Emmet and the gang implement a plan to sneak into Octan Tower (the doomed plan), but walk right into Lord Business's clutches (self-inflicted opposition) while trying to put the piece of resistance on the Kragle (the penultimate goal). But when a mortally wounded Vitruvius admits to Emmet he made up the prophecy (the lowpoint), Emmet sacrifices himself to free the others and Wyldstyle concocts a plan to enlist the aid of the citizens of the universe (the newfound resolve).

---

[42] Note the similarity to the appearance of Matt's ghost in Act Four of *Gravity*. Or don't. Whatever.

Act Four begins roughly 60% into the story and like its predecessors, runs for an average of 20%. Once this act ends, we should be about 80% into the story. With two acts remaining and only 20% of the story left, we can see how the pace gains steam as we enter into the climax, and the character makes a final push to defeat the forces of antagonism in the fifth act.

Act Four Examples

The Hunger Games
2008 Novel
Written by Suzanne Collins

Character
Katniss Everdeen

Ultimate Goal
Win the Hunger Games with Peeta

Total Runtime: 27 chapters

The Hunger Games - Act Four: Implementing a Doomed Plan

The character Implements a Doomed Plan and faces Self-Inflicted Opposition in pursuit of a Penultimate Goal. But when an unthinkable Lowpoint occurs, he pulls himself together and discovers a Newfound Resolve.

Katniss forms an alliance with Rue to attack the Careers (the doomed plan) and nearly gets herself blown up (self-inflicted opposition) while trying to destroy the careers supplies (the penultimate goal). But when Rue is trapped in a net and killed by one of the Career (the lowpoint), the Gamemakers announce a rule change allowing Peeta and Katniss to win the Games together (the newfound resolve).

Start Time: After 15 of 27 Chapters (55.5%)
Runtime: Chapter 16 through 18 (3 Chapters)
Run Percentage: 3 of 27 Chapters (11.1%)

The Doomed Plan - Having made the commitment to fight at the Moment of Truth, the character now devises and implements a plan of action that is destined to fail. It may fail outright, or it may seem to succeed only to have grave consequences the character didn't anticipate.

Katniss and Rue plan to attack the Careers by destroying their supplies. While they do succeed in their objective, their plan leads to Rue being captured and murdered at the hands of the Careers.

The Penultimate Goal - The character's goal in this act is one step removed from the Ultimate Goal, but his pursuit of it leads him to realize what he needs to do to end the conflict once and for all.

Katniss and Rue attempt to destroy the supplies the Careers have hoarded.

Self-Inflicted Opposition - The character makes the conscious decision to go up against the forces of antagonism. Because of this, he is the primary cause of the opposition he faces in this act.

Katniss figures out the Careers supplies are guarded by mines. She targets a bag of apples with her arrows to trigger them, nearly blowing herself up in the process. Katniss' plan ends up getting Rue killed. Way to go, Katniss. It's probably for the best since only one of them could have survived anyway.

Turning Point Catalyst: The Lowpoint

The Lowpoint - Something unimaginable happens with grave emotional consequences for the character. He looks back on all his actions over the course of the story and feels he has failed.

Rue gets trapped in a net and killed by another tribute. I nearly shed a tear. Afterward, Katniss wanders about in a fog wondering how she should proceed. It would seem it has all been for naught.

Turning Point Four: The Newfound Resolve

Start Time: After 17 of 27 Chapters (62.9%)
Runtime: Chapter 18 (1 Chapter)
Run Percentage: 1 of 61 Chapters (3.7%)

<u>The Newfound Resolve</u> - After the Lowpoint, something happens to make the character dig deep within himself and rediscover his resolve. He makes the decision to stop the forces of antagonism at any cost.

The announcer, um, announces that not only is Peeta alive, but he and Katniss can win the Games together! She makes the decision that she will do any and everything to find Peeta and win the Games with him. Rue who?!

MARSHALL L. DOTSON

The Silence of the Lambs
1988 Novel
Written by Thomas Harris

Character
Clarice Starling

Ultimate Goal
Stop the serial killer Buffalo Bill before he kills again.

Total Runtime: 61 chapters

The Silence of the Lambs - Act Four: Implementing a Doomed Plan

The character Implements a Doomed Plan and faces Self-Inflicted Opposition in pursuit of a Penultimate Goal. But when an unthinkable Lowpoint occurs, he pulls himself together and discovers a Newfound Resolve.

Clarice follows Lecter to Tennessee to gain more information from him (the doomed plan), upsets Senator Martin and gets herself taken off the case (self-inflicted opposition) while trying to investigate the scene of Catherine Martin's abduction (the Penultimate Goal). But when she learns of Lecter's escape and Crawford tells her to go back to school (the lowpoint), Clarice finds a message from Lecter, realizes Bill lives in Belvedere, Ohio and asks Crawford to be sent there to investigate the first girl's disappearance (the newfound resolve).

Start Time: After 31 of 61 Chapters (50.8%)
Runtime: Chapter 32 through Chapter 48 (17 Chapters)
Run Percentage: 17 of 61 Chapters (27.9%)

The Doomed Plan - Having made the commitment to fight at the Moment of Truth, the character now devises and implements a plan of action that is destined to fail. It may fail outright, or it may seem to succeed only to have grave consequences the character didn't anticipate.

After Chilton's manipulations, Senator Martin agrees to have Lecter moved to Tennessee in exchange for information on Buffalo Bill's identity. This leads to his escape. Fail.

Meanwhile, Clarice's investigation in Tennessee gets her in trouble with the Senator and the local FBI office. As a result, she is sent back to school for a disciplinary hearing. Double fail.

The Penultimate Goal - The character's goal in this act is one step removed from the Ultimate Goal, but his pursuit of it leads him to realize what he needs to do to end the conflict once and for all.

Clarice follows Lecter to Tennessee to investigate the scene of Catherine Martin's abduction.

Self-Inflicted Opposition - The character makes the conscious decision to go up against the forces of antagonism. Because of this, he is the primary cause of the opposition he faces in this act.

Due to the phony offer Clarice made to Lecter, Senator Martin is convinced she is a naive nobody jeopardizing her daughter's life. Clarice goes to Catherine's apartment and deals with the Tennessee HP officers already on the scene. When she finds private, racy photos that may provide a lead, she is interrupted by Sen. Martin who accuses her of stealing. This leads the Tennessee Bureau of Investigations officer on site to order Clarice back to Quantico. Against his orders, Clarice visits Lecter where he is being housed in Tennessee. She lies her way into the building and finishes telling Lecter about her childhood, including the slaughter of the titular lambs.

After Lecter escapes, Crawford tells Clarice her little visit to Lecter has earned her a recommendation for suspension and a reevaluation of her fitness for service.

Turning Point Catalyst: The Lowpoint

The Lowpoint - Something unimaginable happens with grave emotional consequences for the character. He looks back on all his actions over the course of the story and feels he has failed.

Clarice learns of Lecter's escape, and Crawford tells her to go back to school. Soon after, Crawford discovers the Billy Rubin lead provided by Lecter was a poop joke, and all the information he gave them was shit[43]. Now back at Quantico, Clarice and her roommate discuss her failure with the case. Crawford's wife dies. The audience learns what Bill has been doing, and that he plans to kill Catherine Martin the next day to harvest her hide.

Turning Point Four: The Newfound Resolve

Start Time: After 46 of 61 Chapters (75.4%)
Runtime: Chapter 47 through 48 (2 Chapters)
Run Percentage: 2 of 61 Chapters (3.2%)

The Newfound Resolve - After the Lowpoint, something happens to make the character dig deep within himself and rediscover his resolve. He makes the decision to stop the forces of antagonism at any cost.

Clarice deals with her suspension from the case by studying the file Lecter gave her. After finding a message from him, Clarice realizes Bill's pattern isn't random, and he lives in Belvedere, Ohio. She goes to Crawford and begs to be sent to Belvedere to investigate the first girl's disappearance, knowing if she fails she'll be recycled and demoted to an FBI coffee maker in some backwoods office. Crawford agrees, giving her all the money he has on his person in lieu of an official travel card. Clarice has decided to stop Buffalo Bill and save Catherine Martin despite the personal consequences her failure would entail.

---

[43] Bilirubin! Get it?

Star Wars
1977 Film
Written and directed by George Lucas

Character
Luke Skywalker

Ultimate Goal
Destroy the Death Star and save the princess.

Total Runtime: 120 minutes

Star Wars - Act Four: Implementing a Doomed Plan

The character Implements a Doomed Plan and faces Self-Inflicted Opposition in pursuit of a Penultimate Goal. But when an unthinkable Lowpoint occurs, he pulls himself together and discovers a Newfound Resolve.

Luke and Han cosplay as stormtroopers to sneak into the detention area (the doomed plan), but end up alerting the entire station to their presence (self-inflicted opposition) while trying to rescue the prince and escape the Death Star (the penultimate goal). But when Obi-Wan sacrifices himself for the others to escape (the lowpoint), Luke and Han shoot their way through the two Tie Fighters giving pursuit and escape to the Rebel base (the newfound resolve).

Starting Percentage: 72 of 120 minutes (59.9%)
Runtime: 24 minutes of 120 minutes (20%)

The Doomed Plan - Having made the commitment to fight at the Moment of Truth, the character now devises and implements a plan of action that is destined to fail. It may fail outright, or it may seem to succeed only to have grave consequences the character didn't anticipate.

Rescuing the princess and escaping the Death Star will result in Obi-Wan's death and the Empire learning the location of the Rebel base.

The Penultimate Goal - The character's goal in this act is one step removed from the Ultimate Goal, but his pursuit of it leads him to realize what he needs to do to end the conflict once and for all.

Luke, Han and Chewie attempt to rescue the princess and escape the Death Star.

Self-Inflicted Opposition - The character makes the conscious decision to go up against the forces of antagonism. Because of this, he is the primary cause of the opposition he faces in this act.

Luke and Han willingly go into the heart of the Death Star in attempt to rescue the princess. As a result, they bring the wrath of the Empire onto themselves.

Turning Point Catalyst: The Lowpoint

The Lowpoint - Something unimaginable happens with grave emotional consequences for the character. He looks back on all his actions over the course of the story and feels he has failed.

Obi-Wan allows himself to be struck down by Vader so Luke and the gang can escape. Sad music plays.

Turning Point Four: The Newfound Resolve

Start Time: 94 of 120 minutes (78.3%)
Runtime: 2 minutes of 120 minutes (1.6%)

The Newfound Resolve - After the Lowpoint, something happens to make the character dig deep within himself and rediscover his resolve. He makes the decision to stop the forces of antagonism at any cost.

The Falcon *is pursued by Tie Fighters as Luke and the gang exit the space station. They manage to outgun the enemy ships and escape. The audience is pleased.*

Leia points out that by sending their two worst Tie Fighter pilots to pursue them, the Empire has intentionally allowed them to escape. Knowing the Empire is tracking them, they decide to go straight to the Rebel base in hopes the stolen plans will allow them to destroy the Empire's ultimate weapon. They have decided to make this the rebellion's last stand. For some reason.

Titanic
1997 Film
Written and directed by James Cameron

Character
Rose Dawson

Ultimate Goal
Survive the ship and live life on her terms.

Total Runtime: 187 minutes

Titanic - Act Four: Implementing a Doomed Plan

The character Implements a Doomed Plan and faces Self-Inflicted Opposition in pursuit of a Penultimate Goal. But when an unthinkable Lowpoint occurs, he pulls himself together and discovers a Newfound Resolve.

Rose attempts to escape the ship with Jack (the doomed plan), by navigating the bowels of the sinking ship (self-inflicted opposition) and rescuing him from the detention area (the Penultimate Goal). But when the lifeboats are only taking women and Jack convinces Rose to go by herself (the lowpoint), she has a change of heart and jumps onto the lower decks to stay with him (the newfound resolve).

Starting Percentage: 118 of 187 minutes (63.1%)
Runtime: 22 of 187 minutes (11.8%)

<u>The Doomed Plan</u> - Having made the commitment to fight at the Moment of Truth, the character now devises and implements a plan of action that is destined to fail. It may fail outright, or it may seem to succeed only to have grave consequences the character didn't anticipate.

Rose goes to the detention area to save Jack, but there won't be any lifeboats for them to escape aboard. Not to mention he dies at the end anyway. She only manages to add a few extra minutes to his life. Fail.

<u>The Penultimate Goal</u> - The character's goal in this act is one step removed from the Ultimate Goal, but his pursuit of it leads him to realize what he needs to do to end the conflict once and for all.

Rose attempts to save Jack from the detention area in the bowels of the ship.

<u>Self-Inflicted Opposition</u> - The character makes the conscious decision to go up against the forces of antagonism. Because of this, he is the primary cause of the opposition he faces in this act.

Rose's trip into the heart of the sinking ship is her own doing. She could have just gotten on the lifeboat and left. All the hardship she encounters on her way is a result of her own decisions.

Turning Point Catalyst: The Lowpoint

<u>The Lowpoint</u> - Something unimaginable happens with grave emotional consequences for the character. He looks back on all his actions over the course of the story and feels he has failed.

The crewmen start shooting. Jack convinces Rose to board a lifeboat. Cal tells her he has an arrangement with a boat on the other side of the ship he will share with Jack. Rose is sad but agrees. Once Rose is on the boat being lowered into the ocean, Cal reveals to Jack that while he does have an arrangement with a boat, Jack won't benefit from it. In your face, Jack.

Turning Point Four: The Newfound Resolve

Start Time: 138 of 187 minutes (73.7%)
Runtime: 2 minutes of 187 minutes (1%)

<u>The Newfound Resolve</u> - After the Lowpoint, something happens to make the character dig deep within himself and rediscover his resolve. He makes the decision to stop the forces of antagonism at any cost.

Looking up at Jack, Rose decides she cannot leave him and jumps from the lifeboat onto one of the lower decks. They run to each other and embrace. Rose reminds Jack that if he jumps, she jumps, mirroring their initial interaction at the Dilemma. She has decided nothing will come between her love for this guy she just met yesterday.

ACT FIVE: TRYING A LONGSHOT

"Jim… the statistical likelihood that our plan will succeed is less than 4.3 percent."

"Spock. It'll work."

Spock and Kirk ~ Star Trek, Act Five

Approximate Start Time: 80% into the story
Approximate Runtime: 15% of the story

After facing the catastrophic failure of his Domed Plan at the Lowpoint, and finally getting his shit together at the Newfound Resolve, the character realizes the only course of action left at his disposal carries a very low likelihood of success. His only option is to **Try a Longshot**.

The Longshot is an improbable endeavor intended to destroy the antagonist once and for all. At this point in the story, the forces of antagonism have all but won, but the character is reinvigorated by his Newfound Resolve and is ready to give it one last try. He knows this is the last chance he'll ever have to thwart the antagonist, and he must put everything he has into this final effort. Now, with the fate of the world (or underdog coffee shop/fraternity/etc.) on the line, the character throws up a Hail Mary pass.

Because it is a move of desperation, the Longshot often involves the character attempting something so crazy it just might work[44]. While the forces of

---

[44] While this concept originates from a line of dialogue uttered so often in film and television it has become stock, there is actually a form of logic behind it. It involves

antagonism may have the upper hand in terms of resources and capabilities, the character now has an unbreakable determination and the element of surprise on his side. In a reversal of the character's underestimation of the antagonist in Act Four, the forces of antagonism now underestimate the character and his abilities.

In *Star Wars*, Luke and the Rebels use the stolen Death Star schematics to plan an assault on the battle station's only weakness: a two-meter ventilation shaft at the end of a trench lined with laser cannons. Even the Rebel leaders admit their plan is pretty stupid. The Rebels' slim chance of success gives Peter Cushing's Imperial Leader, Grand Moff Tarkin, ample reason to scoff at his subordinate's request to prepare an evacuation shuttle. "Evacuate?" he asks. "In our moment of triumph? I think you overestimate their chances." Famous last words.

In *Avatar*, Jake and the Na'vi are outmatched, outgunned and overpowered by the humans (damn those humans!). The only shot they have is to use the electromagnetic distortion of the Hallelujah Mountains to scramble the sensors on the Company's high-tech airships and level the playing field. Sure, it's a Longshot, but it's so crazy it just might work.

Because the probability of success for the character is so low, there is often an element of martyrdom underlying this act. Many of the character's allies may give their lives for their cause. Having already faced death at the hands of the antagonist in Act Four, the character realizes that his attack on the antagonist may result in his death, but feels it will be a worthy sacrifice if he can put an end to the conflict.

Though the character will generally survive the contest, in rare instances, he will pay the ultimate price, sacrificing his life for his cause. You can find

---

undertaking a course of action so outside the box (i.e. insane) that the opposing forces would never expect it, and therefore have no contingencies in place to counteract it.

examples of this in *Braveheart, Gladiator, Titanic, V for Vendetta, Pan's Labyrinth, Thelma and Louise, Donnie Darko, Terminator, Terminator 2*—actually, now that I think about it, perhaps it's not so rare of an occurrence.

The character's Initial Desire often returns to the forefront of the narrative in this act. When the story began, the character desired one thing more than anything else in the world. By obtaining this thing, he hoped to change his Imperfect Situation. In this act, he is finally given an opportunity to attain or become the thing he always wanted so desperately.

In the beginning of *Star Wars*, Luke desired for adventure, to zip around in space and fight (for) the Empire. Well, here you go, champ. Take an X-Wing and participate in a full-on assault of the Empire's new death weapon from which you aren't likely to return.

In Act Five of *Inception*, Dom confronts Mal in the Limbo world they created, where she tempts him with the promise of reuniting with his children. As was established in Act One, seeing his children is Dom's initial Desire. He knows it, Mal knows it, and you can bet your pimply posterior Christopher Nolan knows it too.

In stories where the character's Initial Desire is *not* to change his situation, he has learned over the course of the story that he must change some facet of himself. In this act, he is given an opportunity to prove he is capable of this change. In the beginning of *Iron Man*, Tony Stark desired to remain the money-hungry weapons monger he had always been. By navigating the story he slowly comes to realize the error of his initial ways, and in Act Five, must demonstrate it by risking his life to stop Obadiah from releasing his death weapon upon the world.

In this act, the pace of the story kicks into overdrive. Everything from here on out is a mad rush to the climax. In fact, the entirety of this act can be considered the **Climax** of the story, culminating in the Climax of the Climax in the fifth act Turning Point, the Final Push.

In Act Five of *The Silence of the Lambs*, Clarice inadvertently tracks down and locates Jame "Buffalo Bill" Gumb in Ohio, and the two face off in his basement funhouse. In *The Empire Strikes Back*, Luke faces Vader for the first time in a lightsaber duel that leads them through the ominous corridors of Cloud City. These examples illustrate how the fifth act is a final showdown between the two sides of the conflict, as well as a Longshot for the character.

Significance of Trying a Longshot

Everyone loves an underdog, and at this point in the story the character is as outmatched, outgunned and outmaneuvered by the antagonist as he could possibly be. The only thing he has on his side is determination (and a general sense of morality), but he's still going to need a little luck for his Longshot to succeed. Lucky for him the story gods are smiling down on him from the story heavens.

If the character were in a position of superiority coming into this act, it would lessen the impact of his ultimate victory over the antagonist. We won't feel surprise or relief in his success if he's simply dispatching a weak and inferior opponent. The belief that the righteous underdog can overcome a powerful, malevolent oppressor is hardwired into our shared psychology (even if it's not entirely true in the real world). The character knows he stands only the slimmest chance of success, but he is motivated by an obligation to a righteous cause.

In *Titanic*, Jack has none of the resources Cal has at his disposal. When Rose shuns Cal for Jack, she too is brought down to his penurious level. The only thing they have going for themselves is that they are good people motivated by arguably the purest of emotions: true love. Against this, from a theological standpoint, the wicked and tyrannical Cal doesn't stand a snowball's chance in somewhere really warm, like Jamaica or Hawaii.

In order for the character to overcome an antagonist with such a drastic level of power, he too must be willing to do so something drastic. He must be willing to let go of his personal convictions and place his faith in the hands of the "higher power" of his righteousness. This is why the Longshot is often so far-fetched. It's a wing and prayer, relying on divine influence to succeed.

Though the divinity of the Longshot is not often stated explicitly, we can see a literal example of this in *Avatar*. On the eve of his battle with the technologically superior humans, Jake visits the Tree of Souls and prays to the Na'vi god, Eywa, for assistance. While Neytiri is initially dismissive of Jake's naiveté, his faith in the power of righteousness pays off when Eywa intervenes in the final battle, unleashing the full power of the native wildlife to triumphant music and cheers from the audience. Eywa has heard you, Jake. Eywa has heard you.

The expectation of the ability of good to triumph over evil is so ingrained in our collective consciousness that for a story to end in a righteous character's failure often comes as a shock to the audience. This is an important thing to understand if one wishes to tell a tragic story. The tragedy in these cases revolves around a powerful moral conflict between the character and the world he lives in, which he fails to properly identify. If you recall from our earlier discussion of the **Conflict of Ideals**, this is not necessarily a matter of good vs. evil, but of what is "right" to the character versus what is "right" to the storyworld he inhabits.

In *A Game of Thrones*, Ned Stark is a steadfastly righteous (i.e.: honorable) man. But the world he inhabits operates upon a core of deception. Ned's inability to let go of his personal "righteousness" to do what it "right" for the realm leads to his downfall (or the falling down of his head. From his body. When it's chopped off by his enemies).

Similarly, in the film *Carlito's Way*, ex-con Carlito Brigante lives by his self-made "code of the streets". In committing to abandoning his former life, Carlito becomes the righteous criminal, struggling to escape the only world he knows. It is his attempt to do the "righteous" thing by not killing a young rival despite the fact it is the "right" thing to do in his world, that ultimately leads to his downfall (when he falls down, riddled by bullets from said rival's gun).

Goal Five: The Ultimate Goal

Coming into Act Five, the character finally "gets it". Having faced death and rebirth at the Lowpoint and Newfound Resolve, he now understands **The Ultimate Goal** he should have been pursuing all along. Granted, he probably didn't have all the information needed to reach this conclusion until now, but the fact remains had he pursued this goal from the beginning, he could have nipped the entire problem in the bud before it ever evolved into the fight he now faces.

In *Iron Man*, Tony Stark's fifth act goal is to stop Obadiah's diabolical, yet not very well-thought-out plan to sell the ultimate weapon to whoever can afford it. Tony could have saved himself a lot of trouble by eliminating Obadiah from his life a long time ago. While the depths of Obadiah's treachery aren't revealed until Act Four, he was the problem all along. Had Tony have known, the story would have ended quickly, and Marvel's own diabolical plan to release seven interwoven, superhero films every year for the next century would never have come to fruition.

The Ultimate Goal is the goal at the heart of the story. While the goal involves the defeat of antagonist, it also encompasses the emotional or psychological realization of the character's arc. It is only by shedding some flawed aspect of himself the character has been holding onto that he is able to overcome the forces of antagonism.

In *Inception*, Dom's fifth act goal is to rescue Fischer from Mal[45] in Limbo and finish the inception. Finishing the inception is a powerful outer goal (it

---

[45] How many times does this guy get kidnapped?

is the name of the movie after all), but confronting Mal is what he should have been doing all along. Instead, he's been carrying his guilt over her death around with him, allowing her to cause all sorts of problems for his team.

Because the character learned in Act Four what the consequences will be should he fail, he now understands just how important his achievement of the Ultimate Goal is. All the stakes alluded to over the course of the story stand on the verge of realization if he is unsuccessful in defeating the forces of antagonism.

In Act Five of *Harry Potter and the Philosopher's Stone*, Harry and the gang now know Voldemort is behind the attempts to steal the Philosopher's Stone from the Dumbledore's obstacle course of death. Should he acquire it, he will be brought back to life, take over the world and presumably ban Quidditch forever. All the horrible things we've learned he's capable of are suddenly brought to the verge of becoming reality. Harry and his gang aren't just trying to stop him to save themselves; they're trying to save the world (and Quidditch).

In Act Four of *The Hunger Games*, Katniss loses her only ally, Rue, when she is killed by another tribute. It is then announced that, as two remaining survivors from the same District, she and Peeta can win the Games together. Having already faced the loss of one ally, Katniss is unwilling and unable to let Peeta suffer the same fate. She realizes if Peeta dies it will be her fault, and she would have to live with that guilt for the rest of her life. It is imperative she succeed in her Ultimate Goal of finding Peeta and winning the Games with him.

Opposition to the Ultimate Goal - Ultimate Opposition

Having learned the Ultimate Goal of the story, the character must demonstrate his commitment to achieving it by facing the strongest opposition he has yet to encounter. The forces of antagonism will now throw everything they have at him in attempt to destroy him once and for all. This is the **Ultimate Opposition**.

Like the character's Longshot, the Ultimate Opposition is the antagonist's last-ditch effort to eliminate the character and achieve his own goal. At this point, the antagonist realizes the character is the only thing standing between him and his objectives, and as such, he is able to direct the full might of his forces toward him. Although the forces of antagonism underestimate the character's abilities, they often recognize his heroic potential. They know exactly who the character is and the specific threat he poses to their plans.

In *Avatar*, the Colonel and the Company realize Jake is amassing an army of Na'vi from around the planet and launch a preemptive strike before the natives can attack. They realize the threat Jake poses and make it their business to eliminate him.

The opposition to the character's goal in this act is the stuff of legend. It is David v. Goliath, Potter v. Voldemort, Kramer v. Kramer, Coke v. Pepsi. The character must face down his opposite on the field of battle with only one of them allowed to walk away. After watching our character attempt to reason or negotiate with the forces of antagonism through the previous four acts, the audience is ready to watch him transform into a stone-cold badass. He must become more than just the character he has been. He must finally *become a hero*.

In *The Lego Movie*, before Emmet can even earn the right to do battle with Lord Business himself, he must overcome The Man Upstairs (i.e. a real life human being). As far as Lego minifigures are concerned, the opposition he faces in pursuit of his Act Five goal is supernatural, man against the gods themselves. It doesn't get any more ultimate than that.

By the time we reach this act, the antagonist has had just about enough of the character meddling in his affairs. Because of this, it is common for the antagonist to lose the calm, collected, composure he has exuded over the course of the story at the character's sudden, unexpected return from the Lowpoint of Act Four. After all of the character's incessant meddling in his plans, the antagonist finally snaps, often leading to a fatal mistake on his part.

Act Five of *Titanic* begins with Cal losing his cool upon seeing Rose and Jack's storybook love when she abandons her lifeboat to stay by his side. In an act of insanity, he snatches Lovejoy's pistol (the existence of which was conveniently Setup in Act Three) and attempts to shoot them both on the promenade of the ship.

In *Iron Man*, Obadiah loses his mind over Tony's interference of his perfectly evil scheme. In this act, he transforms into a homicidal maniac, willing to kill any and everybody to ensure Tony's demise. He even goes so far as to use a car with a family in it as a weapon to bludgeon Tony to death. Eeeeeeevil!!

If the antagonist has a secret weapon he's been holding back, he will likely unleash it upon the character in this act. In *Iron Man*, we don't actually see Obadiah's Iron Monger suit until the fifth act when he activates it in a final effort to escape the agents of Shield and kill Pepper. In *The Hunger Games*, the game coordinators unexpectedly unleash the "muttations", monstrous doglike hybrids created from the remains of all the fallen tributes, to force the remaining combatants into a final showdown at the Cornucopia. In *The Empire Strikes Back*, Vader breaks out the big guns on Luke with the whole "I'm your father" bit. The antagonists of these stories each hold back their ultimate weapon in hopes it will be enough to break the character's resolve.

Turning Point Catalyst: All is Lost

In this act, the character finally meets the antagonist on the literal or metaphorical field of battle. After the tragedy of The Lowpoint in Act Four, the antagonist may believe the character is all but defeated. Because of this, the character's Longshot catches the antagonist off guard, and he uses the element of surprise to get the drop on the antagonist, managing to land a few lucky blows in the process.

Unfortunately, the high probability of failure of the character's plan soon rears its ugly head as the antagonist's physical or tactical superiority turns the tide in his favor. When this happens, the antagonist begins to see the holes in the character's attack and exploits them to gain the upper hand in the conflict. Once again, the character appears to be defeated, and it now seems **All is Lost**.

At the All is Lost Catalyst, the character's Longshot seems to fail completely. His allies may be killed or captured, or the character himself may be wounded or brought to the edge of death. Whatever the case, it appears that despite the righteousness of his cause, his plan was too improbable to succeed, or the antagonist is just too powerful or resourceful to overcome.

In Act Five of *Inception*, Dom and Ariadne implement her plan to follow Mal into Limbo to rescue Fischer while the rest of the team fights off Fischer's projections long enough to finish the inception. It all seems to be going well enough until Saito succumbs to his gunshot wounds and Mal appears to convince Dom to stay in Limbo with her in exchange for Fischer. It now seems All is Lost for our plucky band of thieves.

In stories where the final showdown between the two sides comes down to a hand-to-hand confrontation, this catalyst often involves the character getting his ass handed to him[46] by the antagonist. In the fifth act of *The Empire Strikes Back*, Luke faces off with Darth Vader in lightsaber combat. Though Luke has initial success in the confrontation, and Vader even admits to being impressed by his skills, Luke is revealed to be no match for his more experienced opponent. Using Force telekinesis, Vader pummels Luke with heavy objects pulled from the walls. At this point, Luke's defeat would seem to be a foregone conclusion (and with the tragic nature of the film's ending, I suppose it is).

Titanic has one of the most well-orchestrated examples of the All is Lost beat I've encountered, and for good reason. As Rose Prime informs us, 1,503 people died onboard the ship that fateful night. The tragic loss of all those lives is captured masterfully by Cameron. The decks of the ship are in absolute chaos. We witness the last moments of passengers who have resolved to die, as well as those who are actively fighting to stay alive. And it's all set to the string ensemble's heart-wrenching final rendition of *Nearer, My God, to Thee*, as they too realize their fate is sealed. It's an incredibly tragic sequence that only spurs our passion to see our two star-crossed lovers survive their insurmountable odds. When we finally cut back to them, we see they are caught in all the turmoil, struggling to stay alive together.

This illustrates how the character often has to make peace with his maker at this catalyst. He knew coming into this act death was a possibility, and now he is forced to accept the fact he is about to die. While he may have faced a metaphorical death at the Lowpoint of Act Four, he now faces a very literal one.

---

[46] A colloquialism for being on the receiving end of a proper ass whooping.

Turning Point Five: The Final Push

Approximate Start Time: 90%
Approximate Runtime: 5%

Because Act Five focuses on the character and his allies confronting the forces of antagonism, the entirety of this act can be rightly thought of as the Climax of the story. But if the fifth act is a battle royal for ultimate supremacy between the opposing sides of the conflict, then the Act Five Turning Point is the showdown between the last two men (or women) standing. It is the Climax of the Climax.

Though the character is brought to the edge of defeat when his Longshot seems to fail at the All is Lost catalyst, he must now pull what little he has left from in his stores, or whip out the one trump card he's been holding onto all this time, and push back against the forces of antagonism one last time. At this moment *he decides to make his last stand*. This process of reaching deep within his reserves and mustering a final attempt to stop the antagonist is **The Final Push**.

A surprisingly poignant example of this Turning Point can be found in *The Lego Movie*. At the All is Lost catalyst in the film, Emmet is trapped in the real world with gigantic, sausage-fingered humans, while his claw-handed, Master Builder buddies are overrun by Lord Business' minions in Bricksburg. Emmet, now an immobile plastic toy, digs within himself and manages to flail his little, plastic appendages to escape the Man Upstairs. Seeing this, the Man Upstairs' son distracts his father, rescues Emmet and sends him back through the "magic portal" to Bricksburg. After seeing a cat poster echoing Vitruvius' words to believe in himself, Emmet returns to Bricksburg with the vision of a Master Builder and a renewed sense of purpose. He now makes a Final Push to place the cap on the Kragle and end the conflict for good.

If the character has a team of competent allies around him, they will have all failed during the All is Lost catalyst, leaving the success of their cause up to him. He knows he must now put his life on the line to ensure the success of their cause.

In the Final Push of *The Silence of the Lambs*, Clarice realizes the man occupying the house she just walked into is Buffalo Bill when a Death's-head hawkmoth lands on his back. At this moment, Clarice and the reader know the FBI's Hostage Rescue Team is at the wrong house (in the wrong state for that matter), and the task of stopping Jame Gumb from butchering Catherine Martin is entirely up to young Starling. While every agent in the FBI is aligned with her cause, she is alone in her confrontation with Gumb.

In *Star Wars*, after losing every member of every other strike team at the All is Lost catalyst[47], Luke makes his final run through the canyon of the Death Star. He (and everyone on Yavin) realizes he is the Rebels' only hope[48]. If he doesn't succeed in his Final Push, the Empire will destroy the Rebel base in a fiery, pre-CGI explosion, take over the universe and presumably ban Quidditch forever.

At this Turning Point, the character often reaches the **Razor's Edge of Death**, where he comes within centimeters, milliseconds or some other small metric unit of being killed by the antagonist. In *The Silence of the Lambs*, Jame Gumb comes within a hammer cock of shooting Clarice in the back of the noggin. In *The*

---

[47] They really must have been hurting for pilots if they gave Luke an X-Wing. A single fighter jet costs a hundred million and they don't even have to leave the atmosphere.
[48] There is a bit of motif going on here, mirroring the initial hologram message from Leia which Luke discovered in R2. While Leia did erroneously state that Obi-Wan Kenobi was her "only hope", Luke turns out to be a new hope.

Hunger Game, Katniss and Peeta come within seconds of swallowing the poisonous nightlock berries before the announcer capitulates and declares them both victors. In *Star Wars*, Darth Vader gets Luke locked in his sights mere seconds before Han shows up to blast him into the sequel. All these characters come within a hairsbreadth of sacrificing their lives for their causes.

In stories with a more "chosen one" feel to them[49], there is often a **Messiah Event,** where the character actually dies at the hands of the antagonist, only to be miraculously brought back to life by the righteousness of his cause. In *Avatar*, Colonel Quaritch smashes up the trailer where Jake's worthless human body is lying. As a result of this Jake "dies" from asphyxiation by the noxious Pandoran atmosphere, only to be brought back to life through Neytiri's love (and a gas mask). This demonstrates to the audience that his love for Neytiri is so pure it's capable of resurrecting him from the dead.

In some cases, the character's Christlike return from the dead imbues him with special powers just to drive the point home to the audience. In *The Matrix*, Neo "dies" after being repeatedly shot in the chest by Agent Smith at point blank range. It's only after Trinity confesses her love for him and seals it with a kiss that he is "resurrected", and commences to kick some serious agent booty in a manner unfathomable to this point. By sacrificing himself for something he believes in, Neo is able to become something of a god (at least within the Matrix).

Needless to say, the Final Push culminates in the ultimate defeat of the forces of antagonism (unless we're talking tragedy, in which case, it's the character who's defeated). Because we have been repeatedly told over the course of the story just how indomitable the antagonist is, the moment of his defeat is that much more cathartic for the audience and the character. There is a powerful release of tension at this climactic moment, as the antagonist reaps the just deserts of his villainy, and our character, at last, becomes a hero.

---

[49] Which is a generally frowned upon narrative technique, but obviously those naysayers have never known the pressures of being the chosen-one.

Act Five Summary

So the central pillars of Act Five are: The Longshot, the Ultimate Goal, Ultimate Opposition, All is Lost and the Final Push. We can, therefore, summarize Act Five as...

The character Tries a Longshot and faces Ultimate Opposition while trying to accomplish the Ultimate Goal. But just when it seems All is Lost, he makes a Final Push against the forces of antagonism, and either succeeds or fails.

To illustrate this, let's examine how the Trying a Longshot action was implemented in the fifth act of *Avatar*. In Act Four, Jake Sully bounced back from his Lowpoint of being excommunicated from the Omaticaya clan by becoming the legendary (and foreshadowed) Toruk Makto and regaining the support of the Na'vi at the Newfound Resolve. Now backed by an army of Na'vi from across the planet in Act Five, Jake and his avatar team put together a plan to achieve their Ultimate Goal of defeating the humans and sending their blue jean wearing, light beer sipping asses back to Earth

Although Jake and his team have amassed a formidable army, they are still outmatched by the technologically superior human forces. Because of this, the only course of action they have left is a Longshot with a high probability of failure. Their plan is to lure the company's army into the Hallelujah Mountains, where the naturally occurring electromagnetic field will disrupt all of their fancy targeting gadgetry (which was set up in Act Three). Their hope is that this will at least give them the benefit of launching a surprise attack.

This showdown with the human forces is the most Ultimate Opposition Jake and the Na'vi have faced in the film. Sure, there have been a few skirmishes between the two sides, with the humans destroying sacred monuments and the Na'vi throwing rocks at them, but now the endgame for the humans is the complete annihilation of the native forces. Jake and the Na'vi are fighting for their right to exist.

When the battle for Pandora begins, the Na'vi capitalize on their element of surprise by mounting a successful first strike against the human army. Though the Na'vi suffer casualties of their own, they manage to take out many of the human airships, killing dozens of the company's mercenaries in the process. Once the two sides are engaged in full-on combat, however, the humans quickly use their technological superiority to gain the upper hand in the conflict. No match for the high-tech killing machines they face, key members of the Na'vi forces are gunned down, and dramatic music plays as we witness the seemingly unstoppable destructive power at the human's disposal.

It would seem at this moment that All is Lost for Jake and his Rebel friends. But when the Na'vi god, Eywa, unleashes the full power of the Pandoran fauna the odds are evened out, allowing Jake and the Na'vi to make a Final Push. Jake uses the human's hand grenades against them, destroying the main bomb ship and nearly killing the main antagonist, Colonel Quaritch in the process.

The colonel's last-minute escape sets the stage for the final showdown between him, Jake and Neytiri in the Pandoran jungle. Together our two heroes manage to dispatch of the colonel and end the conflict with the humans once and for all (well, at least until *Avatar 2*[50] is released in 2035).

Here, we can see the summary of the fifth act of *Avatar*.

---

[50] If you're reading this after *Avatar 2* was released, it may be hard to conceive just how long the 9 year delay between the initial film's release and the release of the pre-planned sequel was.

Jake and the Na'vi go to war with the technologically superior humans (the longshot), and must overcome their advanced death machines (ultimate opposition) to send them back to Earth and reclaim Pandora (the ultimate goal). But when the Na'vi and the avatar team are overpowered (all is lost), Eywa calls in the whole planet as reinforcements, and Jake and Neytiri fight against the Colonel to the death (the final push).

Act Five Examples

The Hunger Games
2008 Novel
Written by Suzanne Collins

Character
Katniss Everdeen

Ultimate Goal
Win the Hunger Games with Peeta

Total Runtime: 27 chapters

The Hunger Games - Act Five: Trying a Longshot

The character Tries a Longshot and faces Ultimate Opposition while trying to accomplish the Ultimate Goal. But just when it seems All is Lost, he makes a Final Push against the forces of antagonism, and either succeeds or fails.

Katniss tries to find Peeta and get medicine to nurse him back to health (the longshot) while facing off with the remaining tributes in the Cornucopia (ultimate opposition), so she and Peeta can win the Games together (the ultimate goal). But when the Gamemakers drive them out of their love nest and sick the muttations on them (all is lost), Katniss and Peeta face off with the last remaining tribute and outsmart the Capitol with nightlock berries to win the Games as a team (the final push).

Start Time: After 18 of 27 Chapters (66.6%)
Runtime: Chapter 19 through 25 (7 Chapters)
Run Percentage: 7 of 27 Chapters (25.9%)

<u>The Longshot</u> - The character is reinvigorated by the revelation he received at the Newfound Resolve, but his only chance of success lies in a plan with a high risk of failure.

Katniss attempts to find Peeta and nurse him back to health.

<u>The Ultimate Goal</u> - The character finally understands what the true goal of the story is. The goal the character has in this act is what the story is all about.

Katniss and Peeta will try to win the Games together.

<u>Ultimate Opposition</u> - The forces of antagonism are now out to destroy the character completely. At this point in the story, the antagonist will throw everything he has into eliminating the character.

Katniss manages to find Peeta, but he is badly injured and nearly dead. The Gamemakers try to lure all the remaining tributes into a showdown at the Cornucopia, by offering them each something they need. Peeta refuses to let Katniss go, but knowing he will die from his wounds if she doesn't, Katniss gives him a sleeping elixir and sneaks out.

With Peeta unconscious, Katniss goes to the Cornucopia and faces the other tributes. She is severely wounded in the confrontation and barely makes it back to Peeta. She injects him with the medicine and passes out.

Turning Point Catalyst: All Is Lost

<u>All is Lost</u> - The character may experience some initial success, but the forces of antagonism rally, and it seems the character's Longshot is doomed to fail.

Katniss and Peeta awaken to find the stream outside their cave has dried up. They realize the Gamemakers are driving them toward the lake for a bloody fight to the death, and they can no longer lie around and wait for the other tributes to kill each other. The two resolve to end it all that day. As they approach the lake, the last remaining tribute, Cato, surprises them by bursting into the clearing. Katniss realizes he isn't attacking, but running from creatures the Gamemakers have unleashed to kill them all.

Turning Point Five: The Final Push

Start Time: After 24 of 27 Chapters (88.8%)
Runtime: Chapter 25 (1 Chapter)
Run Percentage: 1 of 61 Chapters (3.7%)

<u>The Final Push</u> - Faced with his imminent destruction, the character decides to put everything he has into one final endeavor. He uses what little he has left in his stores, or the one trump card he's been holding, knowing if he fails he will be destroyed.

Cato bursts into the clearing being chased by creatures Katniss calls muttations. Cato, Katniss and Peeta climb onto the Cornucopia. As Peeta and Katniss fight off the pack, Cato gets Peeta in a headlock. Peeta signals for Katniss to shoot Cato's hand and he knocks Cato over the side into the wolf pack. When the Gamemakers refuse to let the muttations kill Cato, Katniss shoots him with an arrow as an act of mercy.

With only Katniss and Peeta left, the Gamemakers revoke their previous rule change and announce there can now only be one winner. Gambling on a last resort, Katniss and Peeta prepare to eat the poisoned nightlock berries, but the announcer interrupts and declares them both the victors

The Silence of the Lambs
1988 Novel
Written by Thomas Harris

Character
Clarice Starling

Ultimate Goal
Stop the serial killer Buffalo Bill before he kills again.

Total Runtime: 61 chapters

The Silence of the Lambs - Act Five: Trying a Longshot

The character Tries a Longshot and faces Ultimate Opposition while trying to accomplish the Ultimate Goal. But just when it seems All is Lost, he makes a Final Push against the forces of antagonism, and either succeeds or fails.

Knowing she only has hours at best, Clarice attempts to use Bill's first victim (the longshot) to find Buffalo Bill and save Catherine Martin (the ultimate goal). But when the FBI tracks Buffalo Bill to an address in Chicago, and Clarice is told to keep investigating in Ohio despite the fact she may be recycled (all is lost), the trail leads her to Gumb's house just as he is preparing to kill Catherine Martin (the final push).

Start Time: After 48 of 61 Chapters (78.7%)
Runtime: Chapter 49 through Chapter 56 (8 Chapters)
Run Percentage: 8 of 61 Chapters (13.1%)

The Longshot - The character is reinvigorated by the revelation he received at the Newfound Resolve, but his only chance of success lies in a plan with a high risk of failure.

Knowing she only has a few hours, Clarice attempts to use Bill's first victim, Frederica Bimmel, to find Buffalo Bill.

The Ultimate Goal - The character finally understands what the true goal of the story is. The goal the character has in this act is what the story is all about.

Clarice attempts to save Catherine Martin

Ultimate Opposition - The forces of antagonism are now out to destroy the character completely. At this point in the story, the antagonist will throw everything he has into eliminating the character.

On the morning of the fourth day, Jame Gumb is ready to harvest Catherine's hide, but she's smart enough to capture his precious dog, Precious, and use it as leverage.

Clarice tries to unravel the psychology of Frederica Bimmel to get to the bottom of who killed her. In doing so, she figures out Bill is making a girl suit. Meanwhile, the FBI gets a solid name, but an inaccurate address, on Jame Gumb.

Shortly thereafter, Clarice learns the FBI has tracked Bill to Calumet City and is launching a raid to apprehend him. Already in Belvedere, Clarice decides to interview Frederica's obtuse best friend, Stacy. Her investigation leads her directly to Jame Gumb's house where she promptly realizes he is Buffalo Bill. When she tries to arrest him, he leads her into the basement and a game of cat and mouse ensues ending with Clarice shooting him just before he shoots her.

Turning Point Catalyst: All Is Lost

All is Lost - The character may experience some initial success, but the forces of antagonism rally, and it seems the character's Longshot is doomed to fail.

Clarice is told to keep investigating in Ohio despite the fact the FBI has an address on Jame Gumb in Chicago and is moving to apprehend him. She worries over whether or not she will be recycled. Clarice interviews Frederica Bimmel's bestie, Stacy Hubka, while she mentally counts down the time to the Hostage Rescue Team's raid. Meanwhile, the audience receives word that Jame Gumb is not in Calumet City, and the FBI's raid won't save anyone.

Turning Point Five: The Final Push

Start Time: After 54 of 61 Chapters (88.5%)
Runtime: Chapter 55 through 56 (2 Chapters)
Run Percentage: 2 of 61 Chapters (3.3%)

<u>The Final Push</u> - Faced with his imminent destruction, the character decides to put everything he has into one final endeavor. He uses what little he has left in his stores, or the one trump card he's been holding, knowing if he fails he will be destroyed.

Clarice rings the doorbell as Jame Gumb prepares to kill Catherine. She deduces he is Buffalo Bill when a moth lands on his shoulder, but he flees into the basement before she can apprehend him. Knowing Catherine is also down there, Clarice realizes she doesn't have time to call for backup and follows him into the basement. Gumb kills the lights and dons night vision goggles, leaving Clarice at a disadvantage. But when he cocks the hammer of his gun, Clarice's FBI training kicks in and she fires her pistol in the direction of the sound, striking and killing him.

Star Wars
1977 Film
Written and directed by George Lucas

Character
Luke Skywalker

Ultimate Goal
Destroy the Death Star and save the princess.

Total Runtime: 120 minutes

Star Wars - Act Five: Trying a Longshot

The character Tries a Longshot and faces Ultimate Opposition while trying to accomplish the Ultimate Goal. But just when it seems All is Lost, he makes a Final Push against the forces of antagonism, and either succeeds or fails.

Luke and the Rebels use the stolen data tapes to plot their attack on the Death Star (the longshot), and face the full might of the Empire (ultimate opposition), as they try to destroy the Death Star once and for all (the ultimate goal). But when they fail to make the crucial shot and all but a few ships are destroyed (all is lost), Luke makes a final run on the canyon, sinks the shot with an assist from Han, and destroys the Death Star (the final push).

Act Start: 96 of 120 minutes (81.6%)
Runtime: 21 minutes of 120 minutes (17.5%)

The Longshot - The character is reinvigorated by the revelation he received at the Newfound Resolve, but his only chance of success lies in a plan with a high risk of failure.

The Rebels use the stolen data tapes to plot their attack on the Death Star. The approach will not be easy. In fact, some say it's impossible.

The Ultimate Goal - The character finally understands what the true goal of the story is. The goal the character has in this act is what the story is all about.

Luke et al. attempt to destroy the Death Star.

Ultimate Opposition - The forces of antagonism are now out to destroy the character completely. At this point in the story, the antagonist will throw everything he has into eliminating the character.

The Rebels must fly straight up to the most powerful weapon of mass destruction ever created.

Turning Point Catalyst: All Is Lost

All is Lost - The character may experience some initial success, but the forces of antagonism rally, and it seems the character's Longshot is doomed to fail.

Vader deploys the tie fighters and goes to his own ship as Gold team attempts their attack run. Vader's fighters show up and wreck the Rebel's the plan, destroying all of Gold team's ships. Red team attempts to make the run. Red Leader gets off a shot but misses. Way to go, Red Leader. Luke looks on as all his allies are blown away.

Turning Point Five: The Final Push

Start Time: 113 of 120 minutes (94.1%)
Runtime: 4 minutes of 120 minutes (3.3%)

The Final Push - Faced with his imminent destruction, the character decides to put everything he has into one final endeavor. He uses what little he has left in his stores, or the one trump card he's been holding, knowing if he fails he will be destroyed.

Luke takes his team in at full throttle, knowing this run is the rebellion's last chance at success. As they approach the target, both of Luke's wingmen are taken out by Vader and his squadron of TIE fighters. Luke readies his targeting computer, but Obi-Wan tells him to use the Force instead. This prompts Vader to declare "the force is strong with this one". R2 takes a photon torpedo to the head-like portion of his cylindrical body. Just as Vader gets Luke ship in his sights, Han swoops in and blows Vader off into space, giving Luke his chance. Using the Force, Luke sinks the winning shot, blows up the Death Star, and the unlikely underdogs win the state championship!

MARSHALL L. DOTSON

<u>Titanic</u>
1997 Film
Written and directed by James Cameron

<u>Character</u>
Rose Dawson

<u>Ultimate Goal</u>
Survive the ship and live life on her terms.

Total Runtime: 187 chapters

Titanic - Act Five: Trying a Longshot

The character Tries a Longshot and faces Ultimate Opposition while trying to accomplish the Ultimate Goal. But just when it seems All is Lost, he makes a Final Push against the forces of antagonism, and either succeeds or fails.

Rose and Jack must stay aboard the sinking ship as long as possible, and evade the now murderous Cal (the longshot), to survive together (the ultimate goal). But when the decks erupt into pandemonium as the ship breaks in half and sinks (all is lost), Rose and Jack manage to find each other in the ocean and use a piece of wood to get Rose out of the water (the final push).

Starting Percentage: 140 of 187 minutes (74.9%)
Runtime: 38 minutes of 187 minutes (20.3%)

<u>The Longshot</u> - The character is reinvigorated by the revelation he received at the Newfound Resolve, but his only chance of success lies in a plan with a high risk of failure.

Rose and Jack evade Cal and go to the back of the ship in attempt to stay on board as long as possible.

The Ultimate Goal - The character finally understands what the true goal of the story is. The goal the character has in this act is what the story is all about.

Rose wants to survive the sinking ship with Jack.

Ultimate Opposition - The forces of antagonism are now out to destroy the character completely. At this point in the story, the antagonist will throw everything he has into eliminating the character.

Cal tries to shoot the lovebirds with Lovejoy's pistol. I guess if he can't have her no one can. The ship sinks into the deathly cold of the Atlantic. Rose and Jack are separated.

Turning Point Catalyst: All Is Lost

All is Lost - The character may experience some initial success, but the forces of antagonism rally, and it seems the character's Longshot is doomed to fail.

The decks are in chaos as the last lifeboats are loaded. Rose and Jack encounter Mr. Andrews who confesses he wishes to stay aboard the ship. Jack's friend, Tommy is shot by a bastardo as the band plays to the end. Numerous other passengers struggle with the fact they are about to die.

Turning Point Five: The Final Push

Start Time: 154 of 187 minutes (82.3%)
Runtime: 24 minutes of 187 minutes (12.8%)

The Final Push - Faced with his imminent destruction, the character decides to put everything he has into one final endeavor. He uses what little he has left in his stores, or the one trump card he's been holding, knowing if he fails he will be destroyed.

Rose and Jack make their way to the stern of the ship, knowing it is about to go under. Jack pulls Rose up onto the railing as the ship goes vertical. As the ship slowly sinks, Jack tells Rose to hold his hand, kick, and not let go. She let's go anyway. When Rose reaches the surfaces the world is in chaos, but Jack somehow manages to find her.

The reunited lovers swim away from the panicked masses. Rose gets aboard a piece of wood, but Jack can't because he's no good with physics. Rose tells Jack she loves him. He tells her she must live on to make babies and die an old lady. He makes her promise she will survive.

When the lifeboats finally come back, Rose awakens to find Jack is a handsome popsicle. The lifeboats pass her while she is saying her goodbyes to Jack's corpse. She tries to scream for them to come back but has no voice. In a last-ditch effort, she swims over to a dead guy, steals his whistle and blows it. Hearing her, the lifeboats come about.

ACT SIX: LIVING IN A NEW SITUATION

"But the face on the pillow, rosy in the firelight, is certainly that of Clarice Starling, and she sleeps deeply, sweetly, in the silence of the lambs."

— Toy Story, *Act Six*

Approximate Start Time: 95% into the story
Approximate Runtime: 5% of the story

Having vanquished (or failed to vanquish) the forces of evil in the Final Push of Act Five, the character is now shown to be Living (or not living) in a **New Situation** in the sixth and final act. The thrill of his victory (or failure) has subsided, and we are afforded a momentary glimpse of the character enjoying the fruits of his labors.

This act is commonly referred to as the denouement, which I believe is French for obfuscation. In this portion of the story, all the dangling plot threads are tidied up and resolved. While most structural paradigms tack the denouement onto the end of the final act, our definition of acts as courses of action separates the action the character undertakes in this portion of the story from the action of the previous act.

In those happily ever after stories we've all been brainwashed to love since childhood, the New Situation in which the character finds himself is often the polar opposite of his Imperfect Situation in Act One. This is because, through undertaking the journey of the story, the character has achieved his Initial Desire. By overcoming the obstacles and antagonism that stood between him and a seemingly unrelated physical goal, he has obtained the one thing he so desperately wanted all along. Look at that.

In Act One of *Star Wars*, Luke wanted to leave Tatooine and go off on daring space adventures. This is exactly what he does over the course of the film. After destroying the Death Star in Act Five, Luke is awarded the Rebel Alliance's highest honor at a ceremony in Act Six. He has fulfilled his Initial Desire and become a galactic hero in the process. Because the Ultimate Goal in Star Wars is to rescue the princess, it's quite fitting she is the one who awards the medals to him and Han[51]. Not only is Luke a hero to the Rebellion overall, he is also a hero to Princess Leia specifically, having now saved her twice from execution at the hands of the Empire. Not bad for a farm boy from a planet whose entire ecosystem is an uninhabitable desert.

When Christopher Nolan's *Inception* begins, Dom Cobb is an exile who desperately wants to return home to his children in America. In Act Six, he and his team are all smiles as they debark the plane after completing their mission. By undertaking and completing the seemingly impossible inception of Robert Fischer for Mr. Saito, Dom is able to obtain his Initial Desire at the conclusion of the film (depending on your take of the spinning top before the credits). In this new, happier situation, Dom is reunited with his estranged children and no longer a fugitive on the run. Quite a turn of events from his initial Imperfect Situation.

In the beginning of the Hunger Games, Katniss wishes to be free from her poverty-stricken existence and to feed her starving, dirt-poor family. By Act Six she has won the Hunger Games and the lifetime supply of gruel they give the victors, as well as a house in the most, least run-down part of the District. Mission accomplished, Ms. Everdeen. In fact, she was prepared to live moderately-ever-after in these conditions, but for some inexplicable reason, the Capitol decides the best way to quell the revolution her appearance in the

---

[51] Sorry, Chewie. They don't come in Wookie sizes.

first Games sparked is to put her back on TV and have her do it all again. Albeit, they intend for her to die in the Games. Because as we all know, everyone hates a martyr.

In the case of the tragic story, if the character survives the tragedy inflicted by his hubris, the New Situation in which he finds himself is often much worse than his initial Imperfect Situation. *The Empire Strikes Back* ends on a tragic note for Luke and his pals. Not only does Luke now know Darth Vader is his father, he also knows Vader knows that Yoda knows that Obi-Wan knew the whole time. In addition, he's lost a hand, Han is a statue, and the Empire is still running the galaxy exactly the same as they were at the beginning of the film. Not only has Luke failed to impact any change, he and his friends are worse off than they were when the film began. Maybe next time he should heed the advice of his dead Jedi master who can physically project himself from beyond the grave.

Significance of Living in a New Situation

The purpose of the sixth act is to give us a brief glimpse of the character living in, or in an extreme tragedy, *not* living in, his New Situation. It allows us to see how the character's actions have affected his world, giving the story a sense of completion. Having gone on the ride with the character, watched him repeatedly succeed and fail, we are entitled to witness the spoils of his triumph or come to terms with the reasons for his defeat. Whether he is exalted or exiled, reviled or revered, this is the new world he had a hand in creating. The character may have changed the world for the better, or he may have changed it for the worse, but the world he lives/lived in is now fundamentally different as a result of his actions.

Even if the character doesn't survive, we at least get an idea how the lives of those he left behind are affected by the New Situation he created. In *A Game of Thrones*, Ned Stark's death comes as a bit of a shock to the audience as we witness it through his daughter, Arya's eyes. But following this surprising turn of events we also see the repercussions for the surviving characters. This is the moment in which one of the central conflicts of the series, the War of Five Kings, begins.

Act Six is almost always the shortest act[52]. The reason Act Six is so short is because the extent of the character's New Situation need only be implied to the audience. We don't need to see Dom taking his son to little league games or reading his daughter bedtime stories at the end of *Inception*, any more than we need to see Dr. Ryan Stone going back to her mundane job, dropping tools on the hospital floor at the end of *Gravity*. The implication of what happily ever after means for these characters is left to our imaginations. In this act, we are given just enough to nurture our assumption that all has been set right in the storyworld…

Until the sequel.

---

[52] The exception being the theatrical version of *The Lord of the Rings: The Return of the King*, in which the sixth act, by some form of sorcery, is longer than the entire film itself.

Act Six Summary

Having accomplished (or failed to accomplish) the Ultimate Goal, the character is shown living in a New Situation.

For a particularly bittersweet example of Living in a New Situation, let us turn to James Cameron's box-office mastodon, *Titanic*. In the film, our character, Rose Dawson nee DeWitt Bukater's Ultimate Goal is to survive the sinking of the ship and live life on her own terms. While this seemed unlikely at the opening of the film, things appear to turn in her favor once she meets Jack. But when (spoiler alert) the ship hits an iceberg, their burgeoning relationship is put to the ultimate test.

At the Act Five Turning Point, the decks are in chaos as the passengers all realize the inevitable (i.e. they're gonna die). During the Final Push, Rose and Jack make their way to the stern of the ship, stay aboard until the very end, and (somehow) reunite amidst the pandemonium in the water. Unfortunately, the floating plank they find is only large enough to accommodate one, leading Jack to make a gentlemanly sacrifice of his life, so Rose's body temperature can remain above the freezing point of human tissue.

So, that was Act Five. In Act Six, we return to Rose Prime for the first time since the prologue, as a reminder that, not only did she succeed in her Ultimate Goal of surviving the downing of the ship, she also lived to be two hundred years old. The sixth act is told through a combination of past and present scenes as Rose Prime narrates the events that took place after she was plucked from the freezing water that fateful night. When the rescue ship, *RMS Carpathia*, passes under the watchful gaze of the Statue of Liberty and reaches the shores of America where everything is, by necessity, amazing, Rose assumes the surname of Dawson in honor of the now dead Jack. She also explains, with a smirk, how our dastardly antagonist Cal got his just deserts in the form of a tasty bullet he couldn't resist eating.

In the final moments of the film, we also see that, though she might have lost the love of her life in Jack, Rose obtained her Initial Desire of living life on her own terms. The camera pans over a possibly sleeping, but presumably dead Rose, to an assortment of framed pictures with which she apparently always travels. Through these pictures we see she lived a full and happy life, catching fish and flying planes and meeting African tribesmen and riding horses (like a real cowboy too, none of that sidesaddle stuff), all with a great big smile on her face. How's that for an implication of happily ever after? You go Rose. You go.

Having survived the sinking of the ship through Jack's ultimate sacrifice, Rose is shown to have honored her promise to him by not marrying Cal and living a full and happy life on her own terms.

Act Six Examples

<u>The Hunger Games</u>
2008 Novel
Written by Suzanne Collins

<u>Character</u>
Katniss Everdeen

<u>Ultimate Goal</u>
Win the Hunger Games with Peeta

Total Runtime: 27 chapters

The Hunger Games - Act Six: Living in a New Situation

Having accomplished (or failed to accomplish) the Ultimate Goal, the character is shown living in a New Situation.

Having beaten the Capitol at their own game (literally), Katniss and Peeta give TV interviews before being taken back to District 12 to start their new lives.

Start Time: After 25 of 27 Chapters (92.5%)
Runtime: Chapter 26 through 27 (2 Chapters)
Run Percentage: 2 of 27 Chapters (7.4%)

<u>Living in a New Situation</u> - We see the character adapting to the New Situation his actions have created. Whether he is exalted or exiled, this is the new world he helped create.

Haymitch tells Katniss the Capitol is furious over her theatrics with the nightlock berries. She realizes the most dangerous part of the Games has yet to begin, and she will likely have to suffer through a sequel. Katniss and Peeta appear on the reunion show and continue to play up their relationship, attending a bittersweet victory banquet afterward. The pair is taken by train back to their District where they discuss how Peeta thought their love was real and Katniss didn't. Burn.

<u>The Silence of the Lambs</u>
1988 Novel
Written by Thomas Harris

<u>Character</u>
Clarice Starling

<u>Ultimate Goal</u>
Stop the serial killer Buffalo Bill before he kills again.

Total Runtime: 61 chapters

The Silence of the Lambs - Act Six: Living in a New Situation

Having accomplished (or failed to accomplish) the Ultimate Goal, the character is shown living in a New Situation.

Having rescued Catherine Martin and killed Buffalo Bill, Clarice is a hero and all set to graduate from the Academy. She now sleeps deeply, sweetly in the silence of the lambs.

Start Time: After 56 of 61 Chapters (91.8%)
Runtime: Chapter 57 through Chapter 61 (5 Chapters)
Run Percentage: 5 of 61 Chapters (8.2%)

<u>Living in a New Situation</u> - We see the character adapting to the New Situation his actions have created. Whether he is exalted or exiled, this is the new world he helped create.

Catherine Martin is alive. Starling is a hero. Senator Martin owes her a colloquial "one". Dr. Lecter says he isn't coming after her. Everyone lives happily ever after… until the sequel. Except Chilton. Lecter eats him. Nom nom nom.

Star Wars
1977 Film
Written and directed by George Lucas

Character
Luke Skywalker

Ultimate Goal
Destroy the Death Star and save the princess.

Total Runtime: 120 minutes

Star Wars - Act Six: Living in a New Situation

Having accomplished (or failed to accomplish) the Ultimate Goal, the character is shown living in a New Situation.

Having destroyed the Empire's indestructible new weapon with his awesome pilot skills, Luke is the new darling of the rebellion. Even more amazing, Han is no longer a money-grubbing douchebag. All is seemingly set right with the universe.

Act Start: 117 of 120 minutes (99.1%)
Runtime: 3 minutes of 120 minutes (2.5%)

Living in a New Situation - We see the character adapting to the New Situation his actions have created. Whether he is exalted or exiled, this is the new world he helped create.

Luke is the savior of the universe (in your face Flash Gordon). Han is no longer a scumbag. An awards ceremony is held for Luke and Han. Sorry, Chewie (Rrrrrrr-ghghghghgh!) Medals are awarded, and everyone cheers. The galaxy is saved... until the sequel.

Titanic
1997 Film
Written and directed by James Cameron

<u>Character</u>
Rose Dawson

<u>Ultimate Goal</u>
Survive the ship and live life on her terms.

Total Runtime: 187 minutes

Titanic - Act Six: Living in a New Situation

Having accomplished (or failed to accomplish) the Ultimate Goal, the character is shown living in a New Situation.

Having survived the sinking of the ship through Jack's ultimate sacrifice, Rose is shown to have honored her promise to him by not marrying Cal and living a full and happy life on her own terms.

Starting Percentage: 178 of 187 minutes (95.2%)
Runtime: 9 of 187 minutes (4.8%)

<u>Living in a New Situation</u> - We see the character adapting to the New Situation his actions have created. Whether he is exalted or exiled, this is the new world he helped create.

Rose Prime gives the death toll in contrast to the number of survivors. Mr. Lovett, the leader of the expedition to find the missing heart-of-the-ocean diamond, finally "gets it". Rose Prime throws the ridiculously expensive diamond into the ocean and watches it sink. We see Rose has lead a happy life through the pictures she conveniently displays on her nightstand. She either dies or falls asleep and is reunited with Jack and the other passengers aboard Titanic, *who all offer a round of applause at her final kiss with Jack as the screen fades to white.*

In Conclusion

And there you have it. The final page of the novel has been turned, and the movie theater lights have risen. I hope you have enjoyed this presentation of *Actions & Goals: The Story Structure Secret*. More importantly, I hope you walk away from this book with a greater understanding of the structure underlying so many of our (or at least *my*) favorite stories.

Before you jump into the nine additional story outlines, I would like to get my closing remarks out of the way. While the structural paradigm set forth in this book was born of a desire to simplify my own writing process, the excitement of my discovery inspired me to share it with others who may also be looking to expand their understanding of story. It is my sincere belief that we as writers should not simply accept the status quo as universal truth, but should instead use it as a starting point from which we seek out the truth for ourselves.

I also discovered in writing this book that I garner a significant amount of enjoyment from narratology, and as such, will continue to seek a deeper understanding of story structure. If you are interested in more structural analyses of popular films and novels, or to download six act structure templates in Word, Excel or PDF format, visit sixactstructure.com (or you can follow me on the Twitter).

Finally, if you enjoyed this book, then I encourage you to demonstrate your writerly prowess to the world by leaving a review on Amazon. While more than a single sentence would be appreciated, I understand you are a busy individual whose time is a precious commodity. You therefore have my permission to copy and paste the following sample text directly into your review.

This is the greatest book on story structure ever written. I would marry this book if such a thing were possible (a phone call to my local courthouse assured me it's not). Everyone on the planet should buy this book so the author can quit his day job, write more books and finally buy the Lamborghini Diablo he's wanted since he was six.

In all seriousness, I encourage you not to view this paradigm as a rigid formula to be followed blindly, but as a detailed map of the story landscape. Much as one might be able to easily navigate to a neighboring city or state without much difficulty, it still doesn't hurt to familiarize yourself with the general lay of the land before undertaking your excursion. You may even discover a scenic detour you wouldn't have considered otherwise.

Good luck and good writing.

Marshall Dotson

FURTHER EXAMPLES

Now I'd like to take a deeper look at this structural paradigm at work. We will examine the following popular films and novels step by step, analyzing how each structural element was utilized over the course of the story. It should again be noted that with the exception of the act Turning Points, the act elements in these examples aren't listed in any chronological order, but are summarizations of how each element occurs throughout the act. There may be some redundancy and overlap, as all these elements occur simultaneously during the act.

Avatar

2009 film
Written and Directed by James Cameron

<u>Character</u>
Jake "Crazy Legs" Sully

<u>Ultimate Goal</u>
Save the Na'vi and Pandora from those bothersome, little human creatures.

Total Runtime: 155 minutes

In 2009, James Cameron broke his own box-office record for *Titanic* with the release of *Avatar*. The film, while generally praised, proved to be more divisive than his previous blockbuster. You either really loved it or really hated it. Despite one's personal opinions of the film, its resounding success and audience appeal is undeniable. This can primarily be attributed to its groundbreaking use of CGI and 3D technology, but without a properly structured story at its core, the film would have been little more than a $300 million screensaver.

Earlier, we discussed the importance of having the character earn his understanding of the Ultimate Goal over the course of the story and, love it or hate it, few films exemplify this process like *Avatar*. When the story begins, Jake has no investment whatsoever in the preservation or destruction of Na'vi culture. He sides with the humans by default, but everything that happens throughout the first four acts occurs for the sole purpose of teaching Jake how remarkable, important and superior to Earth Pandora is. Jake's character arc of becoming a purposeful warrior also revolves around his arrival at this realization. After all, a warrior who only fights for money is little more than a mercenary (which, surprise, surprise, is the primary motivation of the forces of antagonism).

Avatar - Act One: Dealing with an Imperfect Situation

A character in an Imperfect Situation faces Oppressive Opposition as he pursues an Initial Goal. But when there is a Disturbance to his routine, he faces a Dilemma regarding his situation and must assume a New Role.

Jake Sully, a wheelchair-bound ex-marine, arrives on a hostile alien world (imperfect situation), and is ridiculed for his disability and lack of intelligence (oppressive opposition) while trying to fill in for this recently deceased, scientist brother (initial goal). But when Jake is assigned to Dr. Grace Augustine's avatar team as security detail (the disturbance), The Colonel of the security forces offers to get Jake's legs fixed in exchange for gathering intel on the Na'vi and their weaknesses (the dilemma) by becoming a spy for the company (the new role).

Runtime: 24 minutes
Run Percentage: 24 of 155 minutes (15.5%)

The Inciting Incident - Something happens, often before the story begins, which if it does not occur would prevent the story as it exists from coming to be.

When Jake's scientist brother is killed in a random robbery, he is asked to step into his shoes. So to speak. Though this technically happens before the start of the film, it is shown in a flashback during the first act.

The Imperfect Situation - The character begins the story in a less than ideal situation he would like to change but seemingly cannot.

The wheelchair-bound Jake arrives at the most hostile environment known to man. Due to his disability, he no longer fits in with the soldiers as he once would. He is totally ignorant of life on Pandora, the Na'vi and science in general. Grace despises him because of his lack of knowledge.

We also discover the scientists and the company have poor relations, and the humans and the Na'vi have been fighting each other for quite some time.

The Initial Desire - Deep within himself, the character wants one particular thing more than anything else in the world.

Jake lost his purpose when he was paralyzed in Venezuela. He no longer has anything to stand for. So to speak. He states explicitly he desires a cause worth fighting for.

Initial Desire Type - The character's Initial Desire is either for or against changing his situation.

For Change: Jake wants to get his legs fixed and find a purpose in his life. These desires are what lead him to abandon his directionless life on Earth in search of a greater cause.

Preexisting Conflict - When the story begins, the character is already dealing with personal conflicts as well as the conflicts of the world at large.

Jake has a grudge with the world due to his injury. On Pandora, the humans and the Na'vi frequently clash over the resources of the planet. The scientists and the mercenaries frequently clash over their opposing opinions about the Na'vi. As both a soldier (kinda) and a scientist (kinda), Jake inadvertently finds himself thrust into the middle of their conflict.

<u>Likability/Empathy Factors</u> - The character is shown to be someone the audience would like to see succeed, or would be willing to follow on the journey of the story.

We can sympathize with Jake because he lost the use of his legs, but we respect him for taking control of his life despite his injuries. The Colonel commends him for having the heart to come to Pandora despite his disadvantage. He doesn't back down when Grace tries to insult his intelligence, proving he's not afraid to stand up for himself. So to speak.

<u>The Initial Goal</u> - When the story opens, the character already has a goal he is actively pursuing.

Jake goes to Pandora to fill in as a researcher for his dead, twin brother.

<u>Initial Goal Type</u> - The character's Initial Goal is either a Normal Routine Goal where he is in his regular environment, or a Fish out of Water Goal where he is already in a situation with which he is unfamiliar.

Fish out of Water Goal: The film begins with Jake arriving on Pandora, a planet he has little knowledge of. In addition to being confined to a wheelchair, he doesn't seem to fit in with either group of humans.

<u>Oppressive Opposition</u> - The character's Initial Desire and/or his Initial Goal are being oppressed by the world around him.

Jake is ridiculed by the other mercenaries for being in a wheelchair. They see him as useless. Shortly after, he is chastised by Grace for knowing nothing about Pandora or the Na'vi, unlike his brother. She also sees him as useless. Jake is all like, "I flew halfway across the galaxy for this?"

ACTIONS & GOALS

Turning Point Catalyst: The Disturbance

<u>The Disturbance</u> - An unexpected event with ominous implications occurs, interrupting the character's normal routine. This event pushes the character toward the Dilemma.

Jake meets Grace, whose day-to-day operations are disrupted by his arrival in the place of his more knowledgeable, but less existent brother. She immediately confronts the head company man, Parker Selfridge, about this. Much to her chagrin, Selfridge assigns Jake to her research team as security detail. Grace is displeased. It would appear the company's day-to-day ebb and flow has been disrupted by Jake's arrival.

Turning Point One: The Dilemma

Start Time: 20 of 155 minutes (12.9%)
Runtime: 4 of 155 minutes (2.5%)

<u>Presentation of The Dilemma</u> - The character is placed in a position where he must choose between life as he has known it or taking a new course of action.

At the Disturbance it was established the humans on Pandora are split into two opposing factions: the nature-loving scientists and the money-grubbing company. At the Dilemma, the colonel asks Jake to step into his office. So to speak. He offers Jake "an opportunity both timely and unique". He asks him to spy on the Na'vi, requiring Jake to decide which side of The Preexisting Conflict he will align himself with. He must choose whether he will remain a paralyzed ex-marine "doing science" for Grace, or become a spy for the Colonel and get his legs fixed.

<u>The New Role</u> - If the character takes this new course of action, he will assume a New Role in which he is untested.

If Jake accepts Quaritch's offer, he will become a spy for the Company.

<u>Refusal/Interference to the New Role (Optional)</u> - The character may be reluctant, unready or unwilling to leave his Imperfect Situation and accept the New Role. In other cases, the character may want to accept the New Role, but someone else attempts to prevent him from accepting it.

Not Applicable.

<u>Accepting The New Role</u> - The character makes the decision to take action by accepting the New Role.

Jake jumps all over Quaritch's offer. So to speak. He agrees to spy on the Na'vi for Quaritch, and in exchange, the Colonel will put up the money to get Jake's legs fixed. Oorah!

Avatar - Act Two: Learning the Rules of an Unfamiliar Situation

The character Learns the Rules of an Unfamiliar Situation and faces Incidental Opposition in pursuit of a Transitional Goal. But when he receives a Reality Check, the character makes a Commitment to his New Role.

Jake goes into the Pandoran wilderness for the first time with little knowledge or training (the unfamiliar situation) and is nearly killed by the local wildlife (incidental opposition) while trying to spy on the Na'vi and gain intel on their weaknesses (the transitional goal). But when he is separated from the group by the fauna of Pandora (the reality check), he is rescued by a Na'vi woman and taken to her village where he convinces the Omaticaya clan to teach him their ways (the commitment).

Starting Percentage: 24 of 155 minutes (15.5%)
Runtime: 25 of 155 minutes (16.1%)

Learning the Rules of an Unfamiliar Situation - The character now finds himself in a situation unlike anything he's ever experienced.

Jake goes out to the Pandoran wilderness for the first time with little knowledge or training. Hilarity ensues.

The Hooking Premise - The unique premise at the heart of a story, often involving an intriguing "what if" scenario that piques the audience's interest.

What if in the future, humans on an alien planet use neurally-linked alien bodies to learn about and interact with the indigenous population?

The Transitional Goal - The character receives a new goal that transitions him out of his initial state of inertia and into the main events of the story.

Jake sets out to spy on the Na'vi and gather intel on their weaknesses.

Incidental Opposition - The character learns there are greater forces of opposition in this new world that may not be out to thwart him specifically, but still stand between him and his new goal.

Within minutes of stepping into the Pandoran jungle, Jake earns the ire of a herd of hammerhead titanotheres and one hungry thanator. He's separated from the research group, loses all his equipment and is hunted down by a pack of snarling viperwolves.

Turning Point Catalyst: The Reality Check

The Reality Check - The plan the character had coming into this act hits a major roadblock, and either fails completely or has unintended negative consequences.

Jake is separated from the group and left for dead, as they are forbidden from running night ops to look for him. He is subsequently attacked by a pack of viperwolves.

Turning Point Two: The Commitment

Start Time: 37 of 155 minutes (23.8%)
Runtime: 12 of 155 minutes (7.7%)

<u>The Commitment</u> - The character commits, or finds himself committed, to becoming the epitome of the New Role he accepted at the Dilemma. In doing so, he becomes an active participant in the Central Conflict.

Jake is rescued by the Na'vi female, Neytiri, and taken to her village. There he convinces the Omaticaya clan to teach him their ways. Jake throws himself into his New Role as an Avatar driver for Grace and a spy for Colonel Quaritch. In doing so, he places himself in the middle of the Central Conflict.

Avatar Act Three: Stumbling into the Central Conflict

The character Stumbles into the Central Conflict and faces Intentional Opposition in pursuit of a False Goal. But when there is a grave Turn of events, he has a Moment of Truth.

Jake begins to go against the directives of the colonel and the company (the central conflict) and is antagonized by both the Na'vi and his fellow humans (intentional opposition) as he learns about Na'vi culture in attempt to convince them to leave Hometree (the false goal). But when he mates with Neytiri and Selfridge demolishes Willowglade (the turn), Jake attacks the bulldozer and attempts to come clean to the Omaticaya people about what the humans really want (the moment of truth).

Starting Percentage: 49 of 155 minutes (31.6%)
Runtime: 42 of 155 minutes (27%)

Stumbling into the Central Conflict - The character learns more about the storyworld and develops a new goal that is diametrically opposed to the goal of the antagonist.

Jake and the Na'vi face off with the Colonel and the Company's army of mercenaries.

The Conflict of Ideals - The two sides of the Central Conflict are pursuing opposing ideals of perfection.

Nature and Heritage (Superior Ideal) vs. Money and Technology (Inferior Ideal)

The False Goal - The character receives a new goal he feels will set everything right in his world. Sadly, this isn't the case, and there is still something bigger he must accomplish.

Jake attempts to learn the ways of the Na'vi to convince them to leave Hometree

Intentional Opposition - As a result of his decision at the Commitment, the character comes to the attention of the forces of antagonism. They now begin opposing him with the specific intention of thwarting his plans.

Tsu'tey and the other Na'vi boys give Jake a hard time as he tries to learn how to be Na'vi. When Grace learns Jake is spying for Quaritch, she moves the operation to a secluded outpost in the Hallelujah Mountains. When Selfridge demolishes Willowglade, Jake attacks the bulldozer. Quaritch learns of this and pays Jake a visit... With his fist.

Turning Point Catalyst: The Turn

The Turn - There is a major turn of events that raises the stakes for the character and his allies and makes his situation far more complicated than it had been up to this point. This event is often surprising, coming as a shock to both the character and the audience.

Jake and Neytiri are mated for life. Selfridge demolishes Willowglade prompting Jake to attack the bulldozer. Quaritch watches the surveillance video, realizes it was Jake, and shuts down the avatar project.

Turning Point Three: The Moment of Truth

Start Time: 85 of 155 minutes (54.3%)
Runtime: 6 of 155 minutes (3.8%)

<u>The Moment of Truth</u> - As a result of the Turn, the character must reevaluate his strategy, analyze who he is, and decide to be truthful with himself about the type of person he must become. In figuring out his true nature, he makes the decision to fight for the things he believes in.

Jake attempts to finally be truthful with the Omaticaya "people", giving a heartfelt speech about how he has come to appreciate the beauty of Pandora. Unfortunately, he is interrupted when his connection to his avatar is killed by the Colonel, but he now knows what he believes in and will fight to protect it.

<u>To Change or Not to Change</u> - At the Moment of Truth, the character faces the decision to either change his perspective and who he has been or retain the same outlook in the face of all which has transpired.

To Change: After coming to understand the honor and nobility of the Na'vi way of life, Jake now sees the error in his ways. He makes the decision to fight for the rights of the Na'vi.

Avatar - Act Four: Implementing a Doomed Plan

The character Implements a Doomed Plan and faces Self-Inflicted Opposition in pursuit of a Penultimate Goal. But when an unthinkable Lowpoint occurs, he pulls himself together and discovers a Newfound Resolve.

Jake uses his avatar to return to Hometree (the doomed plan) and is shunned by both the Na'vi and the company (self-inflicted opposition) for trying to convince the Na'vi to leave before Quaritch destroys their village (the penultimate goal). He is excommunicated by the Omaticaya and left for dead (the lowpoint), but rises from the ashes, becomes Toruk Makto and rallies the whole planet to his cause (the newfound resolve).

Starting Percentage: 91 of 155 minutes (58.7%)
Runtime: 35 of 155 minutes (22.5%)

<u>The Doomed Plan</u> - Having made the commitment to fight at the Moment of Truth, the character now devises and implements a plan of action that is destined to fail. It may fail outright, or it may seem to succeed only to have grave consequences the character didn't anticipate.

Jake and Grace reenter their avatars to convince the Na'vi to leave before Quaritch drops the hammer. They are tied up by the Na'vi and forced to watch as Hometree is destroyed.

<u>The Penultimate Goal</u> - The character's goal in this act is one step removed from the Ultimate Goal, but his pursuit of it leads him to realize what he needs to do to end the conflict once and for all.

Jake attempts to save the Omaticaya people by convincing them to leave Hometree.

<u>Self-Inflicted Opposition</u> - The character makes the conscious decision to go up against the forces of antagonism. Because of this, he is the primary cause of the opposition he faces in this act.

Jake rushes back to Hometree to help but is captured and tied up by the Na'vi instead. He nearly dies trying to accomplish his goal but is ultimately powerless to stop the destruction of Hometree. Afterward, he is arrested by the Company and imprisoned along with the rest of the avatar team. With the help of Trudy, the pilot, the group manages to escape but is nearly shot up by the Colonel. Jake next puts himself in mortal danger by attempting to bond with the flying monster and become Toruk Makto.

Turning Point Catalyst: The Lowpoint

<u>The Lowpoint</u> - Something unimaginable happens with grave emotional consequences for the character. He looks back on all his actions over the course of the story and feels he has failed.

Jake arises from the smoldering ashes of Hometree. He realizes he is now "in the place the eye does not see".

Turning Point Four: The Newfound Resolve

Start Time: 115 of 155 minutes (74.1%)
Runtime: 11 of 155 minutes (9.5%)

<u>The Newfound Resolve</u> - After the Lowpoint, something happens to make the character dig deep within himself and rediscover his resolve. He makes the decision to stop the forces of antagonism at any cost.

Jake shows up at the Na'vi sacred place riding the flying monster thing, and all the Na'vi bow before his Caucasoid awesomeness. He has made the decision to side with the Na'vi and stop the Sky People from turning Pandora into Earth.

Avatar - Act Five: Trying a Longshot

The character Tries a Longshot and faces Ultimate Opposition while trying to accomplish the Ultimate Goal. But just when it seems All is Lost, he makes a Final Push against the forces of antagonism, and either succeeds or fails.

Jake and the Na'vi go to war with the technologically superior humans (the longshot), and must overcome their advanced death machines (ultimate opposition) to send them back to Earth and reclaim Pandora (the ultimate goal). But when the Na'vi and the avatar team are overpowered (all is lost), Eywa calls in the whole planet as reinforcements, and Jake and Neytiri fight to the death with the Colonel (the final push).

Starting Percentage: 126 of 155 minutes (81.2%)
Runtime: 26 of 155 minutes (16.7%)

The Longshot - The character is reinvigorated by the revelation he received at the Newfound Resolve, but his only chance of success lies in a plan with a high risk of failure.

The Na'vi are outgunned by the humans, but attempt to use the magnetic distortion of the flux vortex to their advantage. Additionally, Jake solicits the aid of Eywa.

The Ultimate Goal - The character finally understands what the true goal of the story is. The goal the character has in this act is what the story is all about.

Jake and the gang want to defeat the humans and take back Pandora.

Ultimate Opposition - The forces of antagonism are now out to destroy the character completely. At this point in the story, the antagonist will throw everything he has into eliminating the character.

The Company and its mercenaries send all their warships to the last remaining sacred place of the Omaticaya people with intentions of turning it into a smoldering, beautifully rendered CGI crater.

Turning Point Catalyst: All Is Lost

<u>All is Lost</u> - The character may experience some initial success, but the forces of antagonism rally, and it seems the character's Longshot is doomed to fail.

During the battle for Pandora, Quaritch gets Jake and his flying monster in the sights of his warship. The renegade pilot, Trudy, flies between them instead of just shooting the Colonel's ship down while she held the tactical advantage. After flying around Quaritch's ship like an annoying mosquito, she takes an inevitable shot to the engine and is too busy flipping random switches on the control panel to continue whatever it was she was trying to do to in the first place. Neytiri is shot down. Tsu'tey is shot down. Norm is shot down. Trudy is shot down. The whole plan is shot down.

Turning Point Five: The Final Push

Start Time: 139 of 155 minutes (89.6%)
Runtime: 13 of 155 minutes (8.3%)

<u>The Final Push</u> - Faced with his imminent destruction, the character decides to put everything he has into one final endeavor. He uses what little he has left in his stores, or the one trump card he's been holding, knowing if he fails he will be destroyed.

Just as it seems the humans have won, Eywa, the spirit of the planet, sweeps in to even the score with an army of space creatures. Jake destroys the last few warships with his bare hands (albeit, he has grenades in them).

Afterward, Neytiri and Quaritch have a duel, which she loses. Before Quaritch can deliver his death blow, Jake swoops in to save the day. But when Quaritch smashes up the mobile lab where Jake's human body lies, Jake nearly asphyxiates on the atmosphere of the planet he has chosen to call home. Neytiri draws on her last reserves, kills Quaritch, and makes a final effort to revive

Jake. When he awakens, Neytiri still loves him despite seeing his small, pasty, earthling body.

Avatar - Act Six: Living in a New Situation

Having accomplished (or failed to accomplish) the Ultimate Goal, the character is shown living in a New Situation.

Jake and a few "lucky" humans live on Pandora and Jake becomes a Na'vi.

Starting Percentage: 152 of 155 minutes (98.1%)
Runtime: 3 minutes
Run Percentage: 3 of 155 minutes (2%)

<u>Living in a New Situation</u> - We see the character adapting to the New Situation his actions have created. Whether he is exalted or exiled, this is the new world he helped create.

All but a few chosen humans are sent packing. The time of great sorrow has ended. Jake goes to his birthday party and officially becomes one of the people by discarding his useless human body and transferring his consciousness into his avatar. Everyone lives happily ever after… until the sequel.

A Game of Thrones (Ned Stark)

1996 Novel
Written by George RR Martin

Character
Eddard "Ned" Stark, Lord of Winterfell, Warden of the North.

Ultimate Goal
Stop the Lannisters from taking control of the Iron Throne.

Total Runtime: 72 chapters

Contrary to the phenomenal success of HBO's television adaptation of the novels, George RR Martin's first book in the *Song of Fire and Ice* series was released in 1996 to little fanfare. However, the methodical storytelling and grittiness of the series led to the growth of a cult following that eventually rocketed the series to the bestseller list. While ASoIaF is known for being a sprawling multi-character epic, we can still find the Six Acts not only in the overall storyline, but in the individual stories of each character.

Due to Martin's masterful subversion of genre expectations, we are led to believe Ned Stark is the main character of the first book. This is due both to him having the greatest number of chapters, and his being the prototypical "good" guy we are accustomed to seeing succeed. But, *A Game of Thrones* makes prolific use of tragic story elements in the narrative, and characters who make poor decisions in the storyworld face very real, often fatal consequences.

Ned labors to do the right thing throughout the novel, by attempting to expose the conspiracies surrounding the deaths of his friends Jon Arryn and Robert Baratheon, and meets his own demise for failing to see the wood for the trees. He stubbornly avoids deviating from his code of honor and ends up paying the ultimate price for it at the novel's conclusion. We will see in this example how the character's unwillingness to recognize the flaw in his viewpoint affects the structure of the story, therefore deviating (often for the better) from the traditional Six Act paradigm.

A Game of Thrones: Ned Stark - Act One: Dealing with an Imperfect Situation

A character in an Imperfect Situation faces Oppressive Opposition as he pursues an Initial Goal. But when there is a Disturbance to his routine, he faces a Dilemma regarding his situation and must assume a New Role.

Ned Stark deals with life in the North and deserters on the Wall (the imperfect situation) and faces the impending winter and demands from the king (oppressive opposition) as he lords over Winterfell (the initial goal). But when the King's Hand, Jon Arryn, dies (the disturbance), the King visits and asserts that Ned relocate to the Capitol to replace his recently deceased friend (the dilemma) as Hand of the King (the new role).

Runtime: Chapter 1 through 6 (6 Chapters)
Run Percentage: 6 of 72 Chapters (8.3%)

<u>The Inciting Incident</u> - Something happens, often before the story begins, which if it does not occur would prevent the story as it exists from coming to be.

Ned's friend Jon Arryn discovers the truth about Cersei and Jaime's incestuous relationship and is murdered for it.

The Imperfect Situation - The character begins the story in a less than ideal situation he would like to change but seemingly cannot.

Ned worries over the growing number of deserters from the Night's Watch guarding the Wall. He also learns King Robert is coming to visit, and he must make preparations.

The Initial Desire - Deep within himself, the character wants one particular thing more than anything else in the world.

Ned wants to go about his life at Winterfell as the honorable Warden of the North.

Initial Desire Type - The character's Initial Desire is either for or against changing his situation.

Against Change: Ned is wholly contented to stay in Winterfell as Warden of the North.

Preexisting Conflict - When the story begins, the character is already dealing with personal conflicts as well as the conflicts of the world at large.

Where to begin? At the story's open the preexisting conflicts of the Seven Kingdoms are on the verge of reaching their boiling point. The Lannisters and the Starks have a long-standing disdain for one another. King Robert and Queen Cersei despise each other. Tyrion is hated by his own blood simply for being born. The once-royal Targaryens have been exiled and vow to reclaim the throne. And if that weren't enough, the white walkers have returned to settle a thousand-year-old score with humanity. All these conflicts, and many more introduced later, provide the dramatic fuel that propels the story forward.

Likability/Empathy Factors - The character is shown to be someone the audience would like to see succeed, or would be willing to follow on the journey of the story.

We are introduced to Ned through the eyes of his seven-year-old son Bran. Ned gives Bran life lessons by chopping off a deserter's head with his badass Valyrian steel sword, Ice. He also gives him a lecture about the importance of always doing the right thing. On the way home, they come across a dead direwolf and her abandoned puppies, and Ned allows his children to keep them. What a nice guy.

Ned is shown, through conversations with his wife in the Godswood, to be an honorable man with a strong sense of duty. Not only is he good friends with the King, Robert Baratheon, but the two fought victoriously together in the war that overthrew the Mad King and installed Robert to his throne.

Later, after making sexy-time with his wife, it is revealed the only time Ned's honor ever lapsed resulted in his bastard son, Jon. In spite of this, Ned has done right by the little bastard and raised him, much to the chagrin of his protesting wife.

The Initial Goal - When the story opens, the character already has a goal he is actively pursuing.

Ned wants to be the Lord of Winterfell and prep for winter. Because like it or not, it's coming.

Initial Goal Type - The character's Initial Goal is either a Normal Routine Goal where he is in his regular environment, or a Fish out of Water Goal where he is already in a situation with which he is unfamiliar.

Normal Routine Goal: In the opening chapters, Ned Stark does all the things as Lord of Winterfell he would normally do.

Oppressive Opposition - The character's Initial Desire and/or his Initial Goal are being oppressed by the world around him.

Robert Baratheon is the only man in the Seven Kingdoms with the authority to oppress Ned's goals, which is exactly what he does by asking Ned to relocate to

ACTIONS & GOALS

King's Landing and serve as the King's hand. Ned wants to decline, but his wife begs him to investigate the death of their brother-in-law. In addition to this, deserters from the Night's Watch are making his job difficult.

Turning Point Catalyst: The Disturbance

<u>The Disturbance</u> - An unexpected event with ominous implications occurs, interrupting the character's normal routine. This event pushes the character toward the Dilemma.

While in the godswood, Ned and Catelyn Stark discuss deserters from the wall. She breaks the news about Jon Arryn's death and the King's impending visit.

Turning Point One: The Dilemma

Start Time: After 4 of 72 Chapters (5.5%)
Runtime: Chapter 4 through 6 (3 Chapters)
Run Percentage: 3 of 72 Chapters (4.1%)

<u>Presentation of The Dilemma</u> - The character is placed in a position where he must choose between life as he has known it or taking a new course of action.

King Robert Baratheon arrives at Winterfell to offer Ned the position of Hand of the King, as well as the opportunity for Ned's daughter, Sansa, to marry the crown prince, Joffrey. Ned must choose whether he will stay in Winterfell as the Warden of the North, or travel to King's Landing and become the Hand of the King.

<u>The New Role</u> - If the character takes this new course of action, he will assume a New Role in which he is untested.

If Ned accepts the King's offer, he will become the Hand of the King.

<u>Refusal/Interference to the New Role (Optional)</u> - The character may be reluctant, unready or unwilling to leave his Imperfect Situation and accept the New Role. In other cases, the character may want to accept the New Role, but someone else attempts to prevent him from accepting it.

Ned initially turns down Robert's offer in favor of staying in Winterfell and taking care of his responsibilities.

<u>Nudge From Fate (Optional)</u> - In instances where the character has every reason to decline the New Role, he may receive influence from an outside force that drives him to accept it.

After coitus, Ned and his wife, Catelyn, are interrupted by Maester Luwin who has a secret note for Cat. The note is from Catelyn's sister who says the former Hand of the King, Jon Arryn, was poisoned by the Queen and her family.

<u>Accepting The New Role</u> - The character makes the decision to take action by accepting the New Role.

At his wife's request, Ned agrees to go to King's Landing. They also decide Ned's bastard son, Jon, will be allowed to join the Night's Watch so Catelyn will no longer have to look at his stupid face.

A Game of Thrones: Ned Stark - Act Two: Learning the Rules of an Unfamiliar Situation

The character Learns the Rules of an Unfamiliar Situation and faces Incidental Opposition in pursuit of a Transitional Goal. But when he receives a Reality Check, the character makes a Commitment to his New Role.

Ned learns the complexities of navigating the King's court (unfamiliar situation) and faces the manipulations of people around the king (incidental opposition) as he travels to King's Landing to serve as the Hand of the King and investigate the mysterious circumstances of his friend's death (transitional goal). But when animosity between the children of Houses Stark and Lannister stirs up old disdain between the two families, culminating in the discovery the Lannister's attempted to have Brandon Stark assassinated (the reality check), Ned vows to obtain proof of the Lannister's treachery (the commitment).

Start Time: After 6 of 72 Chapters (8.3%)
Runtime: Chapter 7 through 20 (14 Chapters)
Run Percentage: 14 of 72 Chapters (19.4%)

Learning the Rules of an Unfamiliar Situation - The character now finds himself in a situation unlike anything he's ever experienced.

Ned is forced to play politics as he travels to the Capitol as the newly appointed Hand of the King. With Cersei as Queen, the royal court has become a treacherous place.

The Hooking Premise - The unique premise at the heart of a story, often involving an intriguing "what if" scenario that piques the audience's interest.

What if the most honorable Lord in a treacherous kingdom is drawn into a murderous conspiracy to overthrow the king?

The Transitional Goal - The character receives a new goal that transitions him out of his initial state of inertia and into the main events of the story.

Ned wants to go to the Capitol, serve as the Hand of the King, and investigate his friend's death.

Incidental Opposition - The character learns there are greater forces of opposition in this new world that may not be out to thwart him specifically, but still stand between him and his new goal.

Back in Winterfell someone tries and fails to assassinate Ned's comatose son, Bran, in his absence. The assassination attempt is later revealed to have been orchestrated by Petyr "Littlefinger" Baelish in attempt to frame Tyrion Lannister.

A spiteful encounter between the Lannister/Baratheon and Stark children puts a strain on Ned's relationship with the King.

When Ned arrives in King's Landing, he learns of the attack on Bran from Catelyn, and that the assassin's knife belonged to Tyrion Lannister.

Turning Point Catalyst: The Reality Check

<u>The Reality Check</u> - The plan the character had coming into this act hits a major roadblock, and either fails completely or has unintended negative consequences.

On the road to the Capitol, Sansa Stark and Prince Joffrey go riding together. They encounter Sansa's sister Arya play-fighting with a butcher's boy. Joffrey begins tormenting the boy prompting Arya to hit Joffrey with a stick. When Joffrey threatens Arya with his sword, her direwolf attacks him, maiming his arm. With Joffrey distracted, Arya throws his sword in the river and runs off. Joffrey is angry with Arya but takes his anger out on Sansa.

It takes Ned's men four days to find Arya. Cersei has Arya taken before the king. Arya and Joffrey tell King Robert conflicting stories of their encounter. When Sansa claims she doesn't remember, Queen Cersei demands the death of a direwolf. With Arya's wolf gone, Sansa's direwolf is sentenced to death instead. Ned volunteers to do it himself, as opposed to letting the queen's royal executioner do it. Apparently, being the Hand of the King isn't as easy as it sounds.

Turning Point Two: The Commitment

Start Time: After 17 of 72 Chapters (23.6%)
Runtime: Chapter 18 through 20 (3 Chapters)
Run Percentage: 3 of 72 Chapters (4.1%)

<u>The Commitment</u> - The character commits, or finds himself committed, to becoming the epitome of the New Role he accepted at the Dilemma. In doing so, he becomes an active participant in the Central Conflict.

Catelyn Stark arrives in King's Landing by ship. At a secret meeting with Littlefinger and the royal Master of Whisperers, Varys, Catelyn is told the assassin's knife belonged to Tyrion Lannister. Dun dun duhn.

When Ned arrives at King's Landing, he is approached by Littlefinger who leads him to the brothel where Catelyn is hiding. Cat tells Ned about Tyrion's dagger, and together they plot a strategy to find proof the Lannister's killed Jon Arryn. Ned commits himself to remaining in King's Landing in his New Role as the Hand of the King. His plan to reveal the treachery of the Lannisters to King Robert brings him into the Central Conflict.

A Game of Thrones: Ned Stark - Act Three: Stumbling into the Central Conflict

The character Stumbles into the Central Conflict and faces Intentional Opposition in pursuit of a False Goal. But when there is a grave Turn of events, he has a Moment of Truth.

Ned clashes with the Lannisters (the central conflict) and faces opposition from the King and the court (intentional opposition) as he attempts to expose and depose them (the false goal). But when Ned's wife Catelyn captures Tyrion Lannister, prompting Jaime Lannister to take revenge against Ned (the turn), Ned's comes to realize the true reason his friend Jon Arryn was killed: the king's children were actually conceived by Jaime and Cersei Lannister. Ned confronts Cersei, reveals he knows the truth and gives her an ultimatum to leave King's Landing (the moment of truth).

Start Time: After 20 of 72 Chapters (27.7%)
Runtime: Chapter 21 through 45 (25 Chapters)
Run Percentage: 25 of 72 Chapters (34.7%)

Stumbling into the Central Conflict - The character learns more about the storyworld and develops a new goal that is diametrically opposed to the goal of the antagonist.

The honorable Starks face off with the considerably less honorable Lannisters

The Conflict of Ideals - The two sides of the Central Conflict are pursuing opposing ideals of perfection.

Power and Wealth (Superior Ideal) vs. Honor and Duty (Inferior Ideal)

The False Goal - The character receives a new goal he feels will set everything right in his world. Sadly, this isn't the case, and there is still something bigger he must accomplish.

Ned attempts to obtain proof of the Lannister's betrayal.

Intentional Opposition - As a result of his decision at the Commitment, the character comes to the attention of the forces of antagonism. They now begin opposing him with the specific intention of thwarting his plans.

During a celebratory tournament, Ned has to convince the King not to participate in the melee. When the tournament ends, Varys tells Ned that Robert was meant to die in the melee. Later, Ned and Robert argue over a plot to assassinate the fourteen-year-old Daenerys Targaryen across the Narrow Sea. When the small council sides against him, Ned resigns in protest.

Littlefinger takes Ned to the brothel Jon Arryn visited shortly before his death in hopes of finding answers. As they are leaving, Ned's party is ambushed by Jaime Lannister. Jaime has Ned's men killed in retribution for the abduction of his brother. Damn those Lannisters.

Turning Point Catalyst: The Turn

<u>The Turn</u> - There is a major turn of events that raises the stakes for the character and his allies and makes his situation far more complicated than it had been up to this point. This event is often surprising, coming as a shock to both the character and the audience.

Littlefinger leads Ned to the brothel Jon Arryn visited. There he talks to a young whore with a daughter who bears a striking resemblance to King Robert. On their way back to the Red Keep, Ned's small party is ambushed by Jaime Lannister and a large party of Lannister men. Ned's leg is broken in the ensuing scuffle, causing him to lose consciousness.

Ned dreams of the showdown at the Tower of Joy, which happened during Robert's uprising. He awakens to an angry King Robert's complaints about the abduction of Tyrion Lannister. The King demands Ned make peace with the Lannisters. He also reinstates Ned as Hand of the King and orders him to sit the Iron Throne while Robert goes on a hunting trip.

Turning Point Three: the Moment of Truth

Start Time: After 43 of 72 Chapters (59.7%)
Runtime: Chapter 44 through 45 (2 Chapters)
Run Percentage: 2 of 72 Chapters (2.7%)

<u>The Moment of Truth</u> - As a result of the Turn, the character must reevaluate his strategy, analyze who he is, and decide to be truthful with himself about the type of person he must become. In figuring out his true nature, he makes the decision to fight for the things he believes in.

Ned reveals to his daughter Sansa that he is sending her and her sister Arya back to Winterfell. Sansa pleads to stay so she can marry Prince Joffrey, who is nothing like his drunken father, Robert, and will give her children with pretty, blond hair. This statement leads Ned to an epiphany about why Jon Arryn was murdered; none of the royal children came from the King's testicles.

Ned reflects on this before meeting with Queen Cersei. He decides to stay true to himself and give her the option to flee King's Landing before Robert returns from his hunting trip. Cersei laughs in Ned's face before explaining to him, "When you play the game of thrones, you win or you die. There is no middle ground." Despite this warning, Ned remains steadfast in his decision and fights back against anyone who feels he should take a more drastic course of action.

To Change or Not to Change - At the Moment of Truth, the character faces the decision to either change his perspective and who he has been or retain the same outlook in the face of all which has transpired.

Not to Change: To Ned Stark, the abandonment of his honor is unconscionable. To do so would make him no better than the Lannisters he seeks to depose. When faced with the decision to take the quick and easy route to oust them from power, he chooses to remain steadfast on the honorable path.

A Game of Thrones: Ned Stark - Act Four: Implementing a Doomed Plan

The character Implements a Doomed Plan and faces Self-Inflicted Opposition in pursuit of a Penultimate Goal. But when an unthinkable Lowpoint occurs, he pulls himself together and discovers a Newfound Resolve.

Ned elicits the help of Littlefinger and the gold cloaks (the doomed plan) and goes against the wishes of all his advisors (self-inflicted opposition) to install the King's brother, Stannis, as king (the penultimate goal). But when Ned is betrayed by Littlefinger, and taken prisoner (the lowpoint), Varys convinces him he can still save his daughter, Sansa, by swallowing his pride and confessing to treason (the newfound resolve).

Start Time: After 45 of 72 Chapters (62.4%)
Runtime: Chapter 46 through 58 (13 Chapters)
Run Percentage: 13 of 72 Chapters (18.1%)

<u>The Doomed Plan</u> - Having made the commitment to fight at the Moment of Truth, the character now devises and implements a plan of action that is destined to fail. It may fail outright, or it may seem to succeed only to have grave consequences the character didn't anticipate.

Ned plans to reveal the Lannister's incestuous secret and install Stannis Baratheon to the throne.

<u>The Penultimate Goal</u> - The character's goal in this act is one step removed from the Ultimate Goal, but his pursuit of it leads him to realize what he needs to do to end the conflict once and for all.

Ned attempts to expose the Lannisters and install Stannis as the king.

<u>Self-Inflicted Opposition</u> - The character makes the conscious decision to go up against the forces of antagonism. Because of this, he is the primary cause of the opposition he faces in this act.

Ned learns King Robert has been mortally wounded by a boar while hunting. In his will, Robert declares Ned the Regent, giving him temporary control of the throne. Robert's youngest brother, Renly, urges Ned to seize the royal children to secure his power, but Ned refuses. Instead, he writes a letter to Robert's eldest brother, Stannis, proclaiming him the rightful heir. Because he needs manpower to install Stannis to the throne, Ned asks Littlefinger to arrange the support of the City Watch. This ultimately leads to Littlefinger's betrayal and the failure of Ned's plan. Fail.

When Ned convenes the small council to confirm himself as Protector of the Realm, they are interrupted by a summons from "King Joffrey". When they arrive at the throne room, Queen Cersei destroys Robert's will, and Robert's "son" Joffrey declares himself king. Ned reveals Joffrey has no right to the Iron Throne, but when he calls for the City Watch to arrest Cersei and her children, the watchmen instead attack Ned's men, revealing Littlefinger's betrayal.

Turning Point Catalyst: The Lowpoint

<u>The Lowpoint</u> - Something unimaginable happens with grave emotional consequences for the character. He looks back on all his actions over the course of the story and feels he has failed.

Ned is imprisoned in the windowless, urine-scented, black cells. He thinks back to Cersei's words, "When you play the game of thrones, you win or you die," and realizes he has indeed lost. Ned broods over all that has transpired and the mistakes he has made, finally realizing the error in his ways. He is kept in the cells for days with no food and eventually resigns himself to his fate.

Turning Point Four: The Newfound Resolve

Start Time: After 57 of 72 Chapters (79.1%)
Runtime: Chapter 58 (1 Chapter)
Run Percentage: 1 of 72 Chapters (1.3%)

<u>The Newfound Resolve</u> - After the Lowpoint, something happens to make the character dig deep within himself and rediscover his resolve. He makes the decision to stop the forces of antagonism at any cost.

Ned is unexpectedly visited in the black cells by Varys, who brings him news of his family and the state of the outside world. He urges Ned to admit to treason, command his son, Robb, to call off the rebellion he is leading, and denounce Stannis and Renly Baratheon's claims to the Iron Throne.

When Ned declares his life is not worth forsaking his honor, Varys informs him Cersei has Sansa, whose life is still very much at stake. Ned makes the decision to sacrifice his honor to stop Cersei and Joffrey from murdering his family.

A Game of Thrones: Ned Stark - Act Five: Trying a Longshot

The character Tries a Longshot and faces Ultimate Opposition while trying to accomplish the Ultimate Goal. But just when it seems All is Lost, he makes a Final Push against the forces of antagonism, and either succeeds or fails.

Ned publicly confesses to treason (the longshot) and is ridiculed by the Lannisters and the lice ridden peasants of the Capitol (ultimate opposition) after sacrificing his honor to save his daughters (the ultimate goal). He realizes too late the irrelevance of his honor and is subsequently beheaded (all is lost).

Start Time: After 58 of 72 Chapters (80.5%)
Runtime: Chapter 59 through 65 (7 Chapters)
Run Percentage: 7 of 72 Chapters (9.7%)

<u>The Longshot</u> - The character is reinvigorated by the revelation he received at the Newfound Resolve, but his only chance of success lies in a plan with a high risk of failure.

Ned publicly takes responsibility for the plot to overthrow Joffrey, in hopes of saving his daughters and family.

<u>The Ultimate Goal</u> - The character finally understands what the true goal of the story is. The goal the character has in this act is what the story is all about.

Ned wants to set aside his honor to save his innocent children.

Ultimate Opposition - The forces of antagonism are now out to destroy the character completely. At this point in the story, the antagonist will throw everything he has into eliminating the character.

Ned is publicly shamed by the common folk and beheaded by the Lannisters.

Turning Point Catalyst: All Is Lost

All is Lost - The character may experience some initial success, but the forces of antagonism rally, and it seems the character's Longshot is doomed to fail.

Ned is taken to the town Sept and confesses (untruthfully) that he betrayed the trust of King Robert. Against the protest of his mother, the High Septon, and Sansa, Joffrey declares that as long as he is king, treason shall never go unpunished. He calls for one of his goons to bring him Ned's head. Ned's youngest daughter, Arya, watches as he is beheaded. Damn those Lannisters.

Turning Point Five: The Final Push

Start Time: NA
Runtime: NA
Run Percentage: NA

The Final Push - Faced with his imminent destruction, the character decides to put everything he has into one final endeavor. He uses what little he has left in his stores, or the one trump card he's been holding, knowing if he fails he will be destroyed.

NA for Ned, seeing as how he's dead.

A Game of Thrones: Ned Stark - Act Six: Living in a New Situation

ACTIONS & GOALS

Having accomplished (or failed to accomplish) the Ultimate Goal, the character is shown living in a New Situation.

With Ned executed for failing to sacrifice his honor for the good of the realm, Westeros is thrown into a bloody and far-reaching civil war.

Start Time: After 65 of 72 Chapters (90.2%)
Runtime: Chapter 66 through 72 (7 Chapters)
Run Percentage: 7 of 72 Chapters (9.7%)

<u>Living in a New Situation</u> - We see the character adapting to the New Situation his actions have created. Whether he is exalted or exiled, this is the new world he helped create.

This act is definitely NA for Ned, but the uproar caused by his death ignites a chain of events for the rest of the characters that will take George RR Martin a hundred years to finish writing.

A Game of Thrones (Daenerys Targaryen)

1996 Novel
Written by George RR Martin

<u>Character</u>
Daenerys Targaryen.

<u>Ultimate Goal</u>
Become a Queen and the Mother of Dragons.

Total Runtime: 10 chapters

There are several methods for structuring a multi-POV story, two of which are analyzed in the films *Star Trek, Star Wars,* and *The Empire Strikes Back.* But in *A Game of Thrones,* Martin's approach seems to have been to give Daenerys Targaryen's narrative its own individual act structure, independent of the overall story. This allows her storyline to function as separate, but connected story, interlaced with the events unfolding on the other side of the Narrow Sea, to achieve the strongest dramatic effect. So instead of using the overall runtime of the entire story to determine the act lengths for Daenerys' narrative, we will use only the runtimes of her individual chapters.

While not as tragic as Ned's storyline (i.e. she reaches the end of the story with her head attached to her body), Daenerys' narrative is also filled with a great many tough decisions, some of which she gets wrong and pays a hefty price for. For those of you unfamiliar with the series, Daenerys and her older brother Viserys are the last surviving members of the true royal family of

Westeros. The rest of their family was killed during a rebellion in the kingdom when the current King, Robert Baratheon, usurped the throne from Daenerys' father, Aerys "The Mad King" Targaryen.

A Game of Thrones: Daenerys Targaryen - Act One: Dealing with an Imperfect Situation

A character in an Imperfect Situation faces Oppressive Opposition as he pursues an Initial Goal. But when there is a Disturbance to his routine, he faces a Dilemma regarding his situation and must assume a New Role.

Thirteen-year-old Daenerys Targaryen lives off the good graces of foreigners in Essos (the imperfect situation) and has no choice but to submit to her ill-tempered brother's will (oppressive opposition) as they try to regain their royal status (the initial goal). But when the cruel Viserys plans to marry Daenerys off to Dothraki warlord, Khal Drogo (the disturbance), she must choose between angering her brother, or marrying the savage stranger (the dilemma) and becoming a Khaleesi (the new role).

Runtime: Chapters 3 and 11 (2 Chapters)
Run Percentage: 2 of 10 Chapters (20%)

The Inciting Incident - Something happens, often before the story begins, which if it does not occur would prevent the story as it exists from coming to be.

Daenerys' crazy father, the King of Westeros, is killed in an insurrection. Daenerys' brother and their pregnant mother are forced to flee to Dragonstone, where their mother dies giving birth to her. The duo, now the last remaining Targaryens, flee across the Narrow Sea to Essos where they are raised by Ser Willem Darry until shortly before the story begins.

ACTIONS & GOALS

<u>The Imperfect Situation</u> - The character begins the story in a less than ideal situation he would like to change but seemingly cannot.

Only thirteen, Daenerys feels both her family and her childhood were stolen from her. Viserys, her only surviving kin, is cruel and boorish, physically and mentally abusing her. Though once royalty, they now have no money, surviving purely off the strength of their family name. In addition to this, Viserys plans to marry her off to a foreigner in exchange for an army to retake the throne.

<u>The Initial Desire</u> - Deep within himself, the character wants one particular thing more than anything else in the world.

Daenerys wishes she could have her childhood back. She wants to go back to her old life when she and her brother, were safe.

<u>Initial Desire Type</u> - The character's Initial Desire is either for or against changing his situation.

Against Change: Daenerys doesn't want to be where she is or marry Khal Drogo. She would rather things went back to the way they were.

<u>Preexisting Conflict</u> - When the story begins the character is already dealing with personal conflicts as well as the conflicts of the world at large.

As one of the rightful heirs to the Iron Throne of Westeros, Daenerys shares many of the same preexisting conflicts as Ned across the sea. This is exacerbated by the fact King Robert wants all Targaryen's wiped off the face of the Earth (or whatever planet the story takes place on). She also has a strenuous relationship with her brother who is obsessed with retaking the throne.

<u>Likability/Empathy Factors</u> - The character is shown to be someone the audience would like to see succeed, or would be willing to follow on the journey of the story.

Daenerys' plight is a textbook example of Undeserved Misfortune. She's a young, vulnerable, diminutive girl living in a harsh world. None of the misfortune leveled upon her is a result of her own actions, but there are people in the world who want her dead because of her family name.

<u>The Initial Goal</u> - When the story opens, the character already has a goal he is actively pursuing.

Daenerys seeks to appease Viserys by doing whatever he asks of her in his quest to regain the Iron Throne. This includes being presented to the Dothraki horselord, Khal Drogo, to be assessed as a potential bride.

<u>Initial Goal Type</u> - The character's Initial Goal is either a Normal Routine Goal where he is in his regular environment, or a Fish out of Water Goal where he is already in a situation with which he is unfamiliar.

Fish out of Water Goal: Though Daenerys has been on the run for many years now, she is still a Fish out of Water in her current situation. She is in a strange city, living as the guest of a man she does not trust while preparing to meet a stranger she may soon be forced to marry.

<u>Oppressive Opposition</u> - The character's Initial Desire and/or his Initial Goal are being oppressed by the world around him.

Daenerys lives at the mercy of her brother. He controls every aspect of her life with no regard for her opinions.

Turning Point Catalyst: The Disturbance

<u>The Disturbance</u> - An unexpected event with ominous implications occurs, interrupting the character's normal routine. This event pushes the character toward the Dilemma.

When we first meet Daenerys, the threat of her presentation to Khal Drogo looms over her narrative. The chapter culminates in her being approached by her potential husband.

Turning Point One: The Dilemma

Start Time: After 1 of 10 Chapters (10%)
Runtime: Chapter 11 (1 Chapter)
Run Percentage: 1 of 10 Chapters (10%)

<u>Presentation of The Dilemma</u> - The character is placed in a position where he must choose between life as he has known it or taking a new course of action.

Daenerys must choose to either marry the Khal or incur the wrath of Viserys.

<u>The New Role</u> - If the character takes this new course of action, he will assume a New Role in which he is untested.

If Daenerys marries Khal Drogo, she will become a Khaleesi.

<u>Refusal/Interference to the New Role (Optional)</u> - The character may be reluctant, unready or unwilling to leave his Imperfect Situation and accept the New Role. In other cases, the character may want to accept the New Role, but someone else attempts to prevent him from accepting it.

Daenerys doesn't want to marry Drogo, but cannot deny Viserys. When the day of her wedding finally comes, she is terrified.

<u>Accepting The New Role</u> - The character makes the decision to take action by accepting the New Role.

Daenerys and Drogo are wedded in a big, violent Dothraki ceremony. That evening they consummate their marriage. With sex!

A Game of Thrones: Daenerys Targaryen - Act Two: Learning the Rules of an Unfamiliar Situation

The character Learns the Rules of an Unfamiliar Situation and faces Incidental Opposition in pursuit of a Transitional Goal. But when he receives a Reality Check, the character makes a Commitment to his New Role.

Daenerys and her brother travel with her new husband's khalasar (the unfamiliar situation) and struggle to adapt to the ways of the Dothraki (incidental opposition) as they make their way to the Dothraki capital, Vaes Dothrak (the transitional goal). But when Viserys grows petulant over his loss of status among Dany and the Dothraki (the reality check), he publicly attacks her at a feast and is killed by the Khal and his men as Daenerys looks on unsympathetically (the commitment).

Start Time: After 2 of 10 Chapters, 20%
Runtime: Chapters 23, 36 and 46 (3 Chapters)
Run Percentage: 3 of 10 Chapters (30%)

Learning the Rules of an Unfamiliar Situation - The character now finds himself in a situation unlike anything he's ever experienced.

Daenerys and Viserys are ignorant of Dothraki culture and customs. But while Daenerys struggles to learn the ways of her new people, Viserys denigrates and insults them.

The Hooking Premise - The unique premise at the heart of a story, often involving an intriguing "what if" scenario that piques the audience's interest.

What if a timid teenage princess is forced to become a barbarian queen?

The Transitional Goal - The character receives a new goal that transitions him out of his initial state of inertia and into the main events of the story.

Daenerys travels to Vaes Dothrak to be presented to the dosh khaleen, widows of slain khals who serve as the leaders of the Dothraki religion. All prospective wives of khals must be presented to the dosh khaleen for acceptance.

Incidental Opposition - The character learns there are greater forces of opposition in this new world that may not be out to thwart him specifically, but still stand between him and his new goal.

Viserys' refusal to acknowledge Dothraki customs causes him to rapidly lose favor amongst the horselords. This only makes him more impatient with Daenerys and the Khal, creating Daenerys' internal conflict of trying to respect the Dothraki way of life, while also trying to appease her increasingly belligerent brother.

Turning Point Catalyst: The Reality Check

The Reality Check - The plan the character had coming into this act hits a major roadblock, and either fails completely or has unintended negative consequences.

After Viserys physically assaults Daenerys during her attempt to present him a peace offering, it becomes clear he is out of control and will never respect the ordinances of the Dothraki or acknowledge that he can, and will, be held accountable for his actions under their laws.

Turning Point Two: The Commitment

Start Time: After 4 of 10 Chapters (40%)
Runtime: Chapter 46 (1 Chapter)
Run Percentage: 1 of 10 Chapters (10%)

The Commitment - The character commits, or finds himself committed, to becoming the epitome of the New Role he accepted at the Dilemma. In doing so, he becomes an active participant in the Central Conflict.

As part of a Dothraki motherhood ritual, Daenerys eats a raw stallion heart to ensure the health of her unborn child. Completion of this act cements her place within the khalasar. Later that evening, Viserys shows up drunk to the celebratory feast. He wears a sword on his belt, which is forbidden in the Dothraki city and is lampooned by Khal Drogo to the delight of the Dothraki in attendance. When Viserys draws his sword and pricks blood from Daenerys, he commits an unforgivable offense of Dothraki customs and is sentenced to immediate execution at the hands of the Khal. As Drogo prepares a pot of molten gold to be poured over Viserys head, Daenerys refuses to look away as her brother pleads with her to spare him. Like her new Dothraki brethren, she watches him die with little remorse. She has committed herself to her New Role as a Khaleesi. In doing so, she brings herself to the attention of King Robert across the Narrow Sea who vows to have her killed.

A Game of Thrones: Daenerys Targaryen - Act Three: Stumbling into the Central Conflict

The character Stumbles into the Central Conflict and faces Intentional Opposition in pursuit of a False Goal. But when there is a grave Turn of events, he has a Moment of Truth.

In attempt to maintain control of the throne, the king of Westeros, Robert Baratheon (the central conflict), puts a price on the unsuspecting Daenerys' head (intentional opposition) as she tries to convince the Khal to lead his men across the sea to take the Iron Throne (the false goal). But when Khal Drogo is wounded in battle (the turn), Daenerys trusts a practitioner of blood magic whom she saved from rape to heal him (the moment of truth).

Start Time: After 5 of 10 Chapters (50%)
Runtime: Chapters 54 and 61 (2 Chapters)
Run Percentage: 2 of 10 Chapters (20%)

Stumbling into the Central Conflict - The character learns more about the storyworld and develops a new goal that is diametrically opposed to the goal of the antagonist.

On the other side of the narrow sea, King Robert arranges for the pregnant Daenerys to be assassinated. Even after all these years, the Baratheons and the Targaryen's are still at odds over the fate of the Iron Throne.

The Conflict of Ideals - The two sides of the Central Conflict are pursuing opposing ideals of perfection.

Taking What You Want (Superior Ideal) vs. Respecting the Wants of Others (Inferior Ideal)

The False Goal - The character receives a new goal he feels will set everything right in his world. Sadly, this isn't the case, and there is still something bigger he must accomplish.

Daenerys attempts to convince Drogo they need to set their sights on Westeros and take the Iron Throne from the Baratheons. Though she does eventually succeed in convincing him, their plans for invasion are short-lived.

Intentional Opposition - As a result of his decision at the Commitment, the character comes to the attention of the forces of antagonism. They now begin opposing him with the specific intention of thwarting his plans.

While Daenerys tries to convince Drogo to march on Westeros, King Robert sends an assassin to poison her.

Turning Point Catalyst: The Turn

The Turn - There is a major turn of events that raises the stakes for the character and his allies and makes his situation far more complicated than it had been up to this point. This event is often surprising, coming as a shock to both the character and the audience.

After Drogo's khalasar attacks a town, Daenerys interferes with Dothraki traditions by stopping several of the Khal's bloodriders from raping the townswomen. This begins to earn her enemies among the riders. She receives a message that Drogo was slightly injured in the battle. When Daenerys finds him, the extent of his injuries is revealed to be far greater than she was led to believe.

Turning Point Three: The Moment of Truth

Start Time: After 6 of 10 Chapters (60%)
Runtime: Chapter 61 (1 Chapter)
Run Percentage: 1 of 10 Chapters (10%)

<u>The Moment of Truth</u> - As a result of the Turn, the character must reevaluate his strategy, analyze who he is, and decide to be truthful with himself about the type of person he must become. In figuring out his true nature, he makes the decision to fight for the things he believes in.

One of the recently raped and enslaved townswomen offers to aid in Drogo's healing. Daenerys considers who she is at heart and accepts the woman's offer against the protestations of the Khal's bloodriders who call the women a maegi. Daenerys and the Khal do not back down when their decision is repeatedly questioned.

<u>To Change or Not to Change</u> - At the Moment of Truth, the character faces the decision to either change his perspective and who he has been or retain the same outlook in the face of all which has transpired.

Not to Change: Brought face to face with the savagery of Dothraki customs, Dany decides not to change her established values by inhibiting the rape and slaughter of the residents of the village the khalasar has raided.

ACTIONS & GOALS

A Game of Thrones: Daenerys Targaryen - Act Four: Implementing a Doomed Plan

The character Implements a Doomed Plan and faces Self-Inflicted Opposition in pursuit of a Penultimate Goal. But when an unthinkable Lowpoint occurs, he pulls himself together and discovers a Newfound Resolve.

With Drogo's health rapidly deteriorating, Daenerys begs the maegi to perform blood magic (the doomed plan), earning the ire of the Khal's men as well as the consequences imposed by the magic (self-inflicted opposition) in attempt to save Drogo's life (the penultimate goal). But when the blood magic causes her to lose her child, and Drogo is turned into a vegetable, she smothers him with a pillow to put him out of his misery (the lowpoint).

Start Time: After 7 of 10 Chapters, 70%
Runtime: Chapters 64 and 68 (2 Chapters)
Run Percentage: 2 of 10 Chapters (20%)

The Doomed Plan - Having made the commitment to fight at the Moment of Truth, the character now devises and implements a plan of action that is destined to fail. It may fail outright, or it may seem to succeed only to have grave consequences the character didn't anticipate.

When it is revealed Drogo's wounds have become mortally infected, and he only has hours to live, Daenerys begs the maegi woman to perform blood magic to save his life. This plan has disastrous consequences for Daenerys, Drogo, their unborn child and the khalasar as a whole. Angered by the use of forbidden blood magic, Drogo's riders turn on Daenerys. Many Bothans die. The blood magic causes Daenerys' baby to come out a stillborn, monstrosity. It also leaves Drogo in a vegetative state. Like Idaho[53].

---

[53] Potatoes are vegetables, right?

The Penultimate Goal - The character's goal in this act is one step removed from the Ultimate Goal, but his pursuit of it leads him to realize what he needs to do to end the conflict once and for all.

Daenerys wants to save Drogo's life no matter the consequences (or so she thinks). The disastrous outcome of her pursuit of this goal ultimately leads her to realize her true goal in Act Six; become the Mother of Dragons.

Self-Inflicted Opposition - The character makes the conscious decision to go up against the forces of antagonism. Because of this, he is the primary cause of the opposition he faces in this act.

All the terrible things that occur in this act are a result of Daenerys's foolhardy decisions. She realizes too late the cost demanded of her by the maegi is much higher than she is willing to pay.

Turning Point Catalyst: The Lowpoint

The Lowpoint - Something unimaginable happens with grave emotional consequences for the character. He looks back on all his actions over the course of the story and feels he has failed.

When Daenerys awakens after several days of illness, the maegi informs her she gave birth to Bat Boy. She next learns the majority of the khalasar have deserted, and that, while Drogo is still alive, nobody wants to elaborate on his condition. When she goes to him, she finds him blind, deaf and dumb: his mind turned into a lumpy glob of mashed potatoes by the blood magic. After all her attempts to elicit a response from him fail, Daenerys realizes he is truly gone. That night, she smothers him with a pillow as an act of sympathy.

ACTIONS & GOALS

Turning Point Four: The Newfound Resolve

Start Time: NA
Runtime: NA
Run Percentage: NA

The Newfound Resolve - After the Lowpoint, something happens to make the character dig deep within himself and rediscover his resolve. He makes the decision to stop the forces of antagonism at any cost.

Not Applicable. It's going to take Daenerys several novels worth of adventures to bounce back from this one. Even when she does, she will never be the same.

A Game of Thrones: Daenerys Targaryen - Act Five: Trying a Longshot

The character Tries a Longshot and faces Ultimate Opposition while trying to accomplish the Ultimate Goal. But just when it seems All is Lost, he makes a Final Push against the forces of antagonism, and either succeeds or fails.

Daenerys attempts to use blood magic herself (the longshot) by walking into the fire from Drogo's funeral pyre (ultimate opposition) to hatch her dragon eggs (the ultimate goal). But when the pyre collapses around her, and she would seem to have died (all is lost), the fire dies out and she is revealed to have hatched the first dragons in centuries (the final push).

Start Time: After 9 of 10 Chapters (90%)
Runtime: Chapter 72 (1 Chapter)
Run Percentage: 1 of 10 Chapters (10%)

The Longshot - The character is reinvigorated by the revelation he received at the Newfound Resolve, but his only chance of success lies in a plan with a high risk of failure.

Having learned the basic principles of blood magic from the traitorous maegi woman, Daenerys formulates a plan to hatch the three dragon eggs she received as a gift on the day of her wedding. Though she is not sure if it will work, she uses the maegi woman's blood as a sacrifice by killing her in Drogo's funeral pyre.

<u>The Ultimate Goal</u> - The character finally understands what the true goal of the story is. The goal the character has in this act is what the story is all about.

Daenerys attempts to hatch her dragon eggs and become the mother of dragons.

<u>Ultimate Opposition</u> - The forces of antagonism are now out to destroy the character completely. At this point in the story, the antagonist will throw everything he has into eliminating the character.

Neither Daenerys nor any of the clueless Dothraki in attendance have any idea if her plan will succeed. She faces the possibility of death by walking into the fire, but she feels she no longer has anything left to lose.

Turning Point Catalyst: All Is Lost

<u>All is Lost</u> - The character may experience some initial success, but the forces of antagonism rally, and it seems the character's Longshot is doomed to fail.

Daenerys has lost everything she had only so recently acquired: her powerful husband, her would-be chosen-one child and her status as Khaleesi. Once she steps into the fire, the pyre collapses around her, seemingly killing her.

Turning Point Five: The Final Push

Start Time: After 9.5 Chapters (95%)
Runtime: 1/2 of Chapter 72 (0.5 Chapters)
Run Percentage: 0.5 of 10 Chapters (5%)

The Final Push - Faced with his imminent destruction, the character decides to put everything he has into one final endeavor. He uses what little he has left in his stores, or the one trump card he's been holding, knowing if he fails he will be destroyed.

As the fire dies out, Daenerys is revealed to have not only survived, but to have hatched the first dragons in centuries. Her plan has succeeded. She now becomes the Mother of Dragons.

A Game of Thrones: Daenerys Targaryen - Act Six: Living in a New Situation

Having accomplished (or failed to accomplish) the Ultimate Goal, the character is shown living in a New Situation.

Start Time: NA
Runtime: NA

Living in a New Situation - We see the character adapting to the New Situation his actions have created. Whether he is exalted or exiled, this is the new world he helped create.

While we do catch a short glimpse of Daenerys cradling her baby dragons, her life in this New Situation is to be continued in A Clash of Kings. *The benefit of writing series lies in that the story will be continued in the next installment. This allows the author to create powerful cliffhangers by eschewing Act Six entirely. Having said that, individual installments should still include a sense of resolution, lest your audience feel cheated (a recurrent complaint leveled against many series whose authors fail to provide this sense of finality).*

If A Game of Thrones *would have ended with Ned still imprisoned in the black cells, or Daenerys smothering Drogo with a pillow, there would have been no closure to either of their storylines. While their stories may go on in the subsequent books (well, at least for Daenerys), and questions remain unanswered regarding their fates, there is an individual narrative structure of each installment that reaches a conclusion. Although storylines may conclude in each novel, the larger arc of the narrative remains unresolved. The aspiring series author can learn a great many things by studying the way these resolutions are handled in the last few chapters of* A Game of Thrones.

Gravity

2013 film
Written by Alfonso and Jonás Cuarón
Directed by Alfonso Cuarón

<u>Character</u>
Dr. Ryan Stone

<u>Ultimate Goal</u>
Get back to Earth.

Total Runtime: 84 minutes

One of my favorite aspects of Alfonso Cuarón's *Gravity* is its succinctness. At a tight hour and twenty-four minutes, there is little superfluous excess to be found in the film[54]. Sandra Bullock's Dr. Ryan Stone's character arc revolves around coming to terms with the unexpected and senseless death of her young, unnamed daughter. This causes her to question whether she is strong enough, or even willing, to survive her situation.

It is also interesting to note Ryan's surname, Stone, is a metaphor for weight (drop/fall/sink like a stone). The fact she is weighed down by issues from her past while simultaneously being pulled back to Earth by the titular physical force surely could not have been missed by the father and son screenwriting duo.

---

[54] Unlike that sentence

Gravity - Act One: Dealing with an Imperfect Situation

A character in an Imperfect Situation faces Oppressive Opposition as he pursues an Initial Goal. But when there is a Disturbance to his routine, he faces a Dilemma regarding his situation and must assume a New Role.

Dr. Ryan Stone is a first-time astronaut who is struggling in space (the imperfect situation) dealing with a lack of gravity and the subsequent nausea (oppressive opposition) as she tries to fix a piece of equipment on the Hubble Telescope (the initial goal). But when the Russians shoot down a derelict spy satellite (the disturbance), Stone is detached from the shuttle and must decide whether she will succumb to her fate or take action (the dilemma) and become a space disaster survivor (the new role).

Runtime: 17 minutes
Run Percentage: 17 of 84 minutes (20.2%)

<u>The Inciting Incident</u> - Something happens, often before the story begins, which if it does not occur would prevent the story as it exists from coming to be.

Prior to the start of the film, Dr. Stone's daughter dies in a playground accident. This leads Stone to venture into space in search of solitude, as well as to repair a piece of broken equipment on the Hubble telescope.

<u>The Imperfect Situation</u> - The character begins the story in a less than ideal situation he would like to change but seemingly cannot.

Dr. Ryan Stone is uncomfortable in space and struggles to fight through it. She's also sad because her daughter died in a freak accident.

<u>The Initial Desire</u> - Deep within himself, the character wants one particular thing more than anything else in the world.

Stone wants to finish the mission and go back to Earth. She also wants to come to terms with the death of her daughter.

<u>Initial Desire Type</u> - The character's Initial Desire is either for or against changing his situation.

Against Change: Although her motivations aren't revealed until later in the story, Stone has been holding onto the grief of her daughter's death. She has been incapable of moving on.

<u>Preexisting Conflict</u> - When the story begins, the character is already dealing with personal conflicts as well as the conflicts of the world at large.

The principal Preexisting Conflict Stone faces is internal. She is conflicted over the senseless death of her daughter, causing her to question her own desire to live. I suppose you could also make a case for the whole Russia vs. America thing since the downing of a Russian spy satellite is what jump starts the chain event causing the debris field. But that's, admittedly, a stretch.

<u>Likability/Empathy Factors</u> - The character is shown to be someone the audience would like to see succeed, or would be willing to follow on the journey of the story.

Who doesn't like Sandra Bullock? In this particular film we can easily sympathize with her because the movie is directed in such a manner we get a true sense of what it's like to work in space. Despite the hardships Stone faces, she demonstrates her resilience. Even when mission control suggests she go back in the shuttle to recuperate, she declines, opting instead to tough it out and get the job done. This is a subtle way to earn the audience's respect.

<u>The Initial Goal</u> - When the story opens, the character already has a goal he is actively pursuing.

When the film begins, Stone is in the process of fixing the thingamabob on the Hubble telescope.

Initial Goal Type - The character's Initial Goal is either a Normal Routine Goal where he is in his regular environment, or a Fish out of Water Goal where he is already in a situation with which he is unfamiliar.

Fish out of Water Goal: Stone is shown to be very much out of her element in the vast expanse of space.

Oppressive Opposition - The character's Initial Desire and/or his Initial Goal are being oppressed by the world around him.

The title card tells us, "Life in space is impossible." Simply being in space is oppressive. It is the main antagonist to their mission up to this point.

Turning Point Catalyst: The Disturbance

The Disturbance - An unexpected event with ominous implications occurs, interrupting the character's normal routine. This event pushes the character toward the Dilemma.

The Russians destroy a spy satellite, proving that even in a movie without a tangible antagonist, Hollywood can still find a way to blame the Russians.

Turning Point One: The Dilemma

Start Time: 12 of 84 minutes (14.2%)
Runtime: 5 of 84 minutes (5.9%)

Presentation of The Dilemma - The character is placed in a position where he must choose between life as he has known it or taking a new course of action.

ACTIONS & GOALS

It is announced that debris from a destroyed satellite is en route to the shuttle. When the debris field reaches the shuttle, it puts a satisfying end to Shariff's Macarena dancing[55], and sends an untethered Dr. Stone tumbling off into space. Now she must choose between being a victim of circumstance (as she has long felt she is), or becoming a survivor.

<u>The New Role</u> - If the character takes this new course of action, he will assume a New Role in which he is untested.

If she decides to fight for survival, Stone will become a space catastrophe survivor. Or something.

<u>Refusal/Interference to the New Role (Optional)</u> - The character may be reluctant, unready or unwilling to leave his Imperfect Situation and accept the New Role. In other cases, the character may want to accept the New Role, but someone else attempts to prevent him from accepting it.

Not applicable. Stone doesn't get a vote on the unfolding events.

<u>Accepting The New Role</u> - The character makes the decision to take action by accepting the New Role.

Stone regains her wits, catches her breath, and gives Matt her exact coordinates. She makes the decision to become a survivor.

Gravity - Act Two: Learning the Rules of an Unfamiliar Situation

The character Learns the Rules of an Unfamiliar Situation and faces Incidental Opposition in pursuit of a Transitional Goal. But when he receives a Reality Check, the character makes a Commitment to his New Role.

---

[55] Apparently, Macarena dancing in space is tantamount to having sex in a horror movie.

Stone has to survive being untethered in space (the unfamiliar situation) and overcome her initial panic over her catastrophic situation (incidental opposition) to make it back to the ship (the transitional goal). But when she and Matt discover the crew has been killed and the shuttle is destroyed (the reality check), they resolve to travel to the ISS to secure a new ride home (the commitment).

Starting Percentage: 17 of 84 minutes (20.2%)
Runtime: 7 of 84 minutes (8.3%)

Learning the Rules of an Unfamiliar Situation - The character now finds himself in a situation unlike anything he's ever experienced.

Dr. Stone is untethered and floating through space, which I don't believe has ever happened to any human being in the history of human beings.

The Hooking Premise - The unique premise at the heart of a story, often involving an intriguing "what if" scenario that piques the audience's interest.

What if an inexperienced astronaut is separated from her destroyed shuttle and adrift in space?

The Transitional Goal - The character receives a new goal that transitions him out of his initial state of inertia and into the main events of the story.

Stone and Matt attempt to get back to the safety of the ship.

Incidental Opposition - The character learns there are greater forces of opposition in this new world that may not be out to thwart him specifically, but still stand between him and his new goal.

Stone is separated from the shuttle and the rest of the crew. Once Matt saves her, she is still freaked out by her situation. They soon discover the corpse of Shariff and learn their ride home has been obliterated.

Turning Point Catalyst: The Reality Check

<u>The Reality Check</u> - The plan the character had coming into this act hits a major roadblock, and either fails completely or has unintended negative consequences.

Matt and Stone come across Shariff who is too preoccupied with being dead to be of assistance. The Explorer is in even worse shape than he is.

Turning Point Two: The Commitment

Start Time: 22 of 84 minutes (26.1%)
Runtime: 2 of 84 minutes (2.3%)

<u>The Commitment</u> - The character commits, or finds himself committed, to becoming the epitome of the New Role he accepted at the Dilemma. In doing so, he becomes an active participant in the Central Conflict.

Our two attractive leads discover they are the only survivors. Fitting. Seeing the shuttle is destroyed, Matt tells Stone they will travel through the expanse to the ISS and use its Soyuz's to return to Earth. They have no choice but to commit to their New Role of space catastrophe survivors and face the Central Conflict created by space and the returning debris field.

Gravity - Act Three: Stumbling into the Central Conflict

The character Stumbles into the Central Conflict and faces Intentional Opposition in pursuit of a False Goal. But when there is a grave Turn of events, he has a Moment of Truth.

Stone must come to terms with her will to survive (the central conflict) in the face of the returning debris field and her depleted oxygen supply (intentional opposition) as she and Matt travel to the ISS to use its Soyuz to return to Earth (false goal). But when Matt's jetpack runs out of juice, they nearly overshoot the ISS and he has to separate himself from Stone (the turn) for her to survive and board the ISS (the moment of truth).

Starting Percentage: 24 of 84 minutes (28.5%)
Runtime: 16 of 84 minutes (19%)

Stumbling into the Central Conflict - The character learns more about the storyworld and develops a new goal that is diametrically opposed to the goal of the antagonist.

Stone faces off with space and her will to live. How far is she willing to go to survive? Also, Matt tells Stone to set her watch alarm for ninety minutes to mark the return of the debris field, establishing it as a recurrent form of antagonism.

The Conflict of Ideals - The two sides of the Central Conflict are pursuing opposing ideals of perfection.

Life (Superior Ideal) vs. the Absence of Life (Inferior Ideal)

The False Goal - The character receives a new goal he feels will set everything right in his world. Sadly, this isn't the case, and there is still something bigger he must accomplish.

Matt and Stone attempt to reach the ISS and use the Soyuz to return to Earth.

Intentional Opposition - As a result of his decision at the Commitment, the character comes to the attention of the forces of antagonism. They now begin opposing him with the specific intention of thwarting his plans.

Matt explains that the debris field will return every 90 minutes. Despite the fact Stone is running low on oxygen, he insists she tell him her life story. When they overshoot the ISS, Matt deliberately untethers himself to save her. Stone makes it inside the ISS just as her oxygen supply runs out.

Turning Point Catalyst: The Turn

<u>The Turn</u> - There is a major turn of events that raises the stakes for the character and his allies and makes his situation far more complicated than it had been up to this point. This event is often surprising, coming as a shock to both the character and the audience.

Seeing he will pull Stone away from the ISS, Matt untethers himself and tells her to go on without him. She is now on her own.

Turning Point Three: The Moment of Truth

> Start Time: 32 of 84 minutes (38%)
> Runtime: 8 of 84 minutes (9.5%)

<u>The Moment of Truth</u> - As a result of the Turn, the character must reevaluate his strategy, analyze who he is, and decide to be truthful with himself about the type of person he must become. In figuring out his true nature, he makes the decision to fight for the things he believes in.

Stone watches Matt float away before she tumbles back into the station. Still in radio range, Matt tells her she needs to learn to let go. Though she is on the verge of running out of oxygen, with Matt's direction she fights her way into the station and takes off her suit in dramatic fashion.

Now all alone, Stone makes the decision to carry on, and must fight her way through the derelict space station, space, and the returning debris field.

<u>To Change or Not to Change</u> - At the Moment of Truth, the character faces the decision to either change his perspective and who he has been or retain

the same outlook in the face of all which has transpired.

To Change: After the unexpected loss of Matt, Stone must decide whether she will remain the sniveling pessimist she has been, or take her survival into her own hands by acting with competence and purpose. She chooses the latter.

Gravity - Act Four: Implementing a Doomed Plan

The character Implements a Doomed Plan and faces Self-Inflicted Opposition in pursuit of a Penultimate Goal. But when an unthinkable Lowpoint occurs, he pulls himself together and discovers a Newfound Resolve.

Stone attempts to fly the ISS's damaged Soyuz (the doomed plan) and is nearly burned up in a fire and pulverized by the debris field (self-inflicted opposition) while trying to reach the Chinese space station (the penultimate goal). But when she discovers the Soyuz is out of fuel she resolves to die (the lowpoint) until the spirit of Matt pops in and tells her exactly what she needs to do survive (the newfound resolve).

Starting Percentage: 40 of 84 minutes (47.5%)
Runtime: 26 of 84 minutes (30%)

<u>The Doomed Plan</u> - Having made the commitment to fight at the Moment of Truth, the character now devises and implements a plan of action that is destined to fail. It may fail outright, or it may seem to succeed only to have grave consequences the character didn't anticipate.

Flying the Soyuz to the Chinese station is not going to work out as neatly as Stone intends.

<u>The Penultimate Goal</u> - The character's goal in this act is one step removed from the Ultimate Goal, but his pursuit of it leads him to realize what he needs to do to end the conflict once and for all.

ACTIONS & GOALS

Stone attempts to use the escape pod to fly to the Chinese station.

Self-Inflicted Opposition - The character makes the conscious decision to go up against the forces of antagonism. Because of this, he is the primary cause of the opposition he faces in this act.

Stone wastes time trying to contact Matt to no avail. A fire breaks out while she's slacking off. When she tries to extinguish it, she almost knocks herself unconscious. She makes it to the Soyuz and releases it from the station only to get the craft tangled in the parachute cable. She has to go on a spacewalk to release the cables and almost loses her torque wrench. The debris field returns while she is out and about.

Turning Point Catalyst: The Lowpoint

The Lowpoint - Something unimaginable happens with grave emotional consequences for the character. He looks back on all his actions over the course of the story and feels he has failed.

When she discovers the Soyuz is out of fuel, Stone turns off all the life-support systems and resolves to die.

Turning Point Four: The Newfound Resolve

Start Time: 62 of 84 minutes (73.8%)
Runtime: 4 of 84 minutes (4.7%)

The Newfound Resolve - After the Lowpoint, something happens to make the character dig deep within himself and rediscover his resolve. He makes the decision to stop the forces of antagonism at any cost.

Matt miraculously shows up and convinces her to go on living, before telling her how she can use the emergency landing engines to reach the Chinese station. Stone decides that she will not succumb to space and opts instead to live and stuff.

Gravity - Act Five: Trying a Longshot

The character Tries a Longshot and faces Ultimate Opposition while trying to accomplish the Ultimate Goal. But just when it seems All is Lost, he makes a Final Push against the forces of antagonism, and either succeeds or fails.

Stone has to use the Soyuz's soft landing engines and a run-of-the-mill fire extinguisher to reach the Chinese station (the longshot), and must contend with her inability to dock the pod and the impending collapse of the station (the ultimate opposition) as she tries to use their Soyuz to return to Earth (the ultimate goal). But when the space station enters the atmosphere, and the Soyuz's buttons are all in Chinese (all is lost), she manages to undock just in time and must wait helplessly as the pod plummets to Earth (the final push).

Starting Percentage: 66 of 84 minutes (78.5%)
Runtime: 15 of 84 minutes (17.8%)

The Longshot - The character is reinvigorated by the revelation he received at the Newfound Resolve, but his only chance of success lies in a plan with a high risk of failure.

Stone attempts to use the soft landing engines on the Soyuz to reach the Chinese station, and then use their escape pod to return to Earth. To get from the Soyuz to the Chinese station, she has to use the propulsive force of a fire extinguisher. Good thing she saw Wall-E[56].

The Ultimate Goal - The character finally understands what the true goal of the story is. The goal the character has in this act is what the story is all about.

Stone wants to get to the Chinese station and use their escape pod to return to Earth.

---

[56] If you haven't seen this 2008 Pixar film, the titular robot uses a fire extinguisher to the same effect.

Ultimate Opposition - The forces of antagonism are now out to destroy the character completely. At this point in the story, the antagonist will throw everything he has into eliminating the character.

The Chinese station is on the verge of falling into Earth's atmosphere. She can't get the Soyuz all the way to the station, so she has to eject from the pod and use a fire extinguisher to propel herself. She nearly misses the station but catches the last possible handhold. Drama.

Once onboard the station, she realizes the buttons of their Soyuz are all in Chinese. Despite this, she manages to undock, and the craft falls to Earth in a fiery blaze which looks as if it may incinerate her at any moment. The parachute deploys and the pod crashes into a placid lake. An electrical fire fills the pod with smoke and Stone opens the hatch, flooding the pod and sinking it.

Turning Point Catalyst: All Is Lost

All is Lost - The character may experience some initial success, but the forces of antagonism rally, and it seems the character's Longshot is doomed to fail.

The station is pulled back into the Earth's atmosphere, and the escape pod's buttons are all in Chinese. However, the movie gods are smiling down on Stone, and she manages to initiate the undocking protocol.

Turning Point Five: The Final Push

Start Time: 75 of 84 minutes (89.2%)
Runtime: 6 of 84 minutes (7.1%)

The Final Push - Faced with his imminent destruction, the character decides to put everything he has into one final endeavor. He uses what little he has left in his stores, or the one trump card he's been holding, knowing if he fails he will be destroyed.

Stone accepts her fate as the Soyuz undocks. Surrounded by the debris of the space station, the pod burns through the atmosphere and Stone can only wait helplessly to see if she will live or die. When the pod hits the water, she is stuck inside as it sinks. She strips off her space suit and swims to the surface. Decompression sickness be damned.

Gravity - Act Six: Living in a New Situation

Having accomplished (or failed to accomplish) the Ultimate Goal, the character is shown living in a New Situation.

Stone returns to Earth, having fought for and earned her right to live. She emerges from the water a (presumably) changed person.

Starting Percentage: 81 of 84 minutes (96.4 %)
Runtime: 3 of 84 minutes (3.5%)

<u>**Living in a New Situation**</u> - We see the character adapting to the New Situation his actions have created. Whether he is exalted or exiled, this is the new world he helped create.

Stone gently swims to shore and watches the remains of the Chinese station fall to Earth before taking her first shaky steps on land. Cue epic music.

Harry Potter and the Philosopher's Stone

1997 Novel
Written by JK Rowling

<u>Character</u>
Lara Croft

<u>Ultimate Goal</u>
Stop Voldemort from using the Philosopher's Stone to come back to life.

Total Runtime: 17 chapters

JK Rowling's *Harry Potter* series is a phenomenon unto itself. Her imaginative worldbuilding, relatable characters, and intricate storyline have made the eponymous young wizard a household name and propelled him into the pantheon of legendary heroes.

Rowling's skill can be clearly observed in the multiple, tightly woven plotlines of the story. Harry has several concurrent goals he pursues throughout the book. There is, of course, the Ultimate Goal of stopping Voldemort, but also the omnipresent goals of learning magic, passing classes and winning the House Cup.

Harry's internal, psychological conflict revolves around his questioning of his abilities and the purity of his intentions. He feels unworthy of his reputation as "the boy who lived" even as he accomplishes amazing feats over the course of the story. He labors to do the right thing, but his incessant connection to the Dark Lord, Voldemort, causes him to continuously question the righteousness of his own intentions.

Harry Potter - Act One: Dealing with an Imperfect Situation

A character in an Imperfect Situation faces Oppressive Opposition as he pursues an Initial Goal. But when there is a Disturbance to his routine, he faces a Dilemma regarding his situation and must assume a New Role.

10-year-old orphan, Harry Potter, lives with his mean old aunt, uncle and cousin (the imperfect situation) who mistreat him at every turn (oppressive opposition) as he attempts to survive their torments (the initial goal). But when Harry begins receiving hundreds of magical letters which his uncle forbids him from opening (the disturbance), the giant, half-giant, Hagrid informs Harry he's a wizard and offers him the choice to attend Hogwarts (the dilemma) and become a student of magic (the new role).

Runtime: Chapter 1 through 4 (4 Chapters)
Run Percentage: 4 of 17 Chapters (23.5%)

<u>The Inciting Incident</u> - Something happens, often before the story begins, which if it does not occur would prevent the story as it exists from coming to be.

Voldemort kills Harry's parents, attacks baby Harry and is seemingly destroyed.

<u>The Imperfect Situation</u> - The character begins the story in a less than ideal situation he would like to change but seemingly cannot.

Harry's life sucks. The Dursleys are bullies who mistreat him. His bedroom is a spiderweb riddled cupboard. He is frequently babysat by a smelly cat lady.

The Initial Desire - Deep within himself, the character wants one particular thing more than anything else in the world.

Harry wishes he had some kind of family who actually cares about him.

Initial Desire Type - The character's Initial Desire is either for or against changing his situation.

For Change: Harry wants nothing more than to escape his dreadful life with the Dursleys.

Preexisting Conflict - When the story begins, the character is already dealing with personal conflicts as well as the conflicts of the world at large.

Harry and the Dursleys have a mutual disdain for each other. On a much larger scale, the memory of Voldemort is still fresh in the wizarding community, and there are those who fear he may return.

Likability/Empathy Factors - The character is shown to be someone the audience would like to see succeed, or would be willing to follow on the journey of the story.

Much like the young Daenerys Targaryen in ASoIaF, Harry's suffers from Undeserved Misfortune. He is treated poorly for things beyond his control.

The Initial Goal - When the story opens, the character already has a goal he is actively pursuing.

Harry just wants to survive the torments of his family until he's old enough to leave them.

Initial Goal Type - The character's Initial Goal is either a Normal Routine Goal where he is in his regular environment, or a Fish out of Water Goal where he is already in a situation with which he is unfamiliar.

Normal Routine Goal: Harry goes about his normal routine of being mistreated by the Dursleys.

Oppressive Opposition - The character's Initial Desire and/or his Initial Goal are being oppressed by the world around him.

Harry is harassed by his aunt, uncle and cousin[57]. They make him sleep in a cupboard under the stairs, treat him like a servant and never let him do anything enjoyable. He is frequently punished for things he didn't do (well, at least that he didn't do on purpose).

Turning Point Catalyst: The Disturbance

The Disturbance - An unexpected event with ominous implications occurs, interrupting the character's normal routine. This event pushes the character toward the Dilemma.

As his eleventh birthday approaches, Harry begins receiving a queer amount of letters. When his Uncle Vernon prevents Harry from reading them, the number of letters grows exponentially. This drives his uncle mad in his attempts to prevent Harry from seeing them.

Turning Point One: The Dilemma

Start Time: After 3 of 17 Chapters (17.6%)
Runtime: Chapter 4 (1 Chapter)
Run Percentage: 1 of 17 Chapters (5.8%)

Presentation of The Dilemma - The character is placed in a position where he must choose between life as he has known it or taking a new course of action.

---

[57] And Luke thought he had it bad.

ACTIONS & GOALS

Hagrid bursts through the door of the rickety shack at midnight on Harry's eleventh birthday and reveals the truth of his parentage before inviting him to attend Hogwarts. Harry must choose between staying with the Dursleys and going off to wizarding school. A difficult decision to be sure.

The New Role - If the character takes this new course of action, he will assume a New Role in which he is untested.

If Harry decides to attend Hogwarts, he will become a wizard in training.

Refusal/Interference to the New Role (Optional) - The character may be reluctant, unready or unwilling to leave his Imperfect Situation and accept the New Role. In other cases, the character may want to accept the New Role, but someone else attempts to prevent him from accepting it.

In spite of Hagrid's size, Uncle Vernon musters his nerve and declares that Harry is forbidden from attending a wizarding school.

Accepting The New Role - The character makes the decision to take action by accepting the New Role.

After Hagrid gives Dudley a pig tail, sending Uncle Vernon and Aunt Petunia scattering from the room, Harry is all about going to Hogwarts.

Harry Potter - Act Two: Learning the Rules of an Unfamiliar Situation

The character Learns the Rules of an Unfamiliar Situation and faces Incidental Opposition in pursuit of a Transitional Goal. But when he receives a Reality Check, the character makes a Commitment.

Harry takes his first foray into the magical world by visiting Diagon Alley with Hagrid (the unfamiliar situation) and realizes his lack of magical knowledge (incidental opposition) while trying to purchase school supplies in preparation for

attending Hogwarts (the transitional goal). But when he doesn't know how to access the train and has confrontations with some of his fellow students on the ride to school (the reality check), he learns about the House system and subsequently becomes a Gryffindor (the commitment).

Start Time: After 4 of 17 Chapters (23.4%)
Runtime: Chapter 5 through 7 (3 Chapters)
Run Percentage: 3 of 17 Chapters (17.6%)

Learning the Rules of an Unfamiliar Situation - The character now finds himself in a situation unlike anything he's ever experienced.

Harry takes his first steps into the magical world when Hagrid takes him through the Leaky Cauldron into Diagon Alley.

The Hooking Premise - The unique premise at the heart of a story, often involving an intriguing "what if" scenario that piques the audience's interest.

What if a young orphan discovers he is a wizard who is part of a secret wizarding world?

The Transitional Goal - The character receives a new goal that transitions him out of his initial state of inertia and into the main events of the story.

Harry prepares for and travels to Hogwarts to become a wizarding student. His goal in this act doesn't extend beyond that, because he doesn't know what to expect when he arrives at the school.

Incidental Opposition - The character learns there are greater forces of opposition in this new world that may not be out to thwart him specifically, but still stand between him and his new goal.

In Diagon Alley, Harry meets Malfoy, though not by name, who expresses his belief that only the finer Wizarding families should be allowed to attend Hogwarts.

Next, Harry has difficulty finding a wand. When he finally finds one, Mr. Ollivander says it is the brother to the wand that gave Harry his scar. Voldemort.

Later, Harry can't access platform 9¾ to get on the train to school. When he finally boards the train, he encounters the bossy Hermione and dickish Malfoy who calls Ron poor and tries to steal Harry's sweeties. When they arrive at the castle, the first years are sent to an anteroom where they learn they will be sorted into Houses. Harry mistakenly believes this will involve a physical test in front of the whole school and worries he will embarrass himself.

Turning Point Catalyst: The Reality Check

<u>The Reality Check</u> - The plan the character had coming into this act hits a major roadblock, and either fails completely or has unintended negative consequences.

Harry arrives at the train station and gets a crash course in the magical world when he discovers platform 9¾ doesn't exist. Luckily he meets the Weasley family and their son, Ron whom he befriends. He learns of the robbery at Gringotts from Ron, as well as the fact you should never say Voldemort's name. He's like the boogeyman or Candyman. He also meets a few other students aboard the train, including Hermione and Malfoy. This proves life at Hogwarts won't be all fun and games. When the train arrives at the school, Harry stomach lurches with nerves and Ron goes pale beneath his freckles. Hagrid leads the first years by boat to the castle and they marvel in awe.

Turning Point Two: The Commitment

Start Time: After 6 of 17 Chapters (35.2%)
Runtime: Chapter 8 (1 Chapter)
Run Percentage: 1 of 17 Chapters (5.8%)

<u>The Commitment</u> - The character commits, or finds himself committed, to

becoming the epitome of the New Role he accepted at the Dilemma. In doing so, he becomes an active participant in the Central Conflict.

Harry knows nothing of the House system at Hogwarts. Ron tells him he's heard the sorting is administered via test and Harry becomes nervous. After a bit of fuss with the Sorting Hat, Harry becomes more than a mere student. He becomes a Gryffindor, committing himself to his New Role as a student of magic.

Harry Potter - Act Three: Stumbling into the Central Conflict

The character Stumbles into the Central Conflict and faces Intentional Opposition in pursuit of a False Goal. But when there is a grave Turn of events, he has a Moment of Truth.

Harry bumps heads with Snape and Malfoy (the central conflict) who are both out to thwart his attempts (intentional opposition) to pass classes and learn magic (the false goal). But when Malfoy baits Harry into an after-hours duel, leading him to a chamber containing a Cerberus (the turn), Harry tricks Hagrid into revealing the owner of the package the dog is guarding (the moment of truth).

Start Time: After 7 of 17 Chapters (41%)
Runtime: Chapter 8 through 10 (3 Chapters)
Run Percentage: 3 of 17 Chapters (17.6%)

Stumbling into the Central Conflict - The character learns more about the storyworld and develops a new goal that is diametrically opposed to the goal of the antagonist.

Harry contends with Snape/Quirrell/Voldemort, and Draco Malfoy.

The Conflict of Ideals - The two sides of the Central Conflict are pursuing opposing ideals of perfection.

ACTIONS & GOALS

Camaraderie and Altruism (Superior Ideal) vs. Self-Importance and Power (Inferior Ideal)

The False Goal - The character receives a new goal he feels will set everything right in his world. Sadly, this isn't the case, and there is still something bigger he must accomplish.

Harry wants to learn magic and pass classes.

Intentional Opposition - As a result of his decision at the Commitment, the character comes to the attention of the forces of antagonism. They now begin opposing him with the specific intention of thwarting his plans.

Snape obviously has something against young Mr. Potter. Malfoy tries to get Harry detention. Harry has his first Quidditch match and is cursed by Snape/Quirrell.

Turning Point Catalyst: The Turn

The Turn - There is a major turn of events that raises the stakes for the character and his allies and makes his situation far more complicated than it had been up to this point. This event is often surprising, coming as a shock to both the character and the audience.

After a disagreement with Malfoy, Harry agrees to meet him after hours for a duel. When he arrives, the invitation is revealed to be an attempt to set Harry up for expulsion. Harry and his fellow moppets run and hide in the forbidden part of the castle to avoid the school's caretaker, Filch. There they encounter a three-headed dog blocking a trap door, and Harry concludes it is guarding the package Hagrid retrieved from Gringotts Bank. Apparently, there are serious plots afoot at Hogwarts.

Turning Point Three: The Moment of Truth

Start Time: After 9 of 17 Chapters (52.9%)
Runtime: Chapter 10 (1 Chapter)
Run Percentage: 1 of 17 Chapters (5.8%)

<u>The Moment of Truth</u> - As a result of the Turn, the character must reevaluate his strategy, analyze who he is, and decide to be truthful with himself about the type of person he must become. In figuring out his true nature, he makes the decision to fight for the things he believes in.

A troll attack disrupts the Halloween feast. Harry and Ron realize their poor treatment of Hermione lead her to flee into the troll's path. Harry resolves to adhere to his true nature by fighting the troll, leading the trio to become inseparable friends[58].

<u>To Change or Not to Change</u> - At the Moment of Truth, the character faces the decision to either change his perspective and who he has been or retain the same outlook in the face of all which has transpired.

To Change: Harry makes the decision to go from being more than just a trouble-seeking, little imp to becoming someone who looks out for others. This leads Hermione to have her own transformation from a fastidious apple polisher to someone who looks out for her fellow Gryffindors.

Harry Potter - Act Four: Implementing a Doomed Plan

The character Implements a Doomed Plan and faces Self-Inflicted Opposition in pursuit of a Penultimate Goal. But when an unthinkable Lowpoint occurs, he pulls himself together and discovers a Newfound Resolve.

---

[58] Until *The Goblet of Fire*.

ACTIONS & GOALS

Harry tries to help Hagrid smuggle a baby dragon out of Hogwarts (the doomed plan), and risks being caught by repeatedly going out after hours (self-inflicted opposition) while trying to figure out what Snape is trying to steal from the guarded room (the penultimate goal). But when he's caught out after hours, loses Gryffindor the top spot for the House Cup and is shunned by his own house (the lowpoint), Harry discovers Voldemort is trying to come back to life and vows to stop him at all costs (the newfound resolve).

Start Time: After 10 of 17 Chapters (58.8%)
Runtime: Chapter 11 through 15 (5 Chapters)
Run Percentage: 5 of 17 Chapters (29.4%)

<u>The Doomed Plan</u> - Having made the commitment to fight at the Moment of Truth, the character now devises and implements a plan of action that is destined to fail. It may fail outright, or it may seem to succeed only to have grave consequences the character didn't anticipate.

Their pursuit of Snape leads the gang to discover Hagrid is in possession of an illegal dragon egg. Harry helps Hagrid deliver the baby Dragon to Ron's brother, Charlie, to keep Hagrid from getting in trouble. While he does manage to keep Hagrid's secret safe, Harry brings a great deal of trouble upon himself in the process.

<u>The Penultimate Goal</u> - The character's goal in this act is one step removed from the Ultimate Goal, but his pursuit of it leads him to realize what he needs to do to end the conflict once and for all.

Harry and the little rascals try to figure out what Snape is so obviously trying to steal from the locked room.

<u>Self-Inflicted Opposition</u> - The character makes the conscious decision to go up against the forces of antagonism. Because of this, he is the primary cause of the opposition he faces in this act.

Harry runs the risk of being caught when he continues to sneak out every night. He is ultimately busted by Dumbledore while visiting the Mirror of Erised. Later, Harry learns Draco knows of Hagrid's dragon and volunteers to deliver it to Charlie's friends. He is subsequently caught out at night, loses 150 House points and is shunned by his fellow Gryffindors. Way to go, Harry.

Turning Point Catalyst: The Lowpoint

<u>The Lowpoint</u> - Something unimaginable happens with grave emotional consequences for the character. He looks back on all his actions over the course of the story and feels he has failed.

After catching Harry and Hermione returning from delivering Hagrid's dragon to Ron's brother Charlie, Filch escorts them to Professor McGonagall. This earns them all detention and loses them enough house points to put Gryffindor in last place. Because of this, Harry is shunned by the rest of Gryffindor and resolves to avoid any actions that may cost them more house points.

Turning Point Four: The Newfound Resolve

Start Time: After 14 of 17 Chapters (82.3%)
Runtime: Chapter 15 (1 Chapter)
Run Percentage: 1 of 17 Chapters (5.8%)

<u>The Newfound Resolve</u> - After the Lowpoint, something happens to make the character dig deep within himself and rediscover his resolve. He makes the decision to stop the forces of antagonism at any cost.

When Harry goes on his detention with Hagrid in the Forbidden Forest, he is separated from the group and stumbles upon a hooded figure drinking blood from a dead unicorn. He learns from Firenze, the centaur, that unicorn blood can keep someone alive who may be waiting for something stronger to truly bring him back to life. Harry realizes the figure he saw was Voldemort. Dun dun duhn.

When Harry returns to his room, he finds his Invisibility Cloak has been returned with a note reading, "Just in case." Harry makes the decision to stop Snape and Voldemort, even if it means expulsion. Needless to say, Hermione and Ron will help.

Harry Potter - Act Five: Trying a Longshot

The character Tries a Longshot and faces Ultimate Opposition while trying to accomplish the Ultimate Goal. But just when it seems All is Lost, he makes a Final Push against the forces of antagonism, and either succeeds or fails.

Harry and the gang go into the trap door with no adult supervision (the longshot) and face a series of deadly tests (ultimate opposition) while trying to stop Snape from stealing the stone for Voldemort (the ultimate goal). But when Ron is gravely injured and Hermione is forced to get help (all is lost), Harry enters the final chamber alone and faces off with Quirrell and Voldemort (the final push).

Start Time: After 15 of 17 Chapters (88.2%)
Runtime: Chapter 16 through 17.5 (1.5 Chapters)
Run Percentage: 1.5 of 17 Chapters (8.8%)

The Longshot - The character is reinvigorated by the revelation he received at the Newfound Resolve, but his only chance of success lies in a plan with a high risk of failure.

Unable to bring any adults to their aide, Harry, Ron and Hermione go into the trap door by themselves to stop Snape from stealing the Stone.

The Ultimate Goal - The character finally understands what the true goal of the story is. The goal the character has in this act is what the story is all about.

Harry wants to go into the trapdoor and stop Snape from stealing the Stone.

Ultimate Opposition - The forces of antagonism are now out to destroy the character completely. At this point in the story, the antagonist will throw everything he has into eliminating the character.

Harry and the gang have to pass a progressive series of tests set up by the professors and are nearly killed in the process. Harry makes it to the end and faces off with Quirrell and Voldemort. Or at least Voldemort's noseless face on the back of Quirrell's head.

Turning Point Catalyst: All Is Lost

All is Lost - The character may experience some initial success, but the forces of antagonism rally, and it seems the character's Longshot is doomed to fail.

The three urchins must pass several tests to make it into the giant wizard chess room. Ron, being our resident idiot savant, realizes he must sacrifice himself for Harry and Hermione to take the game. Next, Harry discovers there isn't enough magic potion for both he and Hermione to reach the room with the stone and sends her back to tend to Ron. He has lost all his backup.

Turning Point Five: The Final Push

Start Time: After 16 of 17 Chapters (94.1%)
Runtime: Chapter 17 through 17.5 (0.5 Chapters)
Run Percentage: 0.5 Chapters (2.9%)

The Final Push - Faced with his imminent destruction, the character decides to put everything he has into one final endeavor. He uses what little he has left in his stores, or the one trump card he's been holding, knowing if he fails he will be destroyed.

Harry bursts into the final room to find not Snape, but the timid and sniveling Professor Quirrell. Quirrell gives his evil monologue to Harry's detriment, giving Harry sufficient time to figure out how to get the stone from the mirror. Harry meets Voldemort and "faces" off with him for the first of many times to come. Realizing that touching Harry causes Quirrell excruciating pain, Harry grabs him as he prepares to perform a deadly curse. Harry, too, is in pain and passes out.

Harry Potter - Act Six: Living in a New Situation

Having accomplished (or failed to accomplish) the Ultimate Goal, the character is shown Living in a New Situation.

Start Time: After 16.5 of 17 Chapters (97%)
Runtime: 1/2 of Chapter 17 (0.5 Chapters)
Run Percentage: 0.5 of 17 Chapters (2.9%)

<u>Living in a New Situation</u> - We see the character adapting to the New Situation his actions have created. Whether he is exalted or exiled, this is the new world he helped create.

Harry awakens in the hospital wing to Dumbledore's smiling countenance. The Headmaster recounts everything that transpired after Harry passed out like a little bitch, as well as the real reason the Stone was moved to Hogwarts; Voldemort is trying to impersonate Jesus by coming back to life. As a result, Harry's life has just gotten a lot more complicated.

Inception

2010 film
Written and Directed by Christopher Nolan

<u>Character</u>
Dom Cobb

<u>Ultimate Goal</u>
Plant an inception in Robert Fischer's mind. Return home to his kids.

Total Runtime: 141 minutes

I was pleasantly surprised to discover that, despite its intricate, mind-bending plot, Christopher Nolan's *Inception* unwaveringly adheres to the six act paradigm. The central character, Dom Cobb, is a wounded man losing his grip on reality. Initially, he recruits the inexperienced Ariadne to serve as his architect and teaches her the ways of dream manipulation. But Nolan does a masterful job of inverting their mentor/pupil relationship by having the student become the master who ultimately teaches the guilt-ridden Cobb to let go of his past torments and move forward with his life.

Inception - Act One: Dealing with an Imperfect Situation

A character in an Imperfect Situation faces Oppressive Opposition as he pursues an Initial Goal. But when there is a Disturbance to his routine, he faces a Dilemma regarding his situation and must assume a New Role.

Professional dream thief and fugitive on the run (imperfect situation), Dom Cobb, faces interference from the government, his employer and his malicious ex-wife, Mal (oppressive opposition), as he attempts to steal corporate secrets from wealthy businessman, Mr. Saito (initial goal). But when the extraction fails, and Saito recognizes the skill of Dom's deception (the disturbance), he offers to get him pardoned (the dilemma) if Dom performs an Inception on Saito's corporate rival, Robert Fischer (the new role).

Runtime: 22 minutes
Run Percentage: 22 of 141 minutes (15.6%)

The Inciting Incident - Something happens, often before the story begins, which if it does not occur would prevent the story as it exists from coming to be.

Cobol Engineering hires Dom and Arthur to extract information from Mr. Saito's billion-dollar brain.

The Imperfect Situation - The character begins the story in a less than ideal situation he would like to change but seemingly cannot.

Saito suspects something is up. Dom inadvertently brings Mal into the dream, and she quickly ruins everything. It is revealed their employer will kill them for their failure, and they must now go on the run. Again. Additionally, Dom can't return to the States for fear of imprisonment.

The Initial Desire - Deep within himself, the character wants one particular thing more than anything else in the world.

Dom wants to return home to his kids.

Initial Desire Type - The character's Initial Desire is either for or against changing his situation.

For Change: Though Dom is internally against change, by refusing to forgive himself for his wife's death, in a testament to Christopher Nolan's storytelling ability, Dom's external goal is to change the Imperfect Situation barring him from returning to his kids. It is only by abandoning this resistance to internal change and letting go of his guilt that Dom is ultimately able to change his outward situation.

Preexisting Conflict - When the story begins, the character is already dealing with personal conflicts as well as the conflicts of the world at large.

Dom and Arthur are in a bad way with Cobol Engineering. Because of this, they're trying to pull a fast one on Mr. Saito. Mal has been ruining things for them for a while now, and Dom and Arthur have a difference of opinion about her presence. Dom is also wanted by the US authorities.

Likability/Empathy Factors - The character is shown to be someone the audience would like to see succeed, or would be willing to follow on the journey of the story.

Dom Cobb is Leonardo DiCaprio. So he has that going for himself. He unabashedly admits to Mr. Saito he is the best extractor in the world. We see him in action and learn he is knowledgeable and calm under duress. He proves his expertise to Mr. Saito by placing him inside a dream within a dream. Later we learn he has estranged children he cannot see because he is barred from reentering the United States.

The Initial Goal - When the story opens, the character already has a goal he is actively pursuing.

We meet Dom and Arthur as they attempt to extract information from Saito in a dream.

<u>Initial Goal Type</u> - The character's Initial Goal is either a Normal Routine Goal where he is in his regular environment, or a Fish out of Water Goal where he is already in a situation with which he is unfamiliar.

Normal Routine Goal: Dom is the most skilled extractor in the history of the universe. He is completely at home in the dream world, regardless of whose dream world it is.

<u>Oppressive Opposition</u> - The character's Initial Desire and/or his Initial Goal are being oppressed by the world around him.

Saito is skeptical of Dom and Arthur and appears suspicious of what they are selling. Mal shows up and makes it clear she intends to throw around some monkey wrenches. She rats them out to Saito who has them apprehended and shot before they can get the information they were trying to steal

Turning Point Catalyst: The Disturbance

<u>The Disturbance</u> - An unexpected event with ominous implications occurs, interrupting the character's normal routine. This event pushes the character toward the Dilemma.

When their plan to raid the safe fails, they take Saito up to what turns out to be the next dream level. There, Saito reveals he set the whole thing up as an audition for Dom and his team, which they have failed. But as the dreamer's unconscious constructions raid the city with torches, Saito realizes he is still dreaming and is impressed with their abilities, prompting him to consider hiring them for himself.

Turning Point One: The Dilemma

Start Time: 18 of 141 minutes (12.7%)
Runtime: 4 of 141 minutes (2.8%)

Presentation of The Dilemma - The character is placed in a position where he must choose between life as he has known it or taking a new course of action.

Saito tracks down Dom and Arthur. He offers to fix Dom's legal issues and allow him to return home to his children in exchange for performing an Inception. Dom must choose between never seeing his kids again, and performing an impossible inception for Saito. Hmmm.

The New Role - If the character takes this new course of action, he will assume a New Role in which he is untested.

While Dom is a skilled extractor, if he takes Saito's offer he must become an inceptionist.

Refusal/Interference to the New Role (Optional) - The character may be reluctant, unready or unwilling to leave his Imperfect Situation and accept the New Role. In other cases, the character may want to accept the New Role, but someone else attempts to prevent him from accepting it.

Dom initially says no. When Saito sweetens the deal, Arthur tries to talk Dom out of it.

Accepting The New Role - The character makes the decision to take action by accepting the New Role.

Dom accepts the deal.

Inception - Act Two: Learning the Rules of an Unfamiliar Situation

The character Learns the Rules of an Unfamiliar Situation and faces Incidental Opposition in pursuit of a Transitional Goal. But when he receives a Reality Check, the character makes a Commitment.

Dom and his newly assembled team try to figure out how to perform an Inception (the unfamiliar situation) and must contend with Dom's increasingly aggressive projection of his wife and Cobol's murderous goons (incidental opposition) while trying to formulate a plan to implant an Inception in Fischer's mind (the transitional goal). But when Ariadne follows Dom into his self-induced dream, it is revealed he is intentionally storing memories of Mal who is trying to convince him to stay in Limbo (reality check). When they awaken, they learn the elder Fischer has died, and Ariadne demands to come along on the mission for the safety of the team (the commitment).

Starting Percentage: 22 of 141 minutes (15.6%)
Runtime: 39 of 141 minutes (27.6%)

Learning the Rules of an Unfamiliar Situation - The character now finds himself in a situation unlike anything he's ever experienced.

Dom has to convince his father-in-law of the impossible; he has a way to clear his name. In fact, they must do many impossible things: find a new architect, find a chemist with enough skill to fit their needs, and figure out how to perform an inception.

The Hooking Premise - The unique premise at the heart of a story, often involving an intriguing "what if" scenario that piques the audience's interest.

What if an assortment of dream thieves team up in attempt to perform a seemingly impossible dream heist?

The Transitional Goal - The character receives a new goal that transitions him out of his initial state of inertia and into the main events of the story.

Dom wants to assemble a team and figure out how to perform the inception.

ACTIONS & GOALS

<u>Incidental Opposition</u> - The character learns there are greater forces of opposition in this new world that may not be out to thwart him specifically, but still stand between him and his new goal.

Dom is introduced to Ariadne who he initiates in dream sharing. But when Mal shows up and sticks a knife in Ariadne's gut, their new architect reconsiders taking up this new line of work. Later, Dom visits Mombasa to recruit Eames, the forge, and is nearly shot up by Cobol's goons. The team struggles to devise a plan because doing an inception is really hard.

Turning Point Catalyst: The Reality Check

<u>The Reality Check</u> - The plan the character had coming into this act hits a major roadblock, and either fails completely or has unintended negative consequences.

Ariadne follows Dom into his Yusuf induced dream to see what he's been up to. There she learns he is intentionally keeping memories of Mal. Ariadne also learns Mal is trying to convince Dom to stay in Limbo, as well as (a portion of) how she died.

Turning Point Two: The Commitment

Start Time: 60 of 141 minutes (42.5%)
Runtime: 1 of 141 minutes (0.7%)

<u>The Commitment</u> - The character commits, or finds himself committed, to becoming the epitome of the New Role he accepted at the Dilemma. In doing so, he becomes an active participant in the Central Conflict.

When Dom and Ariadne awaken, it is revealed the elder Fischer has died. Knowing the risk Mal poses to the team, Ariadne demands to tag along on the heist. Dom agrees, committing himself to his New Roles as an inceptionist for Saito and psychiatric patient for Ariadne. This brings them into the Central Conflict of Fischer's dream in the following act.

Inception - Act Three: Stumbling into the Central Conflict

The character Stumbles into the Central Conflict and faces Intentional Opposition in pursuit of a False Goal. But when there is a grave Turn of events, he has a Moment of Truth.

Cobb and the team enter into Fischer's protected dream world (the central conflict) and must contend with his unexpectedly weaponized subconscious (intentional opposition) to implement their simple plan for the inception (the false goal). But when Saito is shot, and it is revealed Fischer's subconscious has been militarized to protect itself from extraction (the turn), Cobb realizes the only way to survive to is to complete the mission and comes clean to Ariadne about how Mal died (the moment of truth).

Starting Percentage: 61 of 141 minutes (43.2%)
Runtime: 21 of 141 minutes (14.8%)

Stumbling into the Central Conflict - The character learns more about the storyworld and develops a new goal that is diametrically opposed to the goal of the antagonist.

Dom and his team battle Mal and Fischer's projections.

The Conflict of Ideals - The two sides of the Central Conflict are pursuing opposing ideals of perfection.

Reality (Superior Ideal) vs. the Dream World (Inferior Ideal)

The False Goal - The character receives a new goal he feels will set everything right in his world. Sadly, this isn't the case, and there is still something bigger he must accomplish.

The team enters the dream world and attempts to kidnap Fischer.

Intentional Opposition - As a result of his decision at the Commitment, the character comes to the attention of the forces of antagonism. They now begin opposing him with the specific intention of thwarting his plans.

The team must outsmart a suspicious Fischer by slipping a mickey in his drink. When they enter the dream and kidnap Fischer, it suddenly comes to light that his subconscious has been militarized to protect itself from extraction. Saito is mortally wounded in the ensuing gun battle. The team narrowly escapes with Fischer and meets up at the warehouse rendezvous point where they establish their plan has effectively gone to excrement. Fischer's projections move in on the building as the team tries to convince a resistant Fischer to fall for their ploy.

Turning Point Catalyst: The Turn

The Turn - There is a major turn of events that raises the stakes for the character and his allies and makes his situation far more complicated than it had been up to this point. This event is often surprising, coming as a shock to both the character and the audience.

Ariadne gets in a car with Dom and a freight train immediately smashes into it. Saito is shot. Fischer's subconscious has been militarized to protect itself from extraction. If any member of the team dies they will be stuck in Limbo forever. The only way to survive is to continue the mission.

Turning Point Three: The Moment of Truth

Start Time: 70 of 141 minutes (49.6%)
Runtime: 12 of 141 minutes (8.5%)

The Moment of Truth - As a result of the Turn, the character must reevaluate his strategy, analyze who he is, and decide to be truthful with himself about the type of person he must become. In figuring out his true nature, he makes the decision to fight for the things he believes in.

Ariadne confronts Dom about Mal and the guilt he has brought into the dream. Dom tells Ariadne the (almost) full story of how Mal died. He tells her he and Mal went so deep in the dream levels they landed in their subconsciouses where they were stuck for fifty years. When they finally awoke, Mal believed the real world was a dream, and they needed to wake up. Mal set Dom up on their anniversary and killed herself for him to join her. Now he is on the run.

This effectively explains why Dom is willing to fight, no matter what, to finish the mission. Ariadne tells Dom he needs to forgive himself and confront Mal. She volunteers to confront Mal with him. This is masterful storytelling by Christopher Nolan. Dom has been willing to fight since the beginning, but it is in this moment we learn the (partly) true reason why.

<u>To Change or Not to Change</u> - At the Moment of Truth, the character faces the decision to either change his perspective and who he has been or retain the same outlook in the face of all which has transpired.

To Change: After Dom explains what happened the night Mal committed suicide, Ariadne tells him his guilt is what empowers Mal within the dream world. She tells him he must confront Mal and agrees to help him do it. Dom realizes she is right, and he must change this integral part of himself to move on with his life and ensure the success of their mission.

Inception - Act Four - Implementing a Doomed Plan

The character Implements a Doomed Plan and faces Self-Inflicted Opposition in pursuit of a Penultimate Goal. But when an unthinkable Lowpoint occurs, he pulls himself together and discovers a Newfound Resolve.

The team goes into the next dream to run the Mr. Charles gambit (the doomed plan) and intentionally draws attention to themselves (self-inflicted opposition) to convince Fischer that Browning set him up and trick him into willingly entering the inception room (the penultimate goal). But when Mal appears in the snow fortress and kills Fischer (the lowpoint), Ariadne comes up with the idea to go into Limbo after them and synchronize the kicks to pull everyone out (the newfound resolve).

Starting Percentage: 82 of 141 minutes (58.1%)
Runtime: 33 of 141 minutes (23.4%)

<u>The Doomed Plan</u> - Having made the commitment to fight at the Moment of Truth, the character now devises and implements a plan of action that is destined to fail. It may fail outright, or it may seem to succeed only to have grave consequences the character didn't anticipate.

The Mr. Charles Gambit in the hotel and the trip into the snow fortress level are all for naught when Mal puts a bullet in Fischer.

<u>The Penultimate Goal</u> - The character's goal in this act is one step removed from the Ultimate Goal, but his pursuit of it leads him to realize what he needs to do to end the conflict once and for all.

Dom and the team attempt to convince Fischer that Browning set him up, and trick him into willingly entering the inception room.

<u>Self-Inflicted Opposition</u> - The character makes the conscious decision to go up against the forces of antagonism. Because of this, he is the primary cause of the opposition he faces in this act.

The team attempts to pull off the Mr. Charles gambit, which involves making Fischer aware of the fact he's in a dream. This deliberately brings the wrath of Fischer's subconscious projections on them. Because of this, the team is pursued through the hotel, and Arthur must do battle with the projections while everyone else goes into the next dream level. There, the others storm a heavily fortified fortress. The coup de grâce to their doomed plan occurs when Mal shows up to assassinate Fischer and Dom can't bring himself to shoot her first. This is self-inflicted opposition at its finest.

Turning Point Catalyst: The Lowpoint

<u>The Lowpoint</u> - Something unimaginable happens with grave emotional consequences for the character. He looks back on all his actions over the course of the story and feels he has failed.

Fischer is shot and killed by Mal. Dom and Eames logically conclude this scheme of theirs has failed, Lord Sidious[59].

Turning Point Four: The Newfound Resolve

Start Time: 113 of 141 minutes (80.1%)
Runtime: 2 of 141 minutes (1.4%)

<u>The Newfound Resolve</u> - After the Lowpoint, something happens to make the character dig deep within himself and rediscover his resolve. He makes the decision to stop the forces of antagonism at any cost.

Ariadne comes up with a plan to go into Limbo, rescue Fischer, complete the inception and pull everyone out with a synchronized kick. Good thing she haphazardly decided to tag along.

Dom makes the decision to face his projection of Mal to return to his kids.

---

[59] Star Wars: Episode One - The Phantom Menace.

ACTIONS & GOALS

Inception - Act Five - Trying a Longshot

The character Tries a Longshot and faces Ultimate Opposition while trying to accomplish the Ultimate Goal. But just when it seems All is Lost, he makes a Final Push against the forces of antagonism, and either succeeds or fails.

Dom and Ariadne go into Limbo to rescue Fischer (the longshot) and confront Dom's guilty projection of Mal (ultimate opposition) to finish the inception (the ultimate goal). But when the rest of the team is overrun, and it seems Dom will be overpowered by his guilt for Mal (all is lost), he reveals he was responsible for implanting the inception that drove Mal to suicide, and that he's finally ready to let her go (the final push).

Starting Percentage: 115 of 141 minutes (81.5%)
Runtime: 22 of 141 minutes (15.6%)

<u>The Longshot</u> - The character is reinvigorated by the revelation he received at the Newfound Resolve, but his only chance of success lies in a plan with a high risk of failure.

Dom and Ariadne go into Limbo to stop Mal, save Fischer, and allow the team to finish the inception.

<u>The Ultimate Goal</u> - The character finally understands what the true goal of the story is. The goal the character has in this act is what the story is all about.

Dom wants to confront his projection of Mal, rescue Fischer from Limbo and finish the inception.

<u>Ultimate Opposition</u> - The forces of antagonism are now out to destroy the character completely. At this point in the story, the antagonist will throw everything he has into eliminating the character.

Dom must face Mal and his regret over implanting the inception that led drove her to suicide. Arthur's sets up charges in an elevator for the hotel kick. The projections close in on the snow fortress. Eames sets up charges in the hospital while Saito tries to hold off the projections. Saito repeats the no room for tourists line before kicking the bucket.

Turning Point Catalyst: All Is Lost

All is Lost - The character may experience some initial success, but the forces of antagonism rally, and it seems the character's Longshot is doomed to fail.

Eames is overpowered by Fischer's projections. Saito dies. It appears Dom will be overpowered by his guilt for Mal.

Turning Point Five: The Final Push

Start Time: 127 of 141 minutes (90%)
Runtime: 10 of 141 minutes (7%)

The Final Push - Faced with his imminent destruction, the character decides to put everything he has into one final endeavor. He uses what little he has left in his stores, or the one trump card he's been holding, knowing if he fails he will be destroyed.

All the kicks go off at once. Ariadne leaps to her "death" to awaken to the next dream level. Dom decides to stay behind to find Saito in Limbo, knowing he may end up trapped there as well. Fischer tells Browning/Eames he will break up his father's company. Dom washes up on the now wrinkly Saito's doorstep and convinces him to shoot himself in the head to wake up.

Inception - Act Six - Living in a New Situation

ACTIONS & GOALS

Having accomplished (or failed to accomplish) the Ultimate Goal, the character is shown living in a New Situation.

Having successfully performed the inception, the team (and Fischer) awakens back on the airplane. Saito makes a phone call, and Dom is granted entry to the United States.

Starting Percentage: 137 of 141 minutes (97.2%)
Runtime: 4 of 141 minutes (2.8%)

<u>Living in a New Situation</u> - We see the character adapting to the New Situation his actions have created. Whether he is exalted or exiled, this is the new world he helped create.

The team awakens on the airplane. Everyone is all smiles, while Fischer looks thoughtful, seeming to have taken the Inception. Yay! Saito makes a phone call, and Dom walks through customs without being sent to prison for the rest of his life. Dom's father-in-law, Michael Caine, picks him up at the airport, and the two go to Dom's house. Dom sees his children playing in the backyard and reunites with them… until the sequel.

Iron Man

2008 film
Written by Mark Fergus, Hawk Ostby, Art Marcum & Matt Holloway
Directed by Jon Favreau

Character
Tony Stark

Ultimate Goal
Stop Obadiah from selling weapons to terrorists.

Total Runtime: 117 minutes

While the 2000 film *X-Men*, 2002's *Spider-Man* and 2005's *Batman Begins* could all be attributed with being the first comic book movies to truly capture the complexity of their source material[60], it wasn't until the release of Jon Favreau's *Iron Man* that the genre truly grew the beard[61]. Robert Downey Jr.'s career-resurrecting turn as eccentric, egotistical, billionaire, Tony Stark, changed the way studios and audiences thought about these films, and, for better or worse, made them perennial summer tentpoles at your local multiplex.

---

[60] You could also make a case for 1998's *Blade*, but while the film was both a critical and commercial success, it's more of a vampire hunter movie than a superhero movie.
[61] This term is commonly applied to television shows and denotes a point at which the quality of a subpar series begins to noticeably improve, and the show finds its own identity. At this point, it is said to have "grown the beard". The term originated from *Star Trek: The Next Generation*, which limped through an unimpressive first season, only to experience a marked improvement in quality which coincided with First Officer William Riker's growing a beard in season two. The more you know.

Tony's character arc is played out straightforwardly to the audience. He may remain, at heart, a narcissistic, billionaire asshole, but we watch him go from a narcissistic, billionaire, asshole who builds the ultimate weapons of war for personal profit, to being a narcissistic, billionaire, asshole who builds the ultimate weapon to stop war for the benefit of others. The entire script is built around Tony's character arc. All the action set pieces, dialogue, and plot twist serve the purpose of showing his arc come to fruition. It's superb storytelling wrapped up in a shiny, hot-rod red package. The sequels, not so much.

Iron Man - Act One: Dealing with an Imperfect Situation

A character in an Imperfect Situation faces Oppressive Opposition as he pursues an Initial Goal. But when there is a Disturbance to his routine, he faces a Dilemma regarding his situation and must assume a New Role.

Billionaire, weapons-manufacturer, Tony Stark, is saddled with ceremonies and responsibilities (the imperfect situation) and is reprimanded by his closest friends and advisors (oppressive opposition) because he would rather chase skirts and be awesome (the initial goal). But when he flies to Afghanistan to present his new missile to the military and is kidnapped by the terrorist organization the Ten Rings (the disturbance), Tony is forced to either build them a missile or formulate a complex escape plan (the dilemma) by building a weaponized suit of armor (the new role).

Runtime: 23 minutes
Run Percentage: 23 of 117 minutes (19.6%)

The Inciting Incident - Something happens, often before the story begins, which if it does not occur would prevent the story as it exists from coming to be.

Prior to the start of the film, Obadiah hires terrorists to kill Tony in Afghanistan.

ACTIONS & GOALS

<u>The Imperfect Situation</u> - The character begins the story in a less than ideal situation he would like to change but seemingly cannot.

Tony's lack of responsibility puts him at odds with those around him.

<u>The Initial Desire</u> - Deep within himself, the character wants one particular thing more than anything else in the world.

Tony wants to go about his awesome high-rolling life, making weapons.

<u>Initial Desire Type</u> - The character's Initial Desire is either for or against changing his situation.

Against Change: Tony believes his outlook and lifestyle are beyond reproach. He would rather everyone else accept him as he is than change himself.

<u>Preexisting Conflict</u> - When the story begins, the character is already dealing with personal conflicts as well as the conflicts of the world at large.

Though it isn't revealed to the audience in this act, Obadiah has a massive beef with Tony, leading him to hire a group of terrorists to assassinate him. This is likely due to Tony's complete lack of responsibility, which is the source of all his other preexisting conflicts. He fails to show up for his Apogee award ceremony, which upsets his friend, Colonel Rhodes. He takes no responsibility for his company's warmongering, which infuriates a young, attractive inexplicably single reporter. He attempts to blow off a weapon's presentation in Afghanistan, which annoys his young, hot, inexplicably single personal assistant. In addition to this, America is at war with terror for, like, ever.

<u>Likability/Empathy Factors</u> - The character is shown to be someone the audience would like to see succeed, or would be willing to follow on the journey of the story.

What's not to like about Tony Stark? Well, a lot actually. But we forgive him of his idiosyncrasies because he's a charming, fast-talking, billionaire, playboy, genius and who doesn't love a charming, fast-talking, billionaire, playboy, genius?

The Initial Goal - When the story opens, the character already has a goal he is actively pursuing.

Make weapons. Be awesome.

Initial Goal Type - The character's Initial Goal is either a Normal Routine Goal where he is in his regular environment, or a Fish out of Water Goal where he is already in a situation with which he is unfamiliar.

Normal Routine Goal: Skipping awards ceremonies to gamble and chase women is just another day in the life of the great Tony Stark.

Oppressive Opposition - The character's Initial Desire and/or his Initial Goal are being oppressed by the world around him.

Rhodes scolds Tony for skipping his ceremony. A reporter scolds Tony for war profiteering. Pepper scolds Tony for nearly missing his weapons presentation. Rhodes scolds Tony again for being late.

Turning Point Catalyst: The Disturbance

The Disturbance - An unexpected event with ominous implications occurs, interrupting the character's normal routine. This event pushes the character toward the Dilemma.

Tony goes to Afghanistan to give a weapons presentation. His convoy is ambushed, and Tony is captured by terrorists.

ACTIONS & GOALS

Turning Point One: The Dilemma

Start Time: 16 of 117 minutes (13.6%)
Runtime: 7 of 117 minutes (5.9%)

Presentation of The Dilemma - The character is placed in a position where he must choose between life as he has known it or taking a new course of action.

Tony awakens in a cave with a battery strapped to his chest to keep the shrapnel he was blasted with from entering his heart. The terrorist torture him into building a Jericho missile. Tony must choose between building their missile and plotting his escape.

The New Role - If the character takes this new course of action, he will assume a New Role in which he is untested.

If Tony decides to fight back against the terrorists, he will become an anti-terrorist war machine.

Refusal/Interference to the New Role (Optional) - The character may be reluctant, unready or unwilling to leave his Imperfect Situation and accept the New Role. In other cases, the character may want to accept the New Role, but someone else attempts to prevent him from accepting it.

Tony tells the terrorist no and is subsequently waterboarded.

Accepting The New Role - The character makes the decision to take action by accepting the New Role.

Tony tells his fellow captive, Yinsen, they will be dead in a week. Yinsen tells Tony, "Well then this is a very important week for you, isn't it?" This prompts Tony to begin working on a super, secret project.

Iron Man - Act Two: Learning the Rules of an Unfamiliar Situation

The character Learns the Rules of an Unfamiliar Situation and faces Incidental Opposition in pursuit of a Transitional Goal. But when he receives a Reality Check, the character makes a Commitment to his New Role.

Imprisoned in a cave, Tony builds a weaponized suit of armor to fight terrorists (the unfamiliar situation) who are suspicious of his intentions and threaten to kill him (incidental opposition) in order to escape (transitional goal). But when the terrorists become suspicious of his actions and his fellow prisoner, Yinsen, is killed in their escape attempt (the reality check), Tony returns to the States and announces he will no longer make weapons (the commitment).

Starting Percentage: 23 of 117 minutes (19.6%)
Runtime: 31 of 117 minutes (26.4%)

Learning the Rules of an Unfamiliar Situation - The character now finds himself in a situation unlike anything he's ever experienced.

Tony goes from a rich, pampered billionaire to a dirty, prisoner in a cave.

The Hooking Premise - The unique premise at the heart of a story, often involving an intriguing "what if" scenario that piques the audience's interest.

What if a billionaire weapons manufacturer builds a weaponized suit of armor to fight terrorists?

The Transitional Goal - The character receives a new goal that transitions him out of his initial state of inertia and into the main events of the story.

Tony attempts to escape the cave and his terrorist captors.

ACTIONS & GOALS

<u>Incidental Opposition</u> - The character learns there are greater forces of opposition in this new world that may not be out to thwart him specifically, but still stand between him and his new goal.

When the terrorists figure out Tony Stark is in the convoy they were paid to destroy, they choose not to kill him. Instead, they demand he build a weapon of mass destruction. He's locked in a cave and forced to do whatever they say. Tony begins implementing a mysterious plan while the terrorists watch on surveillance cameras, threatening him at every turn.

Turning Point Catalyst: The Reality Check

<u>The Reality Check</u> - The plan the character had coming into this act hits a major roadblock, and either fails completely or has unintended negative consequences.

The head terrorist sees Tony testing the leg hydraulics for his suit and pays him a visit in his cell. He threatens to burn Yinsen's tongue with a hot coal and tells Tony he has one day to finish the missile. When Tony and Yinsen implement their plan, Yinsen is mortally wounded. He tells Tony to go on without him. Tony destroys the terrorists' stock of weapons before rocketing off into the sky.

Turning Point Two: The Commitment

Start Time: 41 of 117 minutes (35%)
Runtime: 13 of 117 minutes (11.1%)

<u>The Commitment</u> - The character commits, or finds himself committed, to becoming the epitome of the New Role he accepted at the Dilemma. In doing so, he becomes an active participant in the Central Conflict.

Tony stumbles through the desert without water, but is miraculously spotted by a helicopter and rescued. Tony arrives back in the US and is greeted by Pepper at the airport. He then calls a press conference and gives a speech about his father and his legacy before announcing Stark Enterprises will no longer make weapons. Afterward, Obadiah reprimands Tony for his rash actions and tries to talk some sense into him, but Tony has made up his mind. Tony goes to visit Rhodes to show him what he's now working on. Rhodes is upset and disappointed with Tony for no longer making weapons for the military and refuses to hear him out. Tony is now committed to making a better suit to fulfill his New Role as an anti-terrorist war machine, which brings him into the Central Conflict with Obadiah.

Iron Man - Act Three: Stumbling into the Central Conflict

The character Stumbles into the Central Conflict and faces Intentional Opposition in pursuit of a False Goal. But when there is a grave Turn of events, he has a Moment of Truth.

Tony earns the ire of Obadiah (the central conflict), is locked out of his company and targeted by the ne'er-do-wells who would steal his tech (intentional opposition), as he attempts to build an improved version of his suit (the false goal). But when Tony discovers Obadiah has been selling weapons to terrorists under the table (the turn), he decides to put his new suit to use by taking his weapons out of the hands of terrorists (the moment of truth).

Starting Percentage: 54 of 117 minutes (46.1%)
Runtime: 22 of 117 minutes (18.8%)

<u>Stumbling into the Central Conflict</u> - The character learns more about the storyworld and develops a new goal that is diametrically opposed to the goal of the antagonist.

Tony squares off with the terrorists and Obadiah/Iron Monger.

<u>The Conflict of Ideals</u> - The two sides of the Central Conflict are pursuing opposing ideals of perfection.

Responsible Use of Power (Superior Ideal) vs. War Profiteering (Inferior Ideal)

The False Goal - The character receives a new goal he feels will set everything right in his world. Sadly, this isn't the case, and there is still something bigger he must accomplish.

Tony attempts to build an improved suit.

Intentional Opposition – As a result of his decision at the Commitment, the character comes to the attention of the forces of antagonism. They now begin opposing him with the specific intention of thwarting his plans.

Obadiah returns from a board meeting in New York (with pizza!) and tells Tony the board has locked him out of the company. He begs Tony to show him what he's been working on to no avail. Tony continues working on his new suit, but it still has a few humorous bugs to work out.

Turning Point Catalyst: The Turn

The Turn - There is a major turn of events that raises the stakes for the character and his allies and makes his situation far more complicated than it had been up to this point. This event is often surprising, coming as a shock to both the character and the audience.

At a charity event, Tony is confronted by the reporter he shagged in Act One. She has photographic evidence of Afghani terrorists in possession of Stark Enterprise weapons including a Jericho missile. Upset by this, Tony storms off to find Obadiah who gloats that he is the one who filed the injunction that locked Tony out of the company. He thus admits to double-dealing weapons to both sides. Angered by this Tony leaves the party.

Turning Point Three: The Moment of Truth

Start Time: 74 of 117 minutes (63.2%)
Runtime: 2 of 117 minutes (1.7%)

<u>The Moment of Truth</u> - As a result of the Turn, the character must reevaluate his strategy, analyze who he is, and decide to be truthful with himself about the type of person he must become. In figuring out his true nature, he makes the decision to fight for the things he believes in.

Back at his house, Tony watches the news and sees his former captors terrorizing the inhabitants of the village to which the recently deceased Yinsen was a native. He also sees the terrorists have Stark weapons, including Jericho missiles. As the news anchor wonders if there is anyone who can help these people, Tony looks at his reflection in the glass and blows it to bits. He has made his choice. He puts on his new suit and rockets off to save the day. Tony has decided that he can no longer be the warmonger that he was, and opts instead to fight for those who cannot defend themselves.

<u>To Change or Not to Change</u> - At the Moment of Truth, the character faces the decision to either change his perspective and who he has been or retain the same outlook in the face of all which has transpired.

To Change: Up to this point, Tony has been the epitome of self-centeredness. For presumably the first time in his life, Tony decides to change who he is and go to the aid of the powerless villagers of Gulmira.

Iron Man - Act Four - Implementing a Doomed Plan

The character Implements a Doomed Plan and faces Self-Inflicted Opposition in pursuit of a Penultimate Goal. But when an unthinkable Lowpoint occurs, he pulls himself together and discovers a Newfound Resolve.

ACTIONS & GOALS

Tony tries to singlehandedly save the world from terror (the doomed plan) and brings his new suit to the attention of Obadiah and the terrorists (self-inflicted opposition), as he attempts to destroy his stolen weapons (the penultimate goal). But when Obadiah steals Tony's arc reactor to power his own suit, leaving him to die (the lowpoint), Tony uses his old Mark One reactor to save himself and go after Obadiah (the newfound resolve).

Starting Percentage: 76 of 117 minutes (64.9%)
Runtime: 24 of 117 minutes (20.5%)

The Doomed Plan - Having made the commitment to fight at the Moment of Truth, the character now devises and implements a plan of action that is destined to fail. It may fail outright, or it may seem to succeed only to have grave consequences the character didn't anticipate.

Tony tries to take his weapons out of the hands of those who would use them for evil, bringing his new suit to the attention of Obadiah and the terrorists.

The Penultimate Goal - The character's goal in this act is one step removed from the Ultimate Goal, but his pursuit of it leads him to realize what he needs to do to end the conflict once and for all.

Tony attempts to take his weapons out of the hands of terrorists.

Self-Inflicted Opposition - The character makes the conscious decision to go up against the forces of antagonism. Because of this, he is the primary cause of the opposition he faces in this act.

Tony chooses to fight terrorists in Afghanistan and subsequently earns the ire of the US Air Force who tries to kill him with fighter jets. His adventure in Afghanistan also reveals to Obadiah the existence of Tony's new suit. Later, Tony convinces Pepper to sneak into Stark Enterprises and steal information on Obadiah's new project. Obadiah discovers her in the act and realizes she has stolen the schematics for his top-secret suit. Now he'll have to kill her as well.

Turning Point Catalyst: The Lowpoint

<u>The Lowpoint</u> - Something unimaginable happens with grave emotional consequences for the character. He looks back on all his actions over the course of the story and feels he has failed.

Obadiah pays Tony a visit and paralyzes him with a high-tech doodad. With a captive audience, Obie revels in the evilness of his plan and, in true supervillain fashion, leaves Tony to either die slowly or come up with a means to stop him.

Turning Point Four: The Newfound Resolve

Start Time: 99 of 117 minutes (84.6%)
Runtime: 1 of 117 minutes (0.8%)

<u>The Newfound Resolve</u> - After the Lowpoint, something happens to make the character dig deep within himself and rediscover his resolve. He makes the decision to stop the forces of antagonism at any cost.

Tony stumbles down to his lab and gets the old reactor Pepper saved for him. When he is unable to reach it, his pet robot delivers it to him, and Tony dramatically smashes the glass in which the reactor is encased. He has resolved to stop Obadiah at any cost.

Iron Man - Act Five - Trying a Longshot

The character Tries a Longshot and faces Ultimate Opposition while trying to accomplish the Ultimate Goal. But just when it seems All is Lost, he makes a Final Push against the forces of antagonism, and either succeeds or fails.

Tony uses his old Mark One reactor to power his suit (the longshot) and faces off with Obadiah's more advanced suit (ultimate opposition) to stop Obi's sinister plan for world domination or something (the ultimate goal). But when it becomes clear Obadiah's suit is far more powerful than his own (all is lost), Tony enlists the aid of Pepper to blow the reactor powering the building and electrocute Obadiah (the final push).

Starting Percentage: 100 of 117 minutes (85.4%)
Runtime: 13 of 117 minutes (11.1%)

The Longshot - The character is reinvigorated by the revelation he received at the Newfound Resolve, but his only chance of success lies in a plan with a high risk of failure.

Tony attempts to face Obadiah using his old Mark One reactor as a power source. Pepper and the SHIELD agents attempt to apprehend Obadiah, knowing he has built a suit of his own.

The Ultimate Goal - The character finally understands what the true goal of the story is. The goal the character has in this act is what the story is all about.

Tony wants to stop Obadiah's diabolical, illogical, terrorist plan.

Ultimate Opposition - The forces of antagonism are now out to destroy the character completely. At this point in the story, the antagonist will throw everything he has into eliminating the character.

Obadiah, who has now officially gone crazy, fires up his suit and takes it for a test run by destroying a small portion of the city and killing as many innocent bystanders as possible. Without his new reactor, Tony's suit is impotent in comparison.

Turning Point Catalyst: All Is Lost

All is Lost - The character may experience some initial success, but the forces of antagonism rally, and it seems the character's Longshot is doomed to fail.

Tony's suit is nearly out of power, and Obadiah's suit has the clear advantage. Obadiah makes use of this advantage by toying around with Tony instead of killing him while he has the chance.

Turning Point Five: The Final Push

Start Time: 109 of 117 minutes (93.1%)
Runtime: 4 of 117 minutes (3.4%)

<u>The Final Push</u> - Faced with his imminent destruction, the character decides to put everything he has into one final endeavor. He uses what little he has left in his stores, or the one trump card he's been holding, knowing if he fails he will be destroyed.

Obadiah pins Tony on the glass roof above the arc reactor. Realizing he is incapable of defeating Obadiah, Tony tells Pepper to hit the button to overload the reactor (because every reactor should have a button to overload it). Pepper says no, but Tony uses his charm to convince her otherwise.

Iron Man - Act Six - Living in a New Situation

Having accomplished (or failed to accomplish) the Ultimate Goal, the character is shown living in a New Situation.

Tony reconciles with Pepper, partners with SHIELD and finds a new purpose in his life as the Invincible Iron Man.

Starting Percentage: 113 of 117 minutes (96.6%)
Runtime: 4 of 117 minutes (3.4%)

<u>Living in a New Situation</u> - We see the character adapting to the New Situation his actions have created. Whether he is exalted or exiled, this is the new world he helped create.

Colonel Rhodes gives a press conference in defense of Stark Enterprises. Tony is shown to be alive and well, reading a newspaper about the night's events as Pepper bandages his superficial wounds. The newspaper has dubbed the mysterious man in the suit Iron Man, which Tony takes a liking to. Agent Coulson from the Strategic Homeland Intervention, Enforcement, and Logistics Division supplies Tony with index cards delineating the cover story created for the press. He also tells him Obadiah will be said to have died in a small aircraft crash. Tony tries to reignite the passion he and Pepper experienced on the night of his charity event, but she declines and their relationship remains unchanged... until the sequel.

Afterward, Tony goes to the lectern[62] and begins reading from the cards provided by SHIELD, but the reporter he seduced earlier calls into question the plausibility of his story. Tony begins to ramble before finally revealing to the press "I am Iron Man." So I guess now he's Iron Man.

---

[62] While the word podium has been so chronically misused as to now be considered acceptable by most, a lectern and a podium are, historically, two different things. Just because you can sit on a table doesn't make it a chair.

The Lego Movie

2014 film
Written and Directed by Phil Lord & Christopher Miller

Character
Emmet Brickowski

Ultimate Goal
Stop Lord Business from using the Kragle on the universe.

Total Runtime: 93 minutes

The Lego Group, manufacturer of those colorful interlocking plastic blocks the scourge of bare feet everywhere, was as of 2015 rated the "most powerful brand in the world". And it was the release of their critically acclaimed, feature-film length commercial, *The Lego Movie*, which catapulted the company ahead of globally recognized heavyweights like Ferrari and Apple to grab the prestigious position.

Lego's savvy licensing tactics over the years gave Warner Animation Group the freedom to populate the film with instantly recognizable characters from multiple media and genres, often to parodic effect. There are a bevy of guest appearances including, but not limited to, Robin Hood, Superman, Gandalf, Swamp Creature, 1980s Something Space Guy, Millhouse, Wonder Woman, Michelangelo, Michelangelo[63], Dumbledore, Chewbacca, Shaquille O'Neal, and Cleopatra. I mean, in what other major studio film

---

[63] The Ninja Turtle and the polymath respectively.

will you see Batman played as a self-important jerk or Green Lantern as an annoying sycophant?

But without a well-structured storyline to follow, all those big name characters would be window dressing. Despite the numerous cameos, the focus on lovable, dimwit, Emmet's transition from someone remarkably unremarkable to someone whose belief in himself makes him special, gives the story a sense of purpose and provides the audience with a likable protagonist we'd like to see succeed.

The Lego Movie - Act One: Dealing with an Imperfect Situation

A character in an Imperfect Situation faces Oppressive Opposition as he pursues an Initial Goal. But when there is a Disturbance to his routine, he faces a Dilemma regarding his situation and must assume a New Role.

Emmet Brickowski is a lonely, friendless, unimportant, construction guy (the imperfect situation) covertly being manipulated by an oppressive government (oppressive opposition) who just wants to fit in, have everybody like him and always be happy (the initial goal). But when he stumbles upon a mysterious object under a construction site in pursuit of a strange girl (the disturbance), he is mistaken for "the Special" by the authorities and must choose between being executed (the dilemma) and pretending to be the Special (the new role).

Runtime: 18 minutes
Run Percentage: 18 of 93 minutes (19.3%)

The Inciting Incident - Something happens, often before the story begins, which if it does not occur would prevent the story as it exists from coming to be.

ACTIONS & GOALS

In a prologue sequence, Lord Business and his army of robots steal the Kragle from Vitruvius. Vitruvius reveals the prophecy of the Special to Lord Business and the audience.

The Imperfect Situation - The character begins the story in a less than ideal situation he would like to change but seemingly cannot.

Despite Emmet's enthusiasm, none of the people he interacts with seem to know who he is. His only friend is a plant.

The Initial Desire - Deep within himself, the character wants one particular thing more than anything else in the world.

Emmet wants to have friends and be liked.

Initial Desire Type - The character's Initial Desire is either for or against changing his situation.

For Change: The friendless Emmet tries hard to interact with those around him, but he is universally ignored.

Preexisting Conflict - When the story begins, the character is already dealing with personal conflicts as well as the conflicts of the world at large.

It would appear Lord Business and Vitruvius have been fighting each other for quite some time in pursuit of the Kragle. Vitruvius tells of a prophecy. Flashforward to the future and "Lord Business" is now President Business, who mentions in passing he plans to destroy the world on Taco Tuesday.

Likability/Empathy Factors - The character is shown to be someone the audience would like to see succeed, or would be willing to follow on the journey of the story.

Emmet is a sweet-natured simpleton who wouldn't hurt a fly. He is joyfully obtuse. We can sympathize with his lack of friends despite his apparent good nature.

The Initial Goal - When the story opens, the character already has a goal he is actively pursuing.

Emmet follows a set of instructions delineating his goal to fit in, have everybody like him and always be happy.

Initial Goal Type - The character's Initial Goal is either a Normal Routine Goal where he is in his regular environment, or a Fish out of Water Goal where he is already in a situation with which he is unfamiliar.

Normal Routine Goal: Emmet goes about his daily routine and follows his instructions to get ready for work.

Oppressive Opposition - The character's Initial Desire and/or his Initial Goal are being oppressed by the world around him.

Emmet is unwittingly a participant in Lord Business' oppressive scheme to enslave the universe. This is finally brought to his attention when he is sentenced by Bad Cop to be melted to death despite his innocence.

Turning Point Catalyst: The Disturbance

The Disturbance - An unexpected event with ominous implications occurs, interrupting the character's normal routine. This event pushes the character toward the Dilemma.

Emmett loses his instructions, is smitten at the unexpected appearance of the stunning Wyldstyle and falls down a hole chasing after her. There he finds and touches the piece of resistance.

ACTIONS & GOALS

Turning Point One: The Dilemma

Start Time: 10 of 93 minutes (10.7%)
Runtime: 8 of 93 minutes (8.6%)

<u>Presentation of The Dilemma</u> - The character is placed in a position where he must choose between life as he has known it or taking a new course of action.

Emmet wakes up restrained and is interrogated by Good Cop and Bad Cop. He is revealed to have the mythical "piece of resistance" stuck to his back. When Wyldstyle shows up and saves him, he must choose between staying in Bricksburg at the mercy of the police, or becoming the Special and going on the run.

<u>The New Role</u> - If the character takes this new course of action, he will assume a New Role in which he is untested.

If Emmet agrees to go on the run with Wyldstyle, he will become the Special.

<u>Refusal/Interference to the New Role (Optional)</u> - The character may be reluctant, unready or unwilling to leave his Imperfect Situation and accept the New Role. In other cases, the character may want to accept the New Role, but someone else attempts to prevent him from accepting it.

Emmet attempts to come clean to Wyldstyle about not being the Special but decides against it when she makes it sound super cool.

<u>Accepting The New Role</u> - The character makes the decision to take action by accepting the New Role.

Emmet tells Wyldstyle he is the Special. The pair flees Bricksburg through a secret tunnel.

The Lego Movie - Act Two:
Learning the Rules of an Unfamiliar Situation

The character Learns the Rules of an Unfamiliar Situation and faces Incidental Opposition in pursuit of a Transitional Goal. But when he receives a Reality Check, the character makes a Commitment to his New Role.

Emmet tries to blend in in the Old West and learns about the prophecy (the unfamiliar situation) but is ridiculed by Wyldstyle and the locals (incidental opposition) as he attempts to rendezvous with Vitruvius (the transitional goal). But when Bad Cop tracks him down and the locals rat him out (the reality check), Emmet and the gang are forced to escape to another realm before Emmet can receive any training (the commitment).

Starting Percentage: 18 of 93 minutes (19.3%)
Runtime: 19 of 93 minutes (20.4%)

<u>Learning the Rules of an Unfamiliar Situation</u> - The character now finds himself in a situation unlike anything he's ever experienced.

Emmet has no idea what the Old West is. It's a dangerous place, and Wyldstyle has to teach him how to behave. Emmet doesn't know anything about Master Builders or the prophecy or anything in general, and must be brought up to speed.

<u>The Hooking Premise</u> - The unique premise at the heart of a story, often involving an intriguing "what if" scenario that piques the audience's interest.

What if a seemingly ordinary Lego construction guy discovers he is the chosen one who must save the universe?

<u>The Transitional Goal</u> - The character receives a new goal that transitions him out of his initial state of inertia and into the main events of the story.

ACTIONS & GOALS

Emmet and Wyldstyle attempt to rendezvous with Vitruvius.

Incidental Opposition - The character learns there are greater forces of opposition in this new world that may not be out to thwart him specifically, but still stand between him and his new goal.

The duo arrives in the Old West where it is made clear Emmet's ineptitude is likely to get him killed. Not to mention Wyldstyle thinks he's a total spazoid. They go to a saloon where Emmet stands out and is subsequently threatened by the bar's patrons.

Turning Point Catalyst: The Reality Check

The Reality Check - The plan the character had coming into this act hits a major roadblock, and either fails completely or has unintended negative consequences.

Emmet's mind is shown to be prodigiously empty. Bad Cop shows up, and Sheriff Not-A-Robot tells him where Emmet is hiding.

Turning Point Two: The Commitment

Start Time: 32 of 93 minutes (34.4%)
Runtime: 5 of 93 minutes (53.7%)

The Commitment - The character commits, or finds himself committed, to becoming the epitome of the New Role he accepted at the Dilemma. In doing so, he becomes an active participant in the Central Conflict.

Bad Cop and his army of robots attack, and the gang is forced to escape, first in a stagecoach and then in the Batwing with Batman. Like it or not, Emmet is now committed to his New Role as the Special, which pits him against Lord Business in the Central Conflict.

The Lego Movie - Act Three: Stumbling into the Central Conflict

The character Stumbles into the Central Conflict and faces Intentional Opposition in pursuit of a False Goal. But when there is a grave Turn of events, he has a Moment of Truth.

Emmet and the gang try to stop Lord Business' sinister plan (the central conflict), but Emmet's idiocy is realized by both the Master Builders and Octan (intentional opposition) when he tries to rally the Master Builders to attack Octan Tower (the false goal). But when Bad Cop tracks them to Cloud Cuckoo Land and captures all but a few of the Master Builders (the turn), the remaining Master Builders see the benefits of Emmet's seemingly useless ideas and rally behind him to develop a new course of action (the moment of truth).

Starting Percentage: 37 of 93 minutes (39.7%)
Runtime: 18 of 93 minutes (19.3%)

Stumbling into the Central Conflict - The character learns more about the storyworld and develops a new goal that is diametrically opposed to the goal of the antagonist.

Emmet and the Master Builders battle Lord Business' and his plan to Kragle the whole universe on Taco Tuesday.

The Conflict of Ideals - The two sides of the Central Conflict are pursuing opposing ideals of perfection.

Creative Freedom (Superior Ideal) vs. Strict Guidelines (Inferior Ideal)

The False Goal - The character receives a new goal he feels will set everything right in his world. Sadly, this isn't the case, and there is still something bigger he must accomplish.

ACTIONS & GOALS

Emmet and his crew attempt to assemble the Master Builders to attack Octan Tower.

Intentional Opposition - As a result of his decision at the Commitment, the character comes to the attention of the forces of antagonism. They now begin opposing him with the specific intention of thwarting his plans.

It is now clear the bad guys are after them. Batman stands vehemently between Emmet and Wyldstyle. The Master Builders turn on Emmet upon hearing his motivational speech. Bad Cop and the forces of evil crash the party, capture all the Master Builders and level Cloud Cuckoo land.

Turning Point Catalyst: The Turn

The Turn - There is a major turn of events that raises the stakes for the character and his allies and makes his situation far more complicated than it had been up to this point. This event is often surprising, coming as a shock to both the character and the audience.

Bad Cop follows Emmet's crew using a tracking device on Emmet's leg. Cloud Cuckoo land is destroyed. The submarine hastily constructed by Emmet's gang falls apart and seemingly kills everyone aboard. Bad Cop tells Lord Business the only remnant of the Special is a double-decker couch.

Turning Point Three: The Moment of Truth

Start Time: 52 of 93 minutes (55.9%)
Runtime: 3 of 93 minutes (3.2%)

The Moment of Truth - As a result of the Turn, the character must reevaluate his strategy, analyze who he is, and decide to be truthful with himself about the type of person he must become. In figuring out his true nature, he makes the decision to fight for the things he believes in.

Emmet's couch stays together, and everyone uses it to survive. Metal Beard shows up in his pirate ship and rescues them, hailing Emmet's ideas as surprisingly useful. Emmett gives a better speech and gets everyone to devise a cohesive plan.

Emmet decides he is indeed a unique individual who can make a valid contribution. He and the Master Builders devise a plan to bring the fight to Lord Business.

<u>**To Change or Not to Change**</u> - At the Moment of Truth, the character faces the decision to either change his perspective and who he has been or retain the same outlook in the face of all which has transpired.

To Change: Despite Vitruvius' insistence he is the Special, Emmet has never truly believed it himself. As a result of the Moment of Truth, Emmet makes the decision to become more than just a useless nobody and comes up with a plan to lead the Master Builders in an assault on Octan Tower.

The Lego Movie - Act Four - Implementing a Doomed Plan

The character Implements a Doomed Plan and faces Self-Inflicted Opposition in pursuit of a Penultimate Goal. But when an unthinkable Lowpoint occurs, he pulls himself together and discovers a Newfound Resolve.

Emmet and the gang implement a plan to sneak into Octan Tower (the doomed plan), but walk right into Lord Business's clutches (self-inflicted opposition) while trying to put the piece of resistance on the Kragle (the penultimate goal). But when a mortally wounded Vitruvius admits to Emmet he made up the prophecy (the lowpoint), Emmet sacrifices himself to free the others and Wyldstyle concocts a plan to enlist the aid of the citizens of the universe (the newfound resolve).

Starting Percentage: 55 of 93 minutes (59.1%)
Runtime: 19 of 93 minutes (20.4%)

ACTIONS & GOALS

<u>The Doomed Plan</u> - Having made the commitment to fight at the Moment of Truth, the character now devises and implements a plan of action that is destined to fail. It may fail outright, or it may seem to succeed only to have grave consequences the character didn't anticipate.

Emmet and the gang's plan to sneak into Octan tower fails, Vitruvius is killed, and everyone is captured.

<u>The Penultimate Goal</u> - The character's goal in this act is one step removed from the Ultimate Goal, but his pursuit of it leads him to realize what he needs to do to end the conflict once and for all.

Emmet and the Master Builders attempt to sneak into Octan Tower and put the piece of resistance on the Kragle.

<u>Self-Inflicted Opposition</u> - The character makes the conscious decision to go up against the forces of antagonism. Because of this, he is the primary cause of the opposition he faces in this act.

Emmet and the gang willingly go into Octan towers, walking into Lord Business' trap.

Turning Point Catalyst: The Lowpoint

<u>The Lowpoint</u> - Something unimaginable happens with grave emotional consequences for the character. He looks back on all his actions over the course of the story and feels he has failed.

Vitruvius is mortally wounded. Before dying, he confesses to Emmett he made up the prophecy of the Special. Lord Business sets the timer to kill all the Master Builders and Emmett. Emmet is sad because he isn't special after all. Lord Business takes his tower ship to Bricksburg and begins releasing the Kragle.

Turning Point Four: The Newfound Resolve

Start Time: 71 of 93 minutes (76.3%)
Runtime: 3 of 93 minutes (3.2%)

<u>The Newfound Resolve</u> - After the Lowpoint, something happens to make the character dig deep within himself and rediscover his resolve. He makes the decision to stop the forces of antagonism at any cost.

Ghost Vitruvius shows up and tells Emmett he can still be the Special if he just believes in himself. Emmett manages to rock the battery he is attached to free and rolls it into the abyss of infinite nothingness. Emmet's decision to stop Lord Business at all costs gives Wyldstyle an idea to save the universe.

The Lego Movie - Act Five - Trying a Longshot

The character Tries a Longshot and faces Ultimate Opposition while trying to accomplish the Ultimate Goal. But just when it seems All is Lost, he makes a Final Push against the forces of antagonism, and either succeeds or fails.

Wyldstyle hijacks a TV program to convince the citizens of Bricksburg to fight back against President Business (the longshot) and faces an attack by his minions (ultimate opposition) while Emmet gets a new piece of resistance from a human child to put on the Kragle (the ultimate goal). But when the citizens and Master Builders are overrun by Lord Business' micromanagers (all is lost), Emmett returns to Bricksburg with the vision of a Master Builder, fights his way through the city and faces off with Lord Business (the final push).

Starting Percentage: 74 of 93 minutes (79.5%)
Runtime: 17 of 93 minutes (18.2%)

ACTIONS & GOALS

<u>The Longshot</u> - The character is reinvigorated by the revelation he received at the Newfound Resolve, but his only chance of success lies in a plan with a high risk of failure.

Wyldstyle's uses the TV to get the citizens to fight back against Lord Business with their creativity. Meanwhile, Emmet tries to enlist the aid of a human child to get the piece of resistance back.

<u>The Ultimate Goal</u> - The character finally understands what the true goal of the story is. The goal the character has in this act is what the story is all about.

Emmet's motley crew wants to Defeat Lord Business and his minions, put the piece on the Kragle, and save the universe.

<u>Ultimate Opposition</u> - The forces of antagonism are now out to destroy the character completely. At this point in the story, the antagonist will throw everything he has into eliminating the character.

Lord Business releases his micromanagers and the Kragle upon the unsuspecting citizens of Bricksburg. Emmet is detained by The Man Upstairs who is revealed to be behind all this Kragle business. Emmet must face off with Lord Business directly and appeal to his sense of decency.

Turning Point Catalyst: All Is Lost

<u>All is Lost</u> - The character may experience some initial success, but the forces of antagonism rally, and it seems the character's Longshot is doomed to fail.

Wyldstyle and the citizens of Bricksburg are overrun by the micromanagers. Emmet is apprehended by the Man Upstairs who calls him an unimportant construction guy.

Turning Point Five: The Final Push

Start Time: 84 of 93 minutes (90.3%)
Runtime: 7 of 93 minutes (7.5%)

<u>The Final Push</u> - Faced with his imminent destruction, the character decides to put everything he has into one final endeavor. He uses what little he has left in his stores, or the one trump card he's been holding, knowing if he fails he will be destroyed.

With the aid of the human child, Emmett returns to Bricksburg and sees the world with the vision of a Master Builder. He builds a robot suit and fights his way through the city with the help of Princess Unikitty. He faces off with Lord Business but ends up getting his foot Kragled. The man upstairs and his son have a heart to heart, which is mirrored by Emmett and President Business. Emmet/the child convince Lord Business/The Man Upstairs to put the cap on the Kragle and end the conflict.

The Lego Movie - Act Six - Living in a New Situation

Having accomplished (or failed to accomplish) the Ultimate Goal, the character is shown living in a New Situation.

Emmet is liked and respected. He even gets to hold hands with Wyldstyle. President Business is now on the side of good.

Starting Percentage: 91 of 93 minutes (97.8%)
Runtime: 2 of 93 minutes (2.2%)

<u>Living in a New Situation</u> - We see the character adapting to the New Situation his actions have created. Whether he is exalted or exiled, this is the new world he helped create.

In an uncharacteristic act of humility, Batman tells Wyldstyle Emmet is the hero she deserves. Emmet and Wyldstyle finally hold hands. President Business distributes the antidote for the Kragle, and the people are set free. The human and his childling play with Legos together. But now that Finn's sister is also allowed to play, a new threat arises… for the sequel.

Star Trek

2009 film
Written by Roberto Orci & Alex Kurtzman
Directed by JJ Abrams

Character
James T. Kirk
Spock T. Spock

Ultimate Goal
Stop Nero from destroying Earth and every other federation planet.

Total Runtime: 118 minutes

Similar to *Star Wars*, JJ Abrams' 2009 *Star Trek* reboot is another excellent example of an odd-couple buddy story. The major difference between the two films is that where *Star Wars* emphasizes Luke as the central character of the story, *Star Trek* focuses equally on both Kirk and Spock, splitting the narrative evenly between the two.

Kirk and Spock have similar but different goals and very different ways they go about achieving them. It isn't until the penultimate act of the film that their goals and methods align, and they can work harmoniously together. But, because we have forehand knowledge of these characters and their eventual friendship, we are equally invested in both of them, allowing us to root for their inevitable joining of forces despite their initial differences of opinion.

Also of note is that unlike in the original series where William Shatner's Kirk plays the intermediary between the emotion driven McCoy and the logic guided Spock, screenwriting duo Orci and Kurtzman opted to invert the psychological roles[64] of Kirk and McCoy. This served the purpose of placing the conflict of pure emotion vs. pure logic onto the two central characters, Kirk and Spock. While McCoy serves as the character between them who innately understands the two opposing viewpoints they represent, because he has no authority over either of them, he is powerless to arbitrate. It is only through Kirk and Spock joining forces that the harmony depicted between the trio in the original series can be achieved in the film. Fans of the original series may bemoan the change, as Trekkies are notoriously wont to, but all in all, it made for powerful storytelling.

Star Trek - Act One: Dealing with an Imperfect Situation

A character in an Imperfect Situation faces Oppressive Opposition as he pursues an Initial Goal. But when there is a Disturbance to his routine, he faces a Dilemma regarding his situation and must assume a New Role.

Kirk: Fatherless Kirk lives with his mom and wicked stepfather in Iowa (the imperfect situation) and faces interference from the law and his stepdad (oppressive opposition) as he tries to live by his own rules (the initial goal). But when his reckless, flirtatious ways get him into a fight with a group of Starfleet security cadets (the disturbance), he's encouraged by a high-ranking officer to join Starfleet (the dilemma) and becomes a Starfleet cadet (the new role).

---

[64] In the original series of *Star Trek*, McCoy, Spock and Kirk are said to have embodied a Freudian Trio with each character representing the psychological role of the Id (instinct and emotion), Superego (logic and ideals), and Ego (which attempts to reconcile the two), respectively. In the series, Kirk served as the Ego, reconciling the intense emotional arguments of McCoy's Id, and the unfaltering logic of Spock's Superego. While Spock remained the Superego in the reboot film, Kirk assumed the role of the emotional Id, while McCoy became the Ego.

ACTIONS & GOALS

Spock: Spock, a half-human boy being raised on Vulcan (the imperfect situation) is harassed by the Vulcan boys for being different (oppressive opposition) as he attempts to go to school and get good grades (the initial goal). But when his human mother is insulted by the high council at his acceptance into the Vulcan Academy (the disturbance), Spock must choose between the Vulcan life he knows (the dilemma) and enlisting in Starfleet (the new role).

Runtime: 28 minutes
Run Percentage: 28 of 118 minutes (23.7%)

The Inciting Incident - Something happens, often before the story begins, which if it does not occur would prevent the story as it exists from coming to be.

In the future, Spock Prime fails to save Romulus and the planet is consumed by a black hole. Nero's ship comes through the resulting wormhole in space-time and attacks the USS Kelvin, destroying it and killing Kirk Sr.

The Imperfect Situation - The character begins the story in a less than ideal situation that he would like to change but seemingly cannot.

Kirk is an orphan. His life has no purpose, and although he's alright with it, others are not. He does not want to change his situation

Spock is an outcast who is struggling to find his purpose. He wants to change his situation.

The Initial Desire - Deep within himself, the character wants one particular thing more than anything else in the world.

Kirk wants to go about his life as the only genius-level, repeat offender in the Midwest.

Spock wants to make a meaningful contribution to the universe, or something.

Initial Desire Type - The character's Initial Desire is either for or against changing his situation.

Kirk - Against Change: Kirk thinks he's awesome and just wants to continue being awesome.

Spock - For Change: Spock does not understand his place in the universe and wishes to find it.

Preexisting Conflict - When the story begins, the character is already dealing with personal conflicts as well as the conflicts of the world at large.

Nero has a strong disdain for the Federation, though we don't discover exactly why for some time. Kirk has a strained relationship with his stepfather. He is shown to have had run-ins with the law from a young age. Meanwhile, Spock's plans to be a perfect, whiz kid, goody-goody are constantly undermined by a pack of older, larger Vulcan boys who want to prove Vulcan is just like Earth by bullying the different kid.

Likability/Empathy Factors - The character is shown to be someone the audience would like to see succeed, or would be willing to follow on the journey of the story.

Kirk: Even at a young age, Kirk is a badass. He steals his stepdad's antique Corvette, leads a hoverbike cop on a high-speed chase, and drives the car off a cliff before introducing himself as James Tiberius Kirk.

Spock: Boyhood Spock is a genius, doing complex math computations in his head and presumably preparing for an appearance on Jeopardy. *He maintains his composure in the presence of bullies, but after thirty-four failed attempts to elicit an emotional response, the Vulcan boys finally bust out the "yo momma" jokes and*

Spock elicits the typical response of a human boy, assaulting and overpowering a boy much larger than himself.

<u>The Initial Goal</u> - When the story opens, the character already has a goal he is actively pursuing.

Kirk: Live life by his own rules. Screw the universe.

Spock: Find a place in universe. Be smart and logical. At this point, he's already quite adept at it.

<u>Initial Goal Type</u> - The character's Initial Goal is either a Normal Routine Goal where he is in his regular environment, or a Fish out of Water Goal where he is already in a situation with which he is unfamiliar.

Kirk - Normal Routine Goal: Kirk's normal routine is to run around like a juvenile delinquent even though he is now a grown-up.

Spock - Normal Routine Goal: Spock goes about his regular business of studying for and acing tests, garnering acceptance into the academies of his choosing in the process.

<u>Oppressive Opposition</u> - The character's Initial Desire and/or his Initial Goal are being oppressed by the world around him.

Kirk is being oppressed by his stepfather's rules, the law, and Starfleet cadets who don't know how to take a joke.

Spock is oppressed by Vulcan boys who don't know how to appreciate the differences of others, and later by senior ranking Vulcans who also have a profound lack of respect for human beings.

Turning Point Catalyst: The Disturbance

<u>The Disturbance</u> - An unexpected event with ominous implications occurs, interrupting the character's normal routine. This event pushes the character toward the Dilemma.

Kirk: In Iowa, Kirk meets Cadet Uhura at a bar. His flirtatious ways get him into a fight with Starfleet security cadets who are also in attendance.

Spock: Spock goes before the Vulcan high council to request admission into the Vulcan Academy, but his human parentage is insulted during their offer of acceptance.

Turning Point One: The Dilemma

Start Time: 19 of 118 minutes (16%)
Runtime: 9 of 118 minutes (7.6%)

<u>Presentation of The Dilemma</u> - The character is placed in a position where he must choose between life as he has known it or taking a new course of action.

Kirk: When Captain Pike recognizes Kirk's resemblance to his father after his fight with the cadets, he makes him an offer to enlist in Starfleet. Kirk must choose between staying in Iowa and joining Starfleet.

Spock: In Spock's meeting with the Vulcan high council it is revealed he has been accepted into both Starfleet and the Vulcan Academy. Spock must choose between attending the Vulcan Academy and enlisting in Starfleet.

<u>The New Role</u> - If the character takes this new course of action, he will assume a New Role in which he is untested.

ACTIONS & GOALS

If Kirk agrees to join Starfleet, he will become a Starfleet cadet. Ditto for Spock.

Refusal/Interference to the New Role (Optional) - The character may be reluctant, unready or unwilling to leave his Imperfect Situation and accept the New Role. In other cases, the character may want to accept the New Role, but someone else attempts to prevent him from accepting it.

Kirk: Kirk refuses Pike's outlandish offer to join Starfleet.

Nudge From Fate (Optional) - In instances where the character has every reason to decline the New Role, he may receive influence from an outside force that drives him to accept it.

Spock: Spock is all set to matriculate at the Vulcan Academy. But when the high council insults his human mother, Spock rescinds his request for enrollment.

Accepting The New Role - The character makes the decision to take action by accepting the New Role.

Kirk: Kirk mulls it over, and in true Jim Kirk fashion, decides to go all in.

Spock: By declining to attend the Vulcan Academy, Spock is implied to have accepted admission into Starfleet.

Star Trek - Act Two: Learning the Rules of an Unfamiliar Situation

The character Learns the Rules of an Unfamiliar Situation and faces Incidental Opposition in pursuit of a Transitional Goal. But when he receives a Reality Check, the character makes a Commitment to his New Role.

Kirk: Kirk goes to Starfleet Academy (the unfamiliar situation) where they have an abundance of things called rules (incidental opposition) in hopes of graduating from simply being super awesome to being super awesome in space (the transitional goal). But when the fleet is mustered while he is on academic suspension, and he's forced to stow aboard the Enterprise *(reality check), he is recruited by Captain Pike (again) to lead an away team tasked with stopping Romulans from destroying Vulcan (the commitment).*

Spock: *After dealing with a cheating cadet who somehow outsmarted his unbeatable test (the unfamiliar situation), and facing off with the smart mouth kid who questions his authority (incidental opposition), Commander Spock and the* Enterprise *receive an emergency response signal from Vulcan and mount a rescue mission (the transitional goal). But when it is revealed that Romulans are attacking Vulcan because of Spock (the reality check), Captain Pike agrees to negotiate with the Romulans and promotes Spock to captain in his stead (the commitment).*

Starting Percentage: 28 of 118 minutes (23.7%)
Runtime: 23 of 118 minutes (19.4%)

Learning the Rules of an Unfamiliar Situation - The character now finds himself in a situation unlike anything he's ever experienced.

Kirk goes off to the Starfleet Academy. They have a lot of rules there, and he quickly gets himself into serious trouble.

Commander Spock excels at the Starfleet Academy, but we're not reintroduced to him until his superior intellect is brought into question by a brash young cadet named Kirk who manages to beat the unwinnable test Spock personally programmed.

The Hooking Premise - The unique premise at the heart of a story, often involving an intriguing "what if" scenario that piques the audience's interest.

What if, early in their careers, Kirk and Spock don't get along and must learn to work together to stop a common enemy?

The Transitional Goal - The character receives a new goal that transitions him out of his initial state of inertia and into the main events of the story.

Kirk wants to graduate the Academy and be awesome.

Spock wants to live long and prosper.

Incidental Opposition - The character learns there are greater forces of opposition in this new world that may not be out to thwart him specifically, but still stand between him and his new goal.

Kirk runs into several problems just trying to be his usual, womanizing, authority circumventing self. He clashes with Uhura and Bones over his relentless retaking of the Kobayashi Maru exam and later with Spock, Tyler Perry, and the Starfleet Academy because he cheated on said exam.

Spock's unpassable test is defeated by a cheating Kirk. He and Kirk have it out in front of the entire Starfleet Academy at Kirk's academic hearing.

Turning Point Catalyst: The Reality Check

The Reality Check - The plan the character had coming into this act hits a major roadblock, and either fails completely or has unintended negative consequences.

Kirk: Due to his academic suspension, Kirk is grounded when the fleet is mustered. He subsequently gets Mudflees from Bones and has a near-fatal allergic reaction.

Spock: Kirk unexpectedly barges on the bridge and announces Vulcan is under attack by 'Womulans. Spock tries to call him a liar but is ultimately proven wrong.

Turning Point Two: The Commitment

Start Time: 45 of 118 minutes (38.1%)
Runtime: 6 of 118 minutes (5%)

<u>The Commitment</u> - The character commits, or finds himself committed, to becoming the epitome of the New Role he accepted at the Dilemma. In doing so, he becomes an active participant in the Central Conflict.

The Enterprise *comes out of warp to find the fleet destroyed. They are confronted by a garbled transmission of Nero's head, and must come up with a plan to stop the drill. Captain Pike request officers with advanced hand-to-hand combat training and also takes Kirk since he's not supposed to be there in the first place. Spock is logically promoted to captain. Kirk is illogically promoted to first officer. Kirk commits himself to his New Role as a Starfleet officer by leading an away team to stop the drill. Spock commits to his New Role as captain by being all serious. Meanwhile, the Romulans commit to destroying Vulcan by preparing the red matter, setting the stage for the Central Conflict.*

Star Trek - Act Three: Stumbling into the Central Conflict

The character Stumbles into the Central Conflict and faces Intentional Opposition in pursuit of a False Goal. But when there is a grave Turn of events, he has a Moment of Truth.

Kirk: Hoping to stop Nero and whatever it is he's trying to accomplish (the central conflict), Kirk and the away team face off with gun-toting Romulans (intentional opposition) when they HALO jump to the planet to destroy the drill (the false goal). But when Nero destroys the planet by creating a black hole at its center (the turn) and Spock wants to rendezvous with the fleet instead of going after him, Kirk opts to mutiny to lead the ship after Nero (the moment of truth).

Spock: When it is discovered Nero is trying to create a singularity at the center of all Federation planets (the central conflict), Spock beams to the surface of the collapsing Vulcan against Kirk's protests (intentional opposition) to save the council and his family (the false goal). But when his mother is killed and Vulcan is destroyed (the turn), Kirk tries to mutiny, and Spock has him ejected from the ship (the moment of truth).

Starting Percentage: 51 of 118 minutes (43.2%)
Runtime: 21 of 118 minutes (17.7%)

Stumbling into the Central Conflict - The character learns more about the storyworld and develops a new goal that is diametrically opposed to the goal of the antagonist.

The crew of the Enterprise *faces off with Nero and his plan to destroy Starfleet.*

The Conflict of Ideals - The two sides of the Central Conflict are pursuing opposing ideals of perfection.

Peace and Justice (Superior Ideal) vs. Destruction and Revenge (Inferior Ideal)

The False Goal - The character receives a new goal he feels will set everything right in his world. Sadly, this isn't the case, and there is still something bigger he must accomplish.

Kirk and Spock attempt to stop Nero and whatever it is he's doing to Vulcan.

Intentional Opposition - As a result of his decision at the Commitment, the character comes to the attention of the forces of antagonism. They now begin opposing him with the specific intention of thwarting his plans.

Nero and his crew now want the crew of the Enterprise *to watch helplessly as Vulcan is destroyed. The Romulan redshirts[65] try to stop Kirk, Sulu and a Starfleet redshirt from disabling the drill to no avail. Kirk and Sulu destroy the drill to no avail. Spock tries to rescue his mother to no avail. Can we please get some damn avail?!*

Turning Point Catalyst: The Turn

The Turn - There is a major turn of events that raises the stakes for the character and his allies and makes his situation far more complicated than it had been up to this point. This event is often surprising, coming as a shock to both the character and the audience.

Nero launches the red matter into the hole he's drilled. The ground underneath Spock's mom gives way, and Chekov can't beam her aboard the ship because he's not Scotty. She is dead. Vulcan is destroyed in a black hole as the Enterprise *flies away.*

Turning Point Three: The Moment of Truth

Start Time: 64 of 118 minutes (54.2%)
Runtime: 8 of 118 minutes (6.7%)

The Moment of Truth - As a result of the Turn, the character must reevaluate his strategy, analyze who he is, and decide to be truthful with himself about the type of person he must become. In figuring out his true nature, he makes the decision to fight for the things he believes in.

Spock determines from the artificially created black hole that Nero must be from the future. Spock and Kirk argue about their next move. Kirk wants to go after

---

[65] Cannon fodder. A character's whose primary role in the story is to die. The term originates from *Star Trek*, in which the red-shirted security personnel would frequently be killed to illustrate how dangerous the situation was without having to kill anyone important.

Nero. Spock wants to rendezvous with Starfleet. Spock is the captain, so he makes the call. Kirk flips out and attacks Spock who has him ejected from for mutiny.

Both Spock and Kirk make decisions based on their true natures and fight against each other in defense of them.

<u>To Change or Not to Change</u> - At the Moment of Truth, the character faces the decision to either change his perspective and who he has been or retain the same outlook in the face of all which has transpired.

Kirk and Spock - Not to Change: Buoyed by their conflicting outlooks after the destruction of Vulcan, both Spock and Kirk decide not to change in regard to the Enterprise's next move. This causes their already tumultuous relationship to come to a head. Although a decision against change at this Turning Point often leads the story down a tragic path, the film successfully subverts this stereotype. The decision not to change by both character works in the film because Star Trek *tells the story of the budding friendship between the two Starfleet officers, and this final spat leads to their ultimate union of accords at the Act Four Turning Point.*

Star Trek - Act Four: Implementing a Doomed Plan

The character Implements a Doomed Plan and faces Self-Inflicted Opposition in pursuit of a Penultimate Goal. But when an unthinkable Lowpoint occurs, he pulls himself together and discovers a Newfound Resolve.

Kirk deals with the Hoth[66] like atmosphere of Delta Vega (self-inflicted opposition), while trying to reach the Starfleet outpost (the penultimate goal). But when he is nearly eaten by one of the many space beasts of the planet (the lowpoint), he is rescued by Leonard Nimoy who clues him into Nero's backstory and introduces him to Scotty (the newfound resolve)

---

[66] Hoth is the planet Luke, Han and Leia are living on at the beginning of *The Empire Strikes Back*. But I assume you already knew that.

Spock attempts to rendezvous with Starfleet (the doomed plan) but has his decision questioned by his senior officers (self-inflicted opposition) while trying to come up with a way to stop Nero (the penultimate goal). But when that damned Kirk manages to beam back aboard the ship, emotionally compromise him and convince him to resign command (the lowpoint), Spock has a father to son moment with his dad, who tells him humans are better than Vulcans in many ways and makes him *apologize to Kirk (the newfound resolve).*

Starting Percentage: 72 of 118 minutes (61%)
Runtime: 24 of 118 minutes (20.3%)

<u>The Doomed Plan</u> - Having made the commitment to fight at the Moment of Truth, the character now devises and implements a plan of action that is destined to fail. It may fail outright, or it may seem to succeed only to have grave consequences the character didn't anticipate.

The Enterprise's *attempts to rendezvous with the fleet will be unsuccessful.*

<u>The Penultimate Goal</u> - The character's goal in this act is one step removed from the Ultimate Goal, but his pursuit of it leads him to realize what he needs to do to end the conflict once and for all.

Kirk attempts to reach the Starfleet outpost on Delta Vega.

Spock attempts to rendezvous with the rest of Starfleet.

<u>Self-Inflicted Opposition</u> - The character makes the conscious decision to go up against the forces of antagonism. Because of this, he is the primary cause of the opposition he faces in this act.

Due to his choice to overthrow Spock, Kirk must now try to avoid becoming lunch for the space beasts of Hoth. After conveniently meeting future Spock, Scotty, and Deep Roy, Kirk teleports back onto the Enterprise *and is apprehended by Starfleet security officers.*

Meanwhile, Spock's decision to ignore Kirk's advice is what causes the latter to hatch a complex mutiny scheme. Ultimately, Spock's dad leads him to realize all this mess is his fault because he doesn't appreciate his human side.

Turning Point Catalyst: The Lowpoint

<u>The Lowpoint</u> - Something unimaginable happens with grave emotional consequences for the character. He looks back on all his actions over the course of the story and feels he has failed.

Kirk is marooned on Delta Vega.

Spock is emotionally compromised by Kirk and nearly kills him. This prompts Spock to relinquish his command of the Enterprise. *Cue sad music.*

It's interesting to note that in this act, Spock and Kirk's Turning Points diverge. Their clash at their joint Moment of Truth in the previous act immediately leads to Kirk's individual Lowpoint of being marooned on Delta Vega in Act Four. But Kirk's discovery of his Newfound Resolve and his beaming back aboard the ship causes the failure of Spock's Doomed Plan, his Lowpoint of being emotionally compromised, and his subsequent Newfound Resolve of joining forces with Kirk. Their plot points had been aligned, if at odds up until this point, but it's only after this divergence that their actions are harmoniously united under a shared goal at the conclusion of this act.

Turning Point Four: The Newfound Resolve

Start Time: 92 of 118 minutes (77.9%)
Runtime: 4 of 118 minutes (3.3%)

<u>The Newfound Resolve</u> - After the Lowpoint, something happens to make the character dig deep within himself and rediscover his resolve. He makes the decision to stop the forces of antagonism at any cost.

Kirk finds out about Nero from Spock Prime and decides he must be stopped. He also learns he is the rightful captain of the Enterprise. *Kirk joins up with Scotty, and together they beam aboard the* ship.

After Spock loses command of the Enterprise *to Kirk, his dad gives him life lessons on love and other such nonsense. Afterward, Spock returns to the bridge and volunteers to beam aboard Nero's ship. He too has decided Nero must be stopped. Kirk will come with him, because of course.*

Star Trek - Act Five: Trying a Longshot

The character Tries a Longshot and faces Ultimate Opposition while trying to accomplish the Ultimate Goal. But just when it seems All is Lost, he makes a Final Push against the forces of antagonism, and either succeeds or fails.

Spock and Kirk beam aboard Nero's ship (the longshot) and shoot it out with an army of Romulans (ultimate opposition) to rescue Captain Pike, stop the black hole device and save the human planet Human (the ultimate goal). But when Nero activates the drill and Kirk attempts to apprehend him only to beaten senseless (all is lost), Spock destroys the drill, leads Nero toward the awaiting Enterprise, *and crashes a ton of red matter[67] into the Romulan ship (the final push).*

Starting Percentage: 96 of 118 minutes (81.3%)
Runtime: 17 of 118 minutes (14.4%)

The Longshot - The character is reinvigorated by the revelation he received at the Newfound Resolve, but his only chance of success lies in a plan with a high risk of failure.

---

[67] Seriously, a drop of red matter was enough to create a black hole at the center of a planet. I would think a ton of it detonating next to Saturn would be enough to consume our entire solar system. But admittedly, I'm not a Hollywood physicist.

ACTIONS & GOALS

Kirk and the gang devise a plan to beam aboard Nero's ship, rescue Pike, stop the drill and save the world. Simple enough.

The Ultimate Goal - The character finally understands what the true goal of the story is. The goal the character has in this act is what the story is all about.

Kirk and the crew want to stop Nero, rescue Pike and save Earth.

Ultimate Opposition - The forces of antagonism are now out to destroy the character completely. At this point in the story, the antagonist will throw everything he has into eliminating the character.

Kirk and Spock face off against Nero as he attempts to turn Earth into a black hole. The pair beams aboard a highly advanced enemy ship to rescue Pike but inadvertently land in the Romulan target practice room. Kirk and Spock shoot their way through the ship, meet the perpetually angry Nero and his equally angry goons.

Turning Point Catalyst: All Is Lost

All is Lost - The character may experience some initial success, but the forces of antagonism rally, and it seems the character's Longshot is doomed to fail.

Nero activates the drill conveniently close to the Starfleet Academy. Kirk attempts to apprehend Nero, gets knocked silly by one of Nero's goons, and then by Nero himself. It would seem as though he's about to be choked to death. Again.

Turning Point Five: The Final Push

Start Time: 105 of 118 minutes (88.9%)
Runtime: 8 of 118 minutes (6.7%)

<u>The Final Push</u> - Faced with his imminent destruction, the character decides to put everything he has into one final endeavor. He uses what little he has left in his stores, or the one trump card he's been holding, knowing if he fails he will be destroyed.

Spock destroys the drill with Spock Prime's ship. Nero's ship chases Spock and fires everything. The Enterprise, *taking a page from* the Millennium Falcon *in* A New Hope, *shows up and destroys the missiles at the last second. Spock crashes the red matter into Nero's ship as Scotty beams him, Kirk and Pike back aboard the* Enterprise. *Nero's ship is caught in the black hole and destroyed, while* the Enterprise *has to eject the warp core to escape the pull of the black hole.*

Star Trek - Act Six: Living in a New Situation

Having accomplished (or failed to accomplish) the Ultimate Goal, the character is shown living in a New Situation.

Earth is saved, and Kirk and Spock are heroes. Spock meets Spock Prime who tells him he has much to learn from Kirk. Kirk is officially promoted to captain of the Enterprise. *Spock volunteers to be Kirk's first mate as the* Enterprise *sets off on its second maiden voyage.*

Starting Percentage: 113 of 118 minutes (95.7%)
Runtime: 5 of 118 minutes (4.2%)

<u>Living in a New Situation</u> - We see the character adapting to the New Situation his actions have created. Whether he is exalted or exiled, this is the new world he helped create.

Earth is safe. The Starfleet Academy is a happy place to be. Spock meets Spock Prime who convinces him to stay in Starfleet. Kirk is given command of the Enterprise *from Pike, who tells him his father would be proud. Spock boards the* Enterprise *and volunteers to be First Officer. Kirk obliges. The* Enterprise *sets sail.*

Star Wars Episode V: The Empire Strikes Back

1980 Film
Story by George Lucas
Screenplay by Leigh Brackett and Lawrence Kasdan

Character(s)
Luke Skywalker, Han Solo, Princess Leia

Ultimate Goal
Save Han and Leia from the clutches of the Empire

Total Runtime: 122 minutes

I wanted to include *The Empire Strikes Back* in this analysis because there is generally so much emphasis placed on the first film within storytelling and screenwriting manuals it is often overlooked that *Empire* is the darker, more powerful and most popular film in the trilogy. Additionally, it's an example of a story that ends tragically for the character, and frankly, there aren't enough of those pumping out of the Hollywood machine. Luke's failure to rein in his emotions and give in to the guidance of the Force creates a tragic, yet resonant ending and gives the film a lasting poignance.

Differing from the first film and similar to Abrams' *Star Trek*, *Empire* focuses equally on the separate exploits of Luke and Han/Leia as they pursue their different goals. Leigh Brackett and Lawrence Kasdan's screenplay does an excellent job of interweaving the growing peril faced by Han and Leia with

Luke's pursuit of becoming a Jedi to create foreshadowing and suspense. This culminates in the two storylines converging and ultimately reuniting the group for the climax of the fifth act.

My biggest complaint with the film is that Leia goes from being a BAMF warrior princess in the first movie, to essentially Han's nagging girlfriend in the second. Where she was once a tough-as-nails, high-ranking member of the Rebel Alliance, in *Empire*, she just kind of tags along, backseat driving and criticizing plans without offering any real advice or contributions.

Star Wars Episode V: The Empire Strikes Back - Act One: Dealing with an Imperfect Situation

A character in an Imperfect Situation faces Oppressive Opposition as he pursues an Initial Goal. But when there is a Disturbance to his routine, he faces a Dilemma regarding his situation and must assume a New Role.

Luke, Han, and Leia have set up shop on the inhospitable planet, Hoth (the imperfect situation), to elude the relentless pursuit of the Empire (oppressive opposition) while the Rebels figure out their plan of attack (the initial goal). But when Imperial scouting probes land on the planet, Luke receives a message from Obi-Wan, and the Empire attacks the planet (the disturbance), Luke must choose between rendezvousing with the Rebels or going to Dagobah (the dilemma) to become a card-carrying Jedi (the new role).

Runtime: 37 minutes
Run Percentage: 37 of 122 minutes (30.3%)

<u>The Inciting Incident</u> - Something happens, often before the story begins, which if it does not occur would prevent the story as it exists from coming to be.

When Darth Vader discovers the guy who blew up the Death Star is named Luke Skywalker, he resolves to track him down at all costs.

The Imperfect Situation - The character begins the story in a less than ideal situation that he would like to change but seemingly cannot.

Because they are being relentlessly pursued by the Empire, the Rebels are forced to take up residence on a frozen wasteland planet.

The Initial Desire - Deep within himself, the character wants one particular thing more than anything else in the world.

Luke wants to become a Jedi. Han wants to pay off Jabba the Hutt. Leia and the Rebels want to defeat the Empire.

Initial Desire Type - The character's Initial Desire is either for or against changing his situation.

For Change: Luke wants to be more than just a member of the Rebel Alliance; he wants to become a Jedi. Han wants to pay off his debt to Jabba the Hut and escape his old life (which hopefully involves shagging a princess). Leia wants to help the Rebels to defeat the Empire (as well as come to terms with her feelings for Han).

Preexisting Conflict - When the story begins, the character is already dealing with personal conflicts as well as the conflicts of the world at large.

Although the Death Star has been destroyed, the Empire is still very much at large. Vader has a hard-on for finding Luke. Han and Leia have a tumultuous relationship. Jabba wants Han dead[68].

---

[68] And as the Rebel General helpfully points out, "A death mark's not an easy thing to live with."

Likability/Empathy Factors - The character is shown to be someone the audience would like to see succeed, or would be willing to follow on the journey of the story.

Because we've already gone on an adventure with the characters in the first film, we are pleased to see them return. Luke and Han are now "old buddies." Luke uses new Force abilities to defeat a Wampa, demonstrating his skills have increased. We also see the once self-centered Han is now willing to risk his life to rescue Luke.

The Initial Goal - When the story opens, the character already has a goal he is actively pursuing.

Luke and the gang hide out from the Empire and bide their time until the right moment.

Initial Goal Type - The character's Initial Goal is either a Normal Routine Goal where he is in his regular environment, or a Fish out of Water Goal where he is already in a situation with which he is unfamiliar.

Normal Routine Goal: The Rebels are accustomed to hiding out from the Empire. This business on Hoth is just another day at the office.

Oppressive Opposition - The character's Initial Desire and/or his Initial Goal are being oppressed by the world around him.

Despite the events of A New Hope, *the Empire still rules the galaxy with an iron fist. They have the Rebels confined to an icy wasteland.*

Turning Point Catalyst: The Disturbance

The Disturbance - An unexpected event with ominous implications occurs, interrupting the character's normal routine. This event pushes the character toward the Dilemma.

Imperial scouting probes land on the planet, shattering the relative peace. When Luke goes to investigate, he is captured by a Wampa and receives a Force-O'gram from Obi-Wan.

Turning Point One: The Dilemma

Start Time: 18 of 122 minutes (14.7%)
Runtime: 19 of 122 minutes (15.5%)

Presentation of The Dilemma - The character is placed in a position where he must choose between life as he has known it or taking a new course of action.

The Empire arrives at Hoth and launches an all-out assault on the Rebel base. The Rebel forces are scattered in the wind. Luke must decide between staying with the Rebels or going off by himself to follow Ben's instructions and visiting Dagobah. Han and Leia must choose between going their separate ways and leaving together.

The New Role - If the character takes this new course of action, he will assume a New Role in which he is untested.

Luke: If Luke goes to Dagobah, he will once again become a Jedi pupil.
Han/Leia: If the pair leaves together they will become fugitives on the run from the Empire.

Refusal/Interference to the New Role (Optional) - The character may be reluctant, unready or unwilling to leave his Imperfect Situation and accept the New Role. In other cases, the character may want to accept the New Role, but someone else attempts to prevent him from accepting it.

Not Applicable.

Nudge From Fate (Optional) - In instances where the character has every reason to decline the New Role, he may receive influence from an outside force that drives him to accept it.

When falling debris blocks the path to Leia's ship, Han volunteers to get her out on the Falcon.

Accepting The New Role - The character makes the decision to take action by accepting the New Role.

Luke tells R2 they aren't going to meet up with the others but will instead go to Dagobah.
Han and Leia leave aboard the Falcon *just as Darth Vader walks into the hangar bay.*

Star Wars Episode V: The Empire Strikes Back - Act Two: Learning the Rules of an Unfamiliar Situation

The character Learns the Rules of an Unfamiliar Situation and faces Incidental Opposition in pursuit of a Transitional Goal. But when he receives a Reality Check, the character makes a Commitment to his New Role.

Luke travels to Dagobah (the unfamiliar situation), a slimy, mud hole populated with dangerous wildlife (incidental opposition), where he hopes to find the Jedi Master, Yoda, and become his pupil (the transitional goal). But when he crashes his X-wing in the swamp, effectively marooning himself (the reality check), he meets an annoying, green puppet who turns out to be Master Yoda (the commitment).

Han and Leia are chased by Star Destroyers (the unfamiliar situation) as they try to escape the Empire (the transitional goal). But when they discover the ship can't go to lightspeed, and they must navigate an asteroid field (the reality check), they hide inside an asteroid that turns out to be a giant space worm and must recommit to fleeing (the commitment).

ACTIONS & GOALS

Starting Percentage: 37 of 122 minutes (30.3%)
Runtime: 24 of 122 minutes (19.6%)

Learning the Rules of an Unfamiliar Situation - The character now finds himself in a situation unlike anything he's ever experienced.

Luke: Luke arrives at Dagobah. The place gives him the creeps. R2 is nearly eaten.

Han/Leia: Han and Leia are pursued by a formation of Star Destroyers and realize the hyperdrive motivator has been damaged.

The Hooking Premise - The unique premise at the heart of a story, often involving an intriguing "what if" scenario that piques the audience's interest.

What if Luke abandons the Rebellion to learn the Force from a reclusive Jedi Master while Han and Leia are ruthlessly pursued by the Empire?

The Transitional Goal - The character receives a new goal that transitions him out of his initial state of inertia and into the main events of the story.

Luke: After receiving a message from Obi-Wan in Act One, Luke goes to Dagobah to find Yoda and become his student.

Han/Leia: Han and Leia attempt to avoid Imperial capture.

Incidental Opposition - The character learns there are greater forces of opposition in this new world that may not be out to thwart him specifically, but still stand between him and his new goal.

Luke: Luke deals with life on the swampy Dagobah. R2 is eaten by a swamp monster, but ultimately spit out. Luke has to contend with some weird, little, green guy who wrecks his campsite and steals his flashlight.

Han/Leia: Han and Leia take the wrong exit vector and are pursued by a star destroyer. When they realize the hyperdrive has been damaged, they can't escape their predicament.

Turning Point Catalyst: The Reality Check

<u>The Reality Check</u> - The plan the character had coming into this act hits a major roadblock, and either fails completely or has unintended negative consequences.

Luke: Beginning to believe it was a mistake to come to Dagobah, Luke meets an annoying local who says he knows where to find Yoda.

Han/Leia: In their attempt to escape, the pair realize the hyperdrive is broken. No lightspeed. When the Falcon *comes across an asteroid field, Han attempts to navigate through it in search of a hiding place.*

Turning Point Two: The Commitment

Start Time: 54 of 122 minutes (44.2%)
Runtime: 7 of 122 minutes (5.7%)

<u>The Commitment</u> - The character commits, or finds himself committed, to becoming the epitome of the New Role he accepted at the Dilemma. In doing so, he becomes an active participant in the Central Conflict.

Luke: Luke realizes the little puppet he's been so impatient with is actually the great Jedi master, Yoda, he's come in search of. After initially denying Luke, Yoda agrees to take him on as a pupil at Obi-Wan's request. Luke commits to fulfilling his New Role as Yoda's padawan and learning the ways of the Jedi.

Han/Leia: Han and Leia realize the cave they are in is actually the belly of a giant space worm or something. Once again, they go on the run from Darth Vader's Star

Destroyers. They would seem to be stuck in their New Role as fugitives for the duration of the film.

Star Wars Episode V: The Empire Strikes Back - Act Three: Stumbling into the Central Conflict

The character Stumbles into the Central Conflict and faces Intentional Opposition in pursuit of a False Goal. But when there is a grave Turn of events, he has a Moment of Truth.

Luke must contend with and avoid falling victim to the dark side of the Force (the central conflict), and pass Yoda's intense training regimen (intentional opposition) if he is to learn how to become a Jedi (the false goal). But when he sees a vision from the future of Han and Leia being tortured in Cloud City (the turn), Luke goes to rescue them despite Yoda and Obi-Wan's pleas to the contrary (the moment of truth)

Han and Leia are pursued by Darth Vader and the Empire (the central conflict), who have now hired a plenitude of bounty hunters to capture them (intentional opposition), as they travel to Cloud City to elicit help from Han's pirate buddy, Lando (the false goal). But when C3PO is shot and Leia senses there's something sinister afoot (the turn), Lando reveals his treachery by bringing Han and Leia to Sunday brunch with Lord Vader (the moment of truth).

Starting Percentage: 61 of 122 minutes (50%)
Runtime: 28 of 122 minutes (22.9%)

Stumbling into the Central Conflict - The character learns more about the storyworld and develops a new goal that is diametrically opposed to the goal of the antagonist.

Luke goes up against Vader and the Dark side of the force.

Han and Leia contend with the Empire's pursuit.

The Conflict of Ideals - The two sides of the Central Conflict are pursuing opposing ideals of perfection.

Protection of Friends at All Costs (Superior Ideal) vs. Destruction of Enemies at All Costs (Inferior Ideal)

The False Goal - The character receives a new goal he feels will set everything right in his world. Sadly, this isn't the case, and there is still something bigger he must accomplish.

Luke attempts to learn the ways of the Force from Yoda

Han and Leia head to Cloud City to elicit Lando's help in repairing the hyperdrive.

Intentional Opposition - As a result of his decision at the Commitment, the character comes to the attention of the forces of antagonism. They now begin opposing him with the specific intention of thwarting his plans.

Luke: Yoda's training is intentionally designed to test Luke. He faces pseudo-Vader in the cave. Meanwhile, the real Vader captures his friends and tortures them to lure Luke to him.

Han/Leia: Vader hires bounty hunters to track down the Falcon. *His personal star destroyer is now hot on the heels of the* Falcon. *Boba Fett doesn't fall for Han's ruse and follows them to Cloud City. Because he has a working hyperdrive, Vader arrives first and turns Lando against them.*

Turning Point Catalyst: The Turn

The Turn - There is a major turn of events that raises the stakes for the character and his allies and makes his situation far more complicated than it had been up to this point. This event is often surprising, coming as a shock to both the character and the audience.

Luke: Luke sees a vision of Leia and Han being tortured by the Empire in Cloud City. Yoda tells him it is a vision of the future.

Han/Leia: 3PO is shot by an unseen assailant, and Han and Leia get a sense something sinister is going on when Chewbacca finds the droid's dismantled body.

Turning Point Three: The Moment of Truth

Start Time: 82 of 122 minutes (67.2%)
Runtime: 7 of 122 minutes (5.7%)

The Moment of Truth - As a result of the Turn, the character must reevaluate his strategy, analyze who he is, and decide to be truthful with himself about the type of person he must become. In figuring out his true nature, he makes the decision to fight for the things he believes in.

Luke: After listening to Yoda and Obi-Wan's pleas for him not to go to Cloud City, Luke goes anyway. He decides that he is not the kind of person who would let his friends die and opts to fight Darth Vader instead.

Han/Leia: Lando reveals his treachery to Han and Leia when he brings them to Lord Vader.

To Change or Not to Change - At the Moment of Truth, the character faces the decision to either change his perspective and who he has been or retain the same outlook in the face of all which has transpired.

Not to Change: Luke's sense of commitment to his friends, leads him to go after them despite all of Yoda's training. Even with his newfound knowledge of what is expected of a Jedi, Luke decides he cannot fully abandon the part of himself committed to his friends.

Star Wars Episode V: The Empire Strikes Back - Act Four: Implementing a Doomed Plan

The character Implements a Doomed Plan and faces Self-Inflicted Opposition in pursuit of a Penultimate Goal. But when an unthinkable Lowpoint occurs, he pulls himself together and discovers a Newfound Resolve.

Luke travels to Cloud City (the doomed plan), walking right into Vader's trap (self-inflicted opposition) while trying to rescue his friends (the penultimate goal). But when Han is frozen in carbonite by Vader, and Leia is taken prisoner (the lowpoint), Luke arrives and has a shoot-out with Boba Fett and the Imperial Guard (the newfound resolve).

Starting Percentage: 89 of 122 minutes (72.9%)
Runtime: 11 of 122 minutes (9%)

<u>The Doomed Plan</u> - Having made the commitment to fight at the Moment of Truth, the character now devises and implements a plan of action that is destined to fail. It may fail outright, or it may seem to succeed only to have grave consequences the character didn't anticipate.

Luke travels to and arrives at Cloud City in hopes of rescuing his friends.

<u>The Penultimate Goal</u> - The character's goal in this act is one step removed from the Ultimate Goal, but his pursuit of it leads him to realize what he needs to do to end the conflict once and for all.

Luke tries to save Han and Leia from Vader.

Self-Inflicted Opposition - The character makes the conscious decision to go up against the forces of antagonism. Because of this, he is the primary cause of the opposition he faces in this act.

Luke: Having been told he is walking into a trap by Yoda, Obi-Wan, and Leia, Luke walks into the trap anyway.

Han/Leia: Han deals with the repercussions of not listening to Leia about Lando. He is tortured and encased in carbonite.

Turning Point Catalyst: The Lowpoint

The Lowpoint - Something unimaginable happens with grave emotional consequences for the character. He looks back on all his actions over the course of the story and feels he has failed.

Han is frozen in carbonite. Chewbacca warbles dramatically. Sad music plays.

Turning Point Four: The Newfound Resolve

Start Time: 98 of 122 minutes (80.3%)
Runtime: 2 of 122 minutes (1.6%)

The Newfound Resolve - After the Lowpoint, something happens to make the character dig deep within himself and rediscover his resolve. He makes the decision to stop the forces of antagonism at any cost.

Luke arrives at Cloud City and shoots it out with Boba Fett. Heroic music plays. He has made his decision to face Lord Vader despite the protests of his Jedi Masters.

Star Wars Episode V: The Empire Strikes Back - Act Five: Trying a Longshot

The character Tries a Longshot and faces Ultimate Opposition while trying to accomplish the Ultimate Goal. But just when it seems All is Lost, he makes a Final Push against the forces of antagonism, and either succeeds or fails.

Luke attempts to prove he is a Jedi (the longshot) by facing off with the most ruthless villain in the galaxy (ultimate opposition), in hopes of defeating him once and for all (the ultimate goal). But when Vader overpowers him, chops off his hand and reveals himself to be Luke's father (all is lost), Luke jumps into a chasm, is spat out beneath the city and calls for Leia to rescue him (the final push).

Starting Percentage: 100 of 122 minutes (81.9%)
Runtime: 20 of 122 minutes (16.3%)

The Longshot - The character is reinvigorated by the revelation he received at the Newfound Resolve, but his only chance of success lies in a plan with a high risk of failure.

Luke will face off with Vader. Meanwhile, Leia and Lando will attempt to save Han and escape the city.

The Ultimate Goal - The character finally understands what the true goal of the story is. The goal the character has in this act is what the story is all about.

Luke attempts to defeat the baddest dude in the galaxy to save his friends.

Ultimate Opposition - The forces of antagonism are now out to destroy the character completely. At this point in the story, the antagonist will throw everything he has into eliminating the character.

Luke must fight Vader mano-a-mano, until he loses a mano.

ACTIONS & GOALS

Turning Point Catalyst: All Is Lost

<u>All is Lost</u> - The character may experience some initial success, but the forces of antagonism rally, and it seems the character's Longshot is doomed to fail.

Vader lures Luke into the corridor-of-a-thousand-things-hanging-from-the-wall and uses the Force to throw them at him, knocking him out a window. Luke hangs on by a thread. Meanwhile, Lando and Leia fail to save Han and are pursued by stormtroopers, as they make their way to the Falcon.

Turning Point Five: The Final Push

Start Time: 109 of 122 minutes (89.3%)
Runtime: 13 of 122 minutes (10.6%)

<u>The Final Push</u> - Faced with his imminent destruction, the character decides to put everything he has into one final endeavor. He uses what little he has left in his stores, or the one trump card he's been holding, knowing if he fails he will be destroyed.

Vader chops off Luke's hand before revealing himself to be his father. Talk about a bad dad. With no other options left, Luke throws himself into a seemingly bottomless chasm and is ejected from the bottom of the city. He Force-dials Leia, who demands Lando turn the Falcon *around to pick him up. Leia and Lando retrieve him and try to escape, but the* Falcon *still has no light speed. R2 fixes it. R2 fixes everything.*

Star Wars Episode V: The Empire Strikes Back - Act Six: Living in a New Situation

Having accomplished (or failed to accomplish) the Ultimate Goal, the character is shown living in a New Situation.

Having failed to defeat Vader, Luke now has a robot hand and will try to save Han from Jabba the Hut with the help of Chewie and Lando.

Starting Percentage: 120 of 122 minutes (98.3%)
Runtime: 2 of 122 minutes (1.6%)

<u>Living in a New Situation</u> - We see the character adapting to the New Situation his actions have created. Whether he is exalted or exiled, this is the new world he helped create.

Han is a prisoner of the vile gangster[69] Jabba the Hutt. Lando and Chewie set off on a mission to go after him because nobody will miss those two if they don't come back. Luke has a robot hand, just like his dad.

---

[69] Seriously, who writes this stuff?

Quick Reference Guide

ACT ONE: DEALING WITH AN IMPERFECT SITUATION

A character in an Imperfect Situation faces Oppressive Opposition as he pursues an Initial Goal. But when there is a Disturbance to his routine, he faces a Dilemma regarding his situation and must assume a New Role.

Approximate Runtime: 20%

<u>The Inciting Incident</u> - Something happens, often before the story begins, which if it does not occur would prevent the story as it exists from coming to be.

<u>The Imperfect Situation</u> - The character begins the story in a less than ideal situation he would like to change but seemingly cannot.

<u>The Initial Desire</u> - Deep within himself, the character wants one particular thing more than anything else in the world.

<u>Initial Desire Type</u> - The character's Initial Desire is either for or against changing his situation.

<u>Preexisting Conflict</u> - When the story begins, the character is already dealing with personal conflicts as well as the conflicts of the world at large.

<u>Likability/Empathy Factors</u> - The character is shown to be someone the audience would like to see succeed, or would be willing to follow on the journey of the story.

The Initial Goal - When the story opens, the character already has a goal he is actively pursuing.

Initial Goal Type - The character's Initial Goal is either a Normal Routine Goal where he is in his regular environment, or a Fish out of Water Goal where he is already in a situation with which he is unfamiliar.

Oppressive Opposition - The character's Initial Desire and/or his Initial Goal are being oppressed by the world around him.

Turning Point Catalyst: The Disturbance

The Disturbance - An unexpected event with ominous implications occurs, interrupting the character's normal routine. This event pushes the character toward the Dilemma.

Turning Point One: The Dilemma

Approximate Start Time: 15%
Approximate Runtime: 5%

Presentation of The Dilemma - The character is placed in a position where he must choose between life as he has known it or taking a new course of action.

The New Role - If the character takes this new course of action, he will assume a New Role in which he is untested.

Refusal/Interference to the New Role (Optional) - The character may be reluctant, unready or unwilling to leave his Imperfect Situation and accept the New Role. In other cases, the character may want to accept the New Role, but someone else attempts to prevent him from accepting it.

ACTIONS & GOALS

Nudge From Fate (Optional) - In instances where the character has every reason to decline the New Role, he may receive influence from an outside force that drives him to accept it.

Accepting The New Role - The character makes the decision to take action by accepting the New Role.

ACT TWO: LEARNING THE RULES OF AN UNFAMILIAR SITUATION

The character Learns the Rules of an Unfamiliar Situation and faces Incidental Opposition in pursuit of a Transitional Goal. But when he receives a Reality Check, the character makes a Commitment to his New Role.

Approximate Start Time: 20%
Approximate Runtime: 20%

Learning the Rules of an Unfamiliar Situation - The character now finds himself in a situation unlike anything he's ever experienced.

The Transitional Goal - The character receives a new goal that transitions him out of his initial state of inertia and into the main events of the story.

Incidental Opposition - The character learns there are greater forces of opposition in this new world that may not be out to thwart him specifically, but still stand between him and his new goal.

Turning Point Catalyst: The Reality Check

The Reality Check - The plan the character had coming into this act hits a major roadblock, and either fails completely or has unintended negative consequences.

Turning Point Two: The Commitment

Approximate Start Time: 35%
Approximate Runtime: 5%

<u>The Commitment</u> - The character commits, or finds himself committed, to becoming the epitome of the New Role he accepted at the Dilemma. In doing so, he becomes an active participant in the Central Conflict.

ACT THREE: STUMBLING INTO THE CENTRAL CONFLICT

The character Stumbles into the Central Conflict and faces Intentional Opposition in pursuit of a False Goal. But when there is a grave Turn of events, he has a Moment of Truth.

Approximate Start Time: 40%
Approximate Runtime: 20%

<u>Stumbling into the Central Conflict</u> - The character learns more about the storyworld and develops a new goal that is diametrically opposed to the goal of the antagonist.

<u>The Conflict of Ideals</u> - The two sides of the Central Conflict are pursuing opposing ideals of perfection.

<u>The False Goal</u> - The character receives a new goal he feels will set everything right in his world. Sadly, this isn't the case, and there is still something bigger he must accomplish.

<u>Intentional Opposition</u> – As a result of his decision at the Commitment, the character comes to the attention of the forces of antagonism. They now begin opposing him with the specific intention of thwarting his plans.

Turning Point Catalyst: The Turn

<u>The Turn</u> - There is a major turn of events that raises the stakes for the character and his allies and makes his situation far more complicated than it had been up to this point. This event is often surprising, coming as a shock to both the character and the audience.

Turning Point Three: The Moment of Truth

Approximate Start Time: 55%
Approximate Runtime: 5%

<u>The Moment of Truth</u> - As a result of the Turn, the character must reevaluate his strategy, analyze who he is, and decide to be truthful with himself about the type of person he must become. In figuring out his true nature, he makes the decision to fight for the things he believes in.

<u>To Change or Not to Change</u> - At the Moment of Truth, the character faces the decision to either change his perspective and who he has been or retain the same outlook in the face of all which has transpired.

ACT FOUR: IMPLEMENTING A DOOMED PLAN

The character Implements a Doomed Plan and faces Self-Inflicted Opposition in pursuit of a Penultimate Goal. But when an unthinkable Lowpoint occurs, he pulls himself together and discovers a Newfound Resolve.

Approximate Start Time: 60%
Approximate Runtime: 20%

<u>The Doomed Plan</u> - Having made the commitment to fight at the Moment of Truth, the character now devises and implements a plan of action that is

destined to fail. It may fail outright, or it may seem to succeed only to have grave consequences the character didn't anticipate.

<u>The Penultimate Goal</u> - The character's goal in this act is one step removed from the Ultimate Goal, but his pursuit of it leads him to realize what he needs to do to end the conflict once and for all.

<u>Self-Inflicted Opposition</u> - The character makes the conscious decision to go up against the forces of antagonism. Because of this, he is the primary cause of the opposition he faces in this act.

Turning Point Catalyst: The Lowpoint

<u>The Lowpoint</u> - Something unimaginable happens with grave emotional consequences for the character. He looks back on all his actions over the course of the story and feels he has failed.

Turning Point Four: The Newfound Resolve

Approximate Start Time: 75%
Approximate Runtime: 5%

<u>The Newfound Resolve</u> - After the Lowpoint, something happens to make the character dig deep within himself and rediscover his resolve. He makes the decision to stop the forces of antagonism at any cost.

ACT FIVE: TRYING A LONGSHOT

The character Tries a Longshot and faces Ultimate Opposition while trying to accomplish the Ultimate Goal. But just when it seems All is Lost, he makes a Final Push against the forces of antagonism, and either succeeds or fails.

Approximate Start Time: 80%
Approximate Runtime: 15%

<u>The Longshot</u> - The character is reinvigorated by the revelation he received at the Newfound Resolve, but his only chance of success lies in a plan with a high risk of failure.

<u>The Ultimate Goal</u> - The character finally understands what the true goal of the story is. The goal the character has in this act is what the story is all about.

<u>Ultimate Opposition</u> - The forces of antagonism are now out to destroy the character completely. At this point in the story, the antagonist will throw everything he has into eliminating the character.

Turning Point Catalyst: All Is Lost

<u>All is Lost</u> - The character may experience some initial success, but the forces of antagonism rally, and it seems the character's Longshot is doomed to fail.

Turning Point Five: The Final Push

Approximate Start Time: 90%
Approximate Runtime: 5%

<u>The Final Push</u> - Faced with his imminent destruction, the character decides to put everything he has into one final endeavor. He uses what little he has left in his stores, or the one trump card he's been holding, knowing if he fails he will be destroyed.

ACT SIX: LIVING IN AN IMPROVED SITUATION

Having accomplished (or failed to accomplish) the Ultimate Goal, the character is shown living in a New Situation.

Approximate Start Time: 95%
Approximate Runtime: 5%

Living in a New Situation - We see the character adapting to the New Situation his actions have created. Whether he is exalted or exiled, this is the new world he helped create.

Glossary

Act - One of the main divisions of a story in which a character undertakes an action to achieve a goal. Each Act culminates in the character receiving a new or altered goal to pursue.

Audience Surrogate - A character within a story who is as clueless to the workings of the storyworld as the audience. This character often asks the same questions the audience would, allowing backstory events and world mechanics to be convincingly conveyed to the audience in a logical manner. This eliminates instances of "as we all already know" conversations, where two or more knowledgeable characters pointlessly discuss things they are all aware of for the sole purpose of providing exposition to the audience.

Climax - The point of highest tension near the end of a story to which all events of the story have built. The Central Conflict culminates in the two opposing sides meeting one last time to decide whose ideal is superior. This meeting and the subsequent release of escalated tension create the climactic event.

Conflict of Ideals - The moral argument at the heart of the story. The two opposing sides of the Central Conflict have opposing ideals of perfection they are actively pursuing. While the character may not be invested in either ideal initially, over the course of the story he comes to value one ideal over the other and dedicates himself to its achievement.

Dramatic Phases - These are the three traditional literary acts of Setup, Confrontation, and Resolution. These phases provide dramatic context to the portion of the story to which they pertain. In the Setup Phase, characters are introduced, and exposition of world history is provided. In the Confrontation phase, the two opposing sides of the conflict learn about each other in pursuit of their conflicted goals. In the Resolution phase, the conflict comes to a head and is ultimately resolved.

Establish the Character's Likability/Empathy Factors - Early in the story it is demonstrated to the audience that the character is someone they would like to see succeed. He may not necessarily be a good person, but he is shown to be interesting, likable or someone with which the audience can sympathize.

Evolving Goal - The character pursues a goal over the course of the story which grows with his understanding of his world. By pursuing his Initial Goal at the start of the story, he slowly comes to develop an appreciation of the Ultimate Goal of the story and learns to set aside his initial self-centered intentions to achieve a greater goal which benefits his world at large.

Extemporee - Someone who eschews plotting stories in advance in favor of writing "by the seat of their pants". The common term for this is a "pantser", a word I loathe. Extempore, in adjective form, means spoken, performed, done, or composed with little or no preparation (i.e. pantsing). The "ee" suffix is often added to adjectives, nouns, or verbs to refer to a person who exists in that condition or state (e.g. refugee, escapee). So an extemporee is someone who does things extemporaneously. Granted, you lose the cute alliteration of plotter vs. pantser, but I personally have little interest in cute alliteration.

High-Concept - A story premise with a unique, widely appealing, easily understandable concept at its core which can be communicated to a layman in a simple, intriguing summarization. Unlike the meaning of high-concept itself.

Hooking Premise - The unique idea at the heart of a story, separating it from every other story ever told. It is the hooking concept and distinctive selling point that piques the audience's interested in the story and convinces them to spend their hard earned money to learn how the premise is resolved.

Infodump - An exposition technique in which the storyteller ham-handedly provides an excessive amount of backstory information to the audience in a manner both boring and unrealistic within the context of the story. This may come in the form of internal monologue, external dialogue, narrator ramblings or some terrible combination of them all.

Initial Desire - When the story begins, the character has a long-standing, deep-rooted yearning for some seemingly unattainable thing. The thing he desires may be an abstract concept such as love or freedom, or it may be tied to a physical goal. Because this thing is so far out of his grasp, he is often not pursuing it when the story begins, or if he is pursuing it, realizes his chances of achieving it are slim to none. This is because the thing he desires goes against the desires of those controlling his life. While the thing the character desires seem logical and warranted to him, his desire is often seen as juvenile or unrealistic in the eyes of the powers that be. This diametric opposition creates a recognizable conflict of desires at the beginning of the story

MacGuffin - A plot device, typically a physical object, whose attainment is a principal motivator of the plot, but which serves no purpose to the story other than to provide this motivation. A contemporary example can be found in the briefcase in the film *Pulp Fiction*, a heavily sought after item whose contents have no effect on the story.

Mentor - An experienced character who is well versed in the workings of the storyworld and who guides the main character through some part of his journey. The Mentor imparts knowledge on the character, deftly provides exposition, teaches the character the skills he needs to defeat the antagonist and then generally dies.

Messiah Event - In the fifth act of some stories, the character will die momentarily only to be miraculously brought back to life. In doing so, he often gains special godlike powers which allow him to defeat the previously undefeatable antagonist.

Mirror Antagonist - A main antagonist who is the dark reflection of the character. The two characters may share similar occupations, backgrounds, outlooks or objectives, but differ in their moral outlook. While the character holds some sort of morality at his core, the antagonist is amoral in his belief that the means always justify the ends. This type of antagonist exists to demonstrate to the audience the moral danger the character faces. If the character chooses to sacrifice his morals, he will essentially become the same as the antagonist.

Mutually Exclusive Goals - Colloquially referred to as the "unity of opposites" (read: obfuscation), a mutually exclusive goal within a story indicates victory for one side of the conflict results in failure for the other. Mutual exclusivity implies two propositions that cannot both be simultaneously true. Therefore, if the antagonist succeeds in his goal then the ideology of the character is proven false, and vice versa.

Inferior Ideal - One of the two Conflicted Ideals at the center of the story. While not necessarily unconscionable or evil, the Inferior Ideal is ultimately proven to out of accordance with the way the storyworld operates.

The New Role - While the character existed in a state of volatile, yet understood stasis in the first act, in Act Two he takes on an unfamiliar position in which he is completely untested. This New Role brings with it an unexpected change to his position or responsibilities. Though the character has existing skills lending themselves to his New Role, he must now find new ways to use them if he is to succeed in the Unfamiliar Situation of Act Two.

Plotter - The mortal enemy of the extemporee, this is a writer who meticulously plots out every detail of their story in advance. They tend to favor spreadsheets, corkboards covered in thumbtacked index cards and exhaustive upfront interviews of their characters to understand their motivations.

Preexisting Conflict - When the story begins there are several conflicts within the world which already existed. The character is experiencing personal conflicts in his life caused by the denial of his Initial Desire by the powers that be. There are also shown to be conflicts between other characters, as well as the Central Conflict brewing in the world at large.

Razor's Edge of Death - A point near the end of the Act Five Turning Point, The Final Push, where the character comes within inches or seconds of being killed by the antagonist. This event is generally the crescendo of tension within the story. If the fifth act is the climax, and the Final Push is the climax of the climax, then the Razor's Edge of Death is the climax of the climax of the climax.

Setups, Callbacks and Payoffs - A foreshadowing technique in which a seemingly irrelevant piece of information is provided to the audience, disregarded, and called back to later in the story. This can come in the form of a seemingly insignificant line of dialogue, object or course of action which later proves to be of use, or not without meaning.

Story-Specific Actions - Actions the character takes specific to an individual narrative which are subservient to the universal action of an act. These actions are directly influenced by whichever of the Six Acts they fall under.

Superior Ideal - One of the two Conflicted Ideals at the center of the story. While not always morally correct, the Superior Ideal is the ideal proven true to the way the storyworld operates.

Superior Position - Also known as dramatic irony, this literary device occurs when the audience is given knowledge of key events happening within the story which the character has yet to discover for himself. This places the audience in a position of superiority over the character. Because this knowledge will often have a negative impact on the character, this device is used to create tension as the audience anticipates the character's inevitable realization of this negative information.

Turning Point - An occurrence signifying the end of an Act where the character receives a new goal. These are decisive moments in the story when the character makes a decision to revise his course of action.

Turning Point Catalyst - An event, often negative, which precedes a Turning Point. New or shocking information is discovered which leads the character to realize he must alter his course of action.

Undeserved Misfortune - A narrative concept dating back to Aristotle's *Poetics*, in which a character who is established to be generally decent and moral is unjustly slapped around by the hand of fate. Because no one likes to see a good person unfairly punished, Undeserved Misfortune is used to create sympathetic characters the audience would like to see succeed.

Unfolding Plan Montage - A common narrative technique in filmmaking in which the formation and implementation of a plan are edited into a montage which explains the plan to the audience as they watch it being executed. This generally involves the use of voiceover narration detailing each step as it takes place.

Inspirations, Influences and Further Reading

Jeffrey Alan Schechter, *My Story Can Beat Up Your Story* (Michael Wiese Productions, 2011)

Film Crit Hulk, *Screenwriting 101* (Badass Digest, 2013)

Alexandra Sokoloff, *Screenwriting Tricks for Authors* (2010)

K.M. Weiland, *Structuring your Novel* (PenForASword Publishing, 2013)

Michael Hauge, *Writing Screenplays that Sell* (Collins Reference, 2013)

Cited Works

Avatar. Dir. James Cameron. 20th Century Fox, 2009. Film.

Batman Begins. Dir. Christopher Nolan. Warner Bros. Pictures, 2005. Film.

Big. Dir. Penny Marshall. 20the Century Fox, 1988. Film.

A Christmas Carol. Dickens, Charles. London: Chapman & Hall, 1843. Print.

Die Hard. Dir. John McTiernan. 20th Century Fox, 1988. Film

Finding Nemo. Dir. Andrew Stanton. Buena Vista Pictures, 2003. Film.

A Game of Thrones. Martin, George R. R. New York, NY: Bantam, 1996. Print.

Gravity. Dir. Alfonso Cuarón. Warner Bros. Pictures, 2013. Film.

Harry Potter and the Sorcerer's Stone. Rowling, J. K. New York, NY: Scholastic, 1980. Print.

A History of Three Act Structure. Lanouette Jennine. *Screentakes. Publisher of Website,* 24 December 2012. Web. 31 July 2015.

The Hunger Games. Collins, Suzanne. New York, NY: Scholastic, 2008. Print

Inception. Dir. Christopher Nolan. Warner Bros. Pictures, 2010. Film.

Iron Man. Dir. Jon Favreau. Paramount Pictures, 2008. Film.

The Lego Movie. Dir. Phil Lord and Christopher Miller. Warner Bros. Picture, 2014. Film.

The Lord of the Rings: The Fellowship of the Ring. Dir. Peter Jackson. New Line Cinema, 2001. Film.

The Matrix. Dir. The Wachowski Brothers. Warner Bros. Pictures, 1999. Film.

Screenplay: The Foundations of Screenwriting. Field, Syd. New York, NY: Delta Trade Paperbacks, 2005. Print.

The Silence of the Lambs. Harris, Thomas. New York: St. Martin's, 1988. Print.

Spider-Man. Dir. Sam Raimi. Columbia Pictures, 2002. Film.

Star Trek. Dir. JJ Abrams. Paramount Pictures, 2009. Film.

Star Wars: Episode IV A New Hope. Dir. George Lucas. 20th Century Fox, 1977. Film.

Star Wars: Episode V The Empire Strikes Back. Dir. Irvin Kershner. 20th Century Fox, 1980. Film.

Titanic. Dir. James Cameron. 20th Century Fox, 1997. Film.

Toy Story. Dir. John Lasseter. Buena Vista Pictures, 1995. Film.

The Wizard of Oz. Dir. Victor Fleming. Loew's, Inc., 1939. Film.

Printed in Great Britain
by Amazon